Nature and History in Modern Italy

Ohio University Press Series in Ecology and History

James L. A. Webb, Jr., Series Editor

Nature and History in Modern Italy

Edited by Marco Armiero and Marcus Hall
With a foreword by Donald Worster

OHIO UNIVERSITY PRESS

ATHENS

Ohio University Press, Athens, Ohio 45701
www.ohioswallow.com
© 2010 by Ohio University Press
All rights reserved

Printed in the United States of America
Ohio University Press books are printed on acid-free paper ⊗ ™

17 16 15 14 13 12 11 10   5 4 3 2 1

Library of Congress Cataloging-in-Publication Data
Nature and history in modern Italy / edited by Marco Armiero and Marcus Hall ; with a foreword by Donald Worster.
   p. cm. — (Ohio University Press series in ecology and history)
   Includes bibliographical references and index.
   ISBN 978-0-8214-1915-1 (hardcover : alk. paper) — ISBN 978-0-8214-1916-8 (pbk. : alk. paper) — ISBN 978-0-8214-4347-7 (electronic)
   1. Italy—Environmental conditions. 2. Italy—History—19th century. 3. Italy—History—20th century. 4. Landscapes—Social aspects—Italy—History. 5. Nature—Effect of human beings on—Italy—History. 6. Human ecology—Italy—History. 7. Italy—Social conditions. 8. Pollution—Italy—History. 9. Urbanization—Environmental aspects—Italy—History. 10. Environmentalism—Italy—History. I. Armiero, Marco, 1966– II. Hall, Marcus, 1959–
   GE160.I8N38 2010
   304.20945—dc22

2010019101

Contents

Map 0.1. Geographic map of Italy *(Ohio University Cartographic Center)*

Illustrations

Foreword

The carving of nation-states out of the infinite variety of the living planet may seem like a triumph of the human will. In setting their borders, nations often defy the lines that nature draws. When they do conform and a river or mountain range determines a political boundary, they may refuse to accept such limits on their expansion; they may find ways to claim what lies on the other side of the frontier. Like aggressive landowners, they want only what is "theirs"—that is, all the land (and the sea) that adjoins them on every side. By disregarding limits, they challenge nature.

Yet as these essays on the environmental history of Italy, one of the most prominent nation-states of modern times, demonstrate again and again, the natural environment can play an important role in making the nation. In the first place, the political unification of this single peninsula jutting so dramatically into the Mediterranean Sea seems to have followed physical geography. Italy occupies a distinctive landform and its neighboring islands. Only in the north does this nation occupy a more ambiguous space; there in the Alpine mountains, Italian territory has been a more contested terrain to be defended against invaders. Elsewhere down the peninsula, powerful unifying forces have worked to create a fairly stable, independent sovereignty. But just as any landform is a physical unity rived by tension and difference, so any nation-state is a unity that conceals deep internal contradictions and struggles for power. Italy has long been a land of conflict, and many of its conflicts have occurred over natural resources or over the effects of environmental degradation.

Environmental history tries to incorporate nature, defined as the non-human world, into our understanding of social, economic, political, and cultural change over time. Also, by showing that humans are both part of and outsiders to that world, both vulnerable creatures and yet powerful ecological agents, environmental history redefines what it means to be "human."

This view of the past can also redefine what it means to be "Italian" or "American" or "Chinese." It can show how national differences are not simply products of culture or language; they also have important foundations in geology, climate, soils, flora, and fauna. Nation-states may be expressions of human will and human power, but they are also the outcomes of people living in and adapting to particular ecologies.

For outsiders, Italy has long been viewed through a gauzy, romantic veil. It has appeared to be a place where nature always smiles on its inhabitants and offers tourists an inviting destination. The editors call this image *Il Bel Paese,* the beautiful land. Travelers have gone there to find an easy way of life, far away from winter's severities, a place where the grape and olive grow under intensely blue skies and people take a more relaxed, indulgent approach to life. Anyone who has stood on a terrace overlooking the Sea of Naples on a brilliant sunny morning will know there is some truth in those images. Italy is indeed a beautiful land. But the essays in this book warn us that beauty is not the whole story. Italy is also a land of great instability and conflict, and some of its capacity for violence lies in the very land itself.

Despite its cultural aura of antiquity, suggested by its many ruins dating back to the Romans and Etruscans, Italy is one of the youngest physical landscapes on earth. Its geological youth means instability and volatility. There is, for example, the still-active volcano Mount Vesuvius, just ten kilometers from the center of Naples. There is a history of frequent earthquakes, of devastating landslides, of raging floods, and of fatal diseases to put alongside Italy's popular images of peaceful Tuscan villas and outdoor cafés. It was Italians, we should remember, who invented the word *malaria,* even if they did not for a long time understand what caused that disease or how it might be prevented. The historians of this volume have given us an unsettling portrait of nature's Italy that shows just what the human occupants have had to contend with. However deep its cultural roots, this country is still new and in the making, still held in the grip of forces far from being vanquished.

That nature has been a powerful force in the past and remains so today is buttressed by a wealth of modern scientific data. But the data also show just how much damage humans are capable of causing to the environment, especially as they have done over the last century or two. Many essays in this book reveal the dark and dangerous side of modern industrial capitalism, which has remade not only human relationships but also our relationships with water, forests, and other organisms. Italy is not unique in experiencing these new man-made threats to health, of both humans and the land, but it may have reacted to them differently than its neighbors in the rest of Europe.

The definition of *environment* offered by these historians is broad and comprehensive; it includes cities, factories, and oil refineries as they interact with nature. The beautiful land has become, in modern times, one of the most polluted places on earth, sending a toxic plume far out into the Mediterranean. Since 2008 or so, the country has been featured repeatedly in the news for its street corners piled high with garbage that no one seems to know how to dispose of without stirring up protest or endangering people's lives.

This book demonstrates that traditional history, the study of politics and social conflict, must now be rewritten to show that environmental issues have become a significant cause of struggle among social groups. Some of those groups have long led lives of invisibility and exploitation. That tourist-beguiling Italy has historically been underpinned by the people who furnished the labor on which cathedrals, opera houses, splashing fountains, and tables filled with pasta depended. The laboring classes helped build, too, a gritty and noisy industrial landscape, and they have disproportionately suffered from the often toxic consequences of economic growth.

Anyone seeking a more complicated portrait of modern Italy will find this book a superb guide. It showcases the work of long-acclaimed masters along with rising new talents. Its notes are a gold mine of further reading suggestions and demonstrate how well researched these essays are. The writing is clear and vigorous. The scope is comprehensive. Pack this book along with *Baedeker's Italy* or the latest edition of *Fodor's,* and you will have a compelling new perspective on a land that has won the hearts of so many people around the world. You will learn much about what environmental historians do, but also you will see far more clearly what humans and nature have been doing on this narrow, mountainous, and very special place on earth.

Donald Worster

Acknowledgments

Identifying and then selecting the best scholarship about Italy's modern environmental past has not been an easy assignment. This project faced conceptual, disciplinary, and linguistic barriers, and we realize that the process and product have not been perfect—and much too time consuming. Some excellent scholarship did not make it into our book, and some of the following pages might be trimmed further. Still, we are happy to present this sampling of insights to an English-speaking world, and we hope that our collective efforts will linger in readers' minds like a long sip of smooth *barbaresco*, or else deliver that mouth-puckering of *gelato al limone*.

All authors listed in the following chapters deserve special praise for enduring repeated requests to rework, rephrase, and refine. The conversion of Italian into English has been a particularly delicate task, with most chapters undergoing at least four levels of translation: a preliminary effort by authors, many with assistance from professional translators; a chapter-by-chapter smoothing by Carrol Firmage, environmental humanities research assistant at the University of Utah; a complete rereading and smoothing by both of us followed by more author input; and then copyediting by Ricky S. Huard and Joan Sherman. For those who have not tried it, translation is high art, but we are confident that the following pages render most of what should be told.

In later stages, the book received production assistance from Nancy Basmajian, Beth Pratt, Jean Cunningham, and Judy Wilson. Maps of Italy 1.1–1.3 were ably created by Margaret W. Pearce and her team at the Ohio University Cartographic Center. Florence's tourist office, l'Agenzia per il Turismo di Firenze, generously donated the cover image of Giambologna's sculpture in Villa Demidoff, *Il Colosso dell'Appennino*. We are especially grateful to acquisitions editor Gillian Berchowitz and series editor James L. A. Webb, Jr., for seeing value in the project, and without their encouragement the book would never have arrived in your hands. Significant financial assistance covering a variety of costs as well as other support has been derived from the Institute for the Studies of Mediterranean Societies (Italian National Research Council), the Program in Agrarian Studies at Yale University, the University of California Berkeley, and the Bill Lane Center for the American West at Stanford University (to Marco Armiero); and from the University of Utah and University of Zurich (to Marcus Hall). Esteemed mentor and dear friend Donald Worster has been following our sundry ventures for many years, and we are delighted and honored that he could offer his reflections on this latest one. Lastly we are grateful to our families, immediate and extended, far and near, young and old, for continuing to provide the sustenance, inspiration, and love that make it all possible.

Marco Armiero, Barcelona
Marcus Hall, Zurich
June 2010

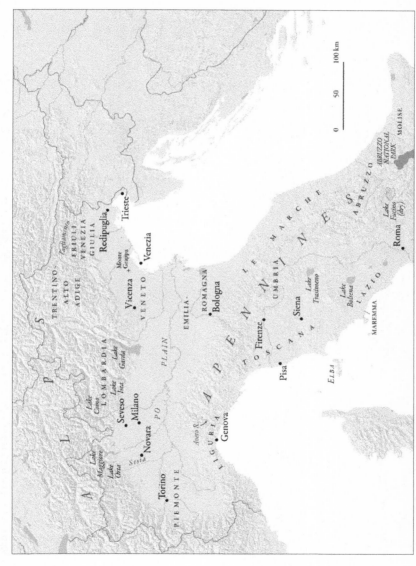

Map 0.2. Geographic map of northern Italy (*Ohio University Cartographic Center*)

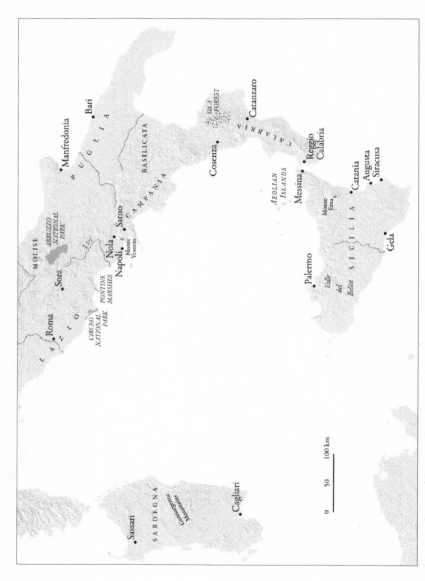

Map 0.3. Geographic map of southern Italy (*Ohio University Cartographic Center*)

Il Bel Paese

An Introduction

Marco Armiero and Marcus Hall

Environmental Boundaries

Relationships between environmental history and boundaries have always been complicated. One might say that environmental history is congenitally uncomfortable with boundaries, no matter what they are meant to delineate. Although definitions of environmental history have been various and even contradictory, there has been one recurring element that most people agree upon: the new discipline should be "trans." Going across traditional borders seems to be an important mission of the discipline if it is to be original: transdisciplinary, transregional, transnational. In the case of transnationalism, however, the individual nation has shown itself to be extraordinarily resilient in analyses of environments through time. For example, national environmental histories have been written about Great Britain (Clapp, Sheail), Israel (Tal), India (Gadgil and Guha), China (Elvin and Liu), Japan (Totman), the United States (Merchant, Steinberg, Petulla, Opie), Spain (González de Molina Navarro and Alier), Germany (Lekan and Zeller, Lekan, Blackbourn, Mauch), Peru (Lizárraga), Costa Rica (Evans), and South Africa (Beinart, Jacobs).[1] The *Encyclopedia of World*

Environmental History includes thirty-four national entries.[2] How can we explain the persistence of *nation* within the history of nature?[3]

The first and perhaps most obvious explanation for this national penchant is the availability of sources. Nations have been crucial entities for documenting, classifying, and surveying the natural world, so when historians sit down to write about it, their geographic limits are already set.[4] Moreover, the land reflects the government and the peoples who have been managing it. A nation's laws, economic policies, and legal systems all shape landscapes, as do the customs and shared habits of the people living there: farming practices, property rights, urban development, transportation systems, national parks, military-industrial complexes. Even though some communities have resisted conforming to larger national trends, one can in many cases still identify such trends. As Richard White points out, nation is a matter of scale, and like any scale, it can enlighten something while hiding something else.[5]

As we set out to explore "Italian" environmental history, we therefore aim to stay within national borders even though we realize such borders may be quite permeable. This book does not dwell on transnational perspectives, yet we firmly believe that Italian environmental history has never been just Italian. We still need studies on Italy's transborder areas and resources: for instance, on seas and fishing, emigration and the creation of ethnic landscapes, illegal traffic of toxic waste, colonial and neocolonial exploitation, the supranational character of the Alps, or the international distribution of scientific knowledge.[6] Nevertheless, the field of Italian environmental history is quite young, and we do not yet have research on those topics. In other words, the book mirrors the state of the discipline as it is rather than as it might become.[7]

In the Scylla-and-Charybdis journey between the dangers of geographic determinism and nationalistic feeling, our goal is to understand how nature has built a nation and how nation has in turn shaped, confined, and rearranged the expressions of the natural world. We believe that in the case of Italy, a nation's nature is not just a matter of discourse. A (re)invention of nation has implied a (re)invention of its landscape even in very materialistic terms. The Italian nation has carved its physical spaces with cities, railroads, highways, canals, dams, harbors, mines, and parks. Yet Italian nature has not been merely raw material for building a state and inventing a common identity. Nature and nation have shaped each other.

An Artificial Homeland

It is therefore less easy than we might imagine to separate Tuscany's hillsides from Dante, Chianti wines from the Uffizi Gallery. In this central Italian landscape, sedimented in its rolling terrain as well as in its medieval and classical imprint, work, nature, and culture have combined to produce the hybrid environment that tourists are looking for. And the same can be said for all parts of the country, even those less touristy. From the high Alps to the Sicilian shores, Italy's landscapes have always been fragments of nature and projections of our idea about Nature. Even if Italy became a nation only in 1860, the process of nationalizing the country and its land took much longer. Indeed, observers spoke of an Italian landscape long before Italy became a nation. Early travelers on Europe's Grand Tour—tourists—had very clear ideas about what they would find in the peninsula: no one could contemplate an Italian nature without ruins, shepherds, farms, or villages on the backstage.[8] Such human presence has always been integral to understanding Dante's home. How else could one understand a thousand village bell towers nestled under a thousand terraced hills? Few countries have as much history as Italy, a sharp tongue of land jutting down the Mediterranean, inhabited since ancient times and scarce in "natural spaces" if this expression means nature apart from ourselves. The idea of wilderness is controversial everywhere, and it sounds even stranger in Italy. This country seems too little, too crowded, too "old" for that. Italy is the place that Petrarch in the fourteenth century and the abbot Antonio Stoppani in the nineteenth called *Il Bel Paese,* the beautiful country. Italy is where George Perkins Marsh crafted his 1864 conservation classic, entitling it simply *Man and Nature.*

Italian patriot and philosopher Carlo Cattaneo sought to express this idea of hybrid landscapes. In the 1840s, he described the wide Po Plain (or Val Padana) as an immense by-product of human activities rather than as a gift from nature: "Since human fate has been to live by working hard, each civilized region can be distinguished from wild ones by the fact it becomes an immense repository of human labor. It is for this reason that nine-tenths of our country is not derived from nature, but from our own hands; ours is an artificial homeland."[9]

Cattaneo was probably wrong about the proportion of natural and artificial, as nature has been inseparable from Italian civilization, but this is not the point. His idea of an artificial homeland—an archive of its inhabitants' daily lives—is significant. Cattaneo may have been focusing on work and technology, especially of irrigation and drainage, but we can enlarge his metaphor to include all human traces on the land. The dichotomy of artificial and natural, cultural and material is inadequate for interpreting the Italian landscape and insufficient for understanding either one separately or the relationships between the two.

This idea of a hand-forged homeland stresses the concept of a hybrid place, but it says little about the origins of this hybridization or the characteristics of its components. For instance, though Cattaneo emphasized people's ingenuity in confronting natural constraints, Marsh warned about the dark side of this hybridization, which he believed could be more disruptive than beneficial. Was nature ally or enemy in fashioning Italy's heritage?[10]

In an effort to simplify, one can consider those two extremes—heaven and hell, Dante's *Paradiso* and *Inferno*—as one of the most basic ways to classify Italian nature. Italy is a sun-kissed land where crops grow with little labor, where climate is benign, where people have the leisure to enjoy friendships, food, and places; it is a country rich in history and art, where ingenuity substitutes for scarce raw materials so that water turbines can replace coal-fired power. Conversely, this heaven can become the hell that villagers face in a land harboring malaria, floods, earthquakes, and volcanic eruptions. The nature of Italy is also marked by little coal or oil or other valuable minerals and by rugged hills and mountains but few plains, a nature as dangerous and tarnished as it is luxurious and romantic. These competing narratives, rather than describing natures outside the observer, serve to construct that nature through the observer's perceptions.

Bringing Environment to Italian History

Unlike the "silent spring" of some environmentalist traditions, ecological concerns were hardly represented in Italian social movements of the sixties. In most instances, such concerns were depicted largely as hobbies for the well-to-do.[11] According to the vocabulary of that period, ecology was a middle-class science, and efforts to protect animals and plants were a diversion for members of the nobility, who were insensitive to messages being promoted by blue-collar workers and radical students. This does not mean that everyone involved in unions and leftist parties (such as the Italian Communist Party, or PCI) was uninterested in environmental issues.[12] Indeed, it was precisely in this cultural milieu that Italian environmentalism experimented with new discourses and new concerns, such as occupational health and environmental justice;[13] moreover, pacifist movements involving outcries against nuclear weapons found some of their most passionate manifestations in the Italian Left. Although these early concerns for health and pacifism, for example, offer clues to interpreting Italy's environmentalist past, we can also realize that its brand of environmentalism had to negotiate a complicated path between a powerful communist party and an elite protectionist culture.[14]

Such political realities are reflected in recent elections, in which the Green vote oscillated from just 2.79 percent in 1992 to 3 percent in 2008 (in this last case, the Green vote was in coalition with other leftist parties, which ushered in a dramatic defeat for the whole coalition). Although there has been progress in understanding Italian environmental movements, there is a rising need to explore the broader background of Italian attitudes toward nature.[15]

The relationships between Italy's historical profession and the environment can offer some explanatory power to understanding the historiography of Italian environmental history. Idealistic historians—Benedetto Croce's disciples—and Marxist historians have both been more attuned to segregating rather than uniting the histories of society and of nature, but the latter have been more willing to blend them. In particular, Italian agricultural history has been deeply influenced by the Marxist approach, becoming a fertile substratum of the new environmental history.[16] Thus, modes of production, property rights, and social relations have long been crucial to understanding the historical relationships of Italians with nature. There has never been a "wilderness" debate in Italy, and Italian environmental historians have always seen the object of their study as a combination of landscape and humanscape, natural and artificial.

IN CONSIDERING the many topics and approaches that one might choose to represent Italian relationships between nature and people through time, we have opted for breadth over depth in this volume. Rather than establishing disciplinary borders and fixing canons, we have involved scholars from several backgrounds and visions. We believe that the essays collected in this work show the richness of the field and point the way toward the range of questions being asked. The following pages explore policies and sensibilities, laws and practices, microanalyses and large pictures, slow processes and sudden events. In both scale and methodology, we consider our authors to be challenging the view that environment be confined to the "sidebar" of Italian history.

This message is evidently the core of Piero Bevilacqua's introductory essay, which provides a trail map for the book. Indeed, his essay gives a bird's-eye view of the main features of the Italian environment, useful for those familiar and unfamiliar with the peninsula's bays, rivers, plains, and mountains. Bevilacqua dwells on relations of causality between nonhuman and human events of national history by considering how nature can serve as historical agency, a contentious issue among historians. Just as Ted Steinberg and Carolyn Merchant craft their environmental histories of the United States, Piero Bevilacqua starts from the ground, quite literally: what can geology tell us about Italian settlement patterns or nature perceptions? Yet Bevilacqua does not propose monocausal, deterministic explanations but instead focuses on searching for reciprocal relationships between nature and society. The mosquito, for instance, has been a powerful agent in shaping Italian history, but is this insect simply "nature"? What were the other root causes of disease epidemics and their effects on human societies? What were the human agencies contributing to such hydrographical disasters as floods and landslides? And how have humans coped with these events, manifested as they are as environmental transformations and changing perceptions? For Bevilacqua, environmental change is geological, climatological, and hydrographical, as well as social and political.

Many of Bevilacqua's themes are the focus of other essays. The patterns of ownership and access that Bevilacqua mentions, along with their consequences for the management of Italy's natural resources, are enriched in Gabriella Corona's essay. She seeks to identify patterns between ecosystem functions and ownership models during the last two hundred years when common property was increasingly privatized across Italy. Her central subject of the commons is also central to Wilko von Hardenberg's explanation of Fascist conservation policies and local resistance, as it is to Bruno Vecchio's consideration of perceptions about eighteenth- and nineteenth-century forest degradation. Vecchio's essay does not examine the material state of the forest but narratives about them, asserting that the "forest question" was a reflection of rhetorical judgments even more than ecological disruption. All of these essays require us to look again at collectively owned properties and go beyond viewing the commons as courting inevitable tragedy in the style taught by Garret Hardin.

Several authors push deeper into the issue of nature's agency in human history. Emanuela Guidoboni and Walter Palmieri are the most sensitive to the raw power of nature. In their essays on earthquakes and landslides, respectively, they remind us that Italy is a geologically youthful land with frequent seismic and hydrologic events. But they are careful to point out that as soon as humans enter the scene, such natural disasters are not very natural at all. Blame for the disaster or inadequacy of emergency response can be traced to moods of deities, political decisions, and architectural features, all of which depend on place and century according to a range of cultural factors.

Combinations of human agency and natural agency form the core of other essays presented in this volume. Marcus Hall's contribution expounds on Bevilacqua's mention of the mosquito by looking at how humans chose to battle this malaria vector with powerful new pesticides on the island of Sardinia. The eradication project that followed World War II adapted a warlike metaphor, and more important for Hall's purpose, such metaphors delineated the imperial overtones of this struggle. What the Rockefeller Foundation masterminded in their Sardinian Project was probably not the best choice from the Italian perspective.

How narratives and discourses affected ecological relationships is at the core of several other essays, including Roberta Cevasco's microanalysis of alder woods and their management. The alder patches she studies in the northern Apennines are more than cultural landscapes, being dependent on and crucial to human societies. The Alps also present rich cultural spaces, especially in times of warfare, as shown by Marco Armiero. He analyzes the ways in which World War I shaped the Alpine landscape, offering a compelling example of a historical approach inclusive of cultural and ecological dynamics. In these rugged mountains, narratives and bombs changed the landscape and the national perception of it; here, the Great War was a dramatic process of nationalization of nature and its representation. Industrial landscapes are taken up by Stefania Barca, who tells of the tension between ecological and social changes resulting from work. The Liri Valley in the nineteenth century becomes a perfect case study for illustrating the effects of a rapid and brutal conversion of primary materials to secondary products. The history of Italian industrialization turns from energy production (in Barca's chapter) to the manufacture of hazardous products (in Serneri's), the economic boom of the sixties (in Adorno's), and finally the collective memory of the Seveso dioxin spill (in Centemeri's). To offer a vision of Italy as a polluted country is a mixed metaphor because it is hard to imagine chimneys looming on any Italian horizon or gray smoke wafting over the Mediterranean blue.

Simone Neri Serneri examines the first wave of Italian industrialization, choosing to focus on unhealthy factories. The limited knowledge of chemical hazards, the political choice to protect private interests, and the priority for sustaining economic development did not foster rigorous legal methods for protecting public health and the common good. Salvatore Adorno picks up the thread fifty years later in Sicily's post–World War II petrochemical age, when the state was investing massively in the country's southern regions, leaving a grisly heritage of pollution and illness.

Although the transformation of the Sicilian village of Gela was only one small instance of the usual devil's bargain of trading health for salary and sacrificing aesthetics for progress, the events at Seveso brought these trends to a head. The toxic horrors happening just north of Milan pushed Italy to the world stage, in an incident on a par with Three Mile Island, Bhopal, Chernobyl, and the *Exxon Valdez*. Though Seveso's dioxin spill is generally remembered as the starting point for the European Union's policies to minimize chemical hazards, Laura Centemeri offers an insightful interpretation of how this dramatic spill required a complex negotiation between the Catholic tradition of the affected community and the Marxist views of the activists demanding retribution. We are still unsure how the associated toxic exposures were distributed according to class and gender, for instance, but understanding Gela and Seveso in terms of political ecology suggests fresh directions for further research.

Wilko von Hardenberg also adopts a class analysis in his essay on Fascist conservation policies and local resistance. He tells of the inconsistencies of Fascist practices that celebrated rural life and agriculture together with corporate industrialization while neglecting local interests and access to natural resources. In turn, Luigi Piccioni places this story in wider environmentalist context by stressing two main points: the special concerns for Italy's cultural landscape and the irreversible damages inflicted by the Fascist regime. Piccioni does not cover the last decades of Italian environmentalism, which saw several new developments, practices, and organizations.[17]

Since the turn of the twenty-first century, Italy, like other countries, has seen a new kind of environmentalism surfacing that revolves around the topic of justice. This was the case for the dramatic garbage wars in Naples from 2006 to 2008, which were, at their core, issues of environmental justice.[18] But the same can be said for other local conflicts involving incinerators, new railways for high-speed trains, and toxic spills.[19] You will not find much mention of these last stories in the following pages, and to be sure, they are not the only missing pieces of Italy's modern environmental puzzle. Nevertheless, this book paints many rich pictures of nature and history across this very complicated land. We invite you to join us for a new grand tour.

AS WE COMPILED this group of essays, Italy confronted its usual emergencies: in the south, forest fires in Calabria set by arsonists, hoping to remove restrictions on building construction, or other fires smoldering in hills of garbage on the outskirts of Naples; in the north, melting glaciers near Monte Rosa that were shifting ridgelines and thus the boundary with Switzerland; and in the center, a cruel earthquake that rolled through cities and over people who asked not only for solidarity but also for justice. In the same period, urban and rural environments emptied and then filled with tourists, ourselves included, hailing from distant lands to enjoy the beauties of this country. Once again, this heaven and this hell—with picturesque beaches and alpine cirques, with real fire and real ruins—are fitting images of Italy's genius loci. Instead of seeing just one of these images, we think it wiser to view them together, coexisting in the same place, neither cursed nor blessed but a hybrid landscape fashioned by history as well as nature.

Notes

1. Brian W. Clapp, *An Environmental History of Britain since the Industrial Revolution* (London: Longman, 1994); John Sheail, *An Environmental History of Twentieth-Century Britain* (New York: Palgrave, 2002); Alon Tal, *Pollution in a Promised Land: An Environmental History of Israel* (Berkeley: University of California Press, 2002); Madhav Gadgil and Ramachandra Guha, *This Fissured Land: An Ecological History of India* (Delhi: Oxford University Press, 1992); Mark Elvin and Ts'ui-jung Liu, *Sediments of Time: Environment and Society in Chinese History* (New York: Cambridge University Press, 1998); Conrad Totman, *History of Japan* (Malden, MA: Blackwell, 2005); Carolyn Merchant, *The Columbia Guide to American Environmental History* (New York: Columbia University Press, 2002); Ted Steinberg, *Down to Earth: Nature's Role in American History* (New York: Oxford University Press, 2002); Joseph M. Petulla, *American Environmental History: The Exploitation and Conservation of Natural Resources* (San Francisco: Boyd and Fraser, 1977); John Opie, *Nature's Nation: An Environmental History of the United States* (Fort Worth, TX: Harcourt Brace College Publishers, 1998); Manuel González de Molina Navarro and Joan Martínez Alier, *Naturaleza transformada: Estudios de historia ambiental en España* (Barcelona: Icaria Editorial, 2001); Thomas Lekan and Thomas Zeller, eds., *Germany's Nature: Cultural Landscapes and Environmental History* (New Brunswick, NJ: Rutgers University Press, 2005); Thomas M. Lekan, *Imagining the Nation in Nature: Landscape Preservation and German Identity* (Cambridge, MA: Harvard University Press, 2004); David Blackbourn, *The Conquest of Nature: Water, Landscape and the Making of Modern Germany* (New York: W. W. Norton, 2006); Christof Mauch, *Nature in German History* (New York: Berghahn Books, 2004); Lizardo Seiner Lizárraga, *Estudios de historia medioambiental: Perú, siglos XVI–XX* (Lima: Universidad de Lima, 2002); Sterling Evans, *The Green Republic: A Conservation History of Costa Rica* (Austin: University of Texas Press, 1999); William Beinart, *The Rise of Conservation in South Africa: Settlers, Livestock, and the Environment, 1770–1950* (New York: Oxford University Press, 2003); Nancy J. Jacobs, *Environment, Power, and Injustice: A South African History* (New York: Cambridge University Press, 2003).

2. Shepard Krech III, John R. McNeill, and Carolyn Merchant, eds., *Encyclopedia of World Environmental History,* 3 vols. (New York: Berkshire Publishing Group, 2004).

3. We might say that environmental history was born with a special transnational mission, as Donald Worster wrote in his seminal essay "World without Borders: The Internationalizing of Environmental History," in *Environmental*

History: Critical Issues in Comparative Perspective, ed. Kendal E. Bailes (Lanham, MD: University Press of America, 1985), 661–69.

4. See James Scott, *Seeing Like a State: How Certain Schemes to Improve the Human Condition Have Failed* (New Haven, CT: Yale University Press, 1998).

5. Richard White, "The Nationalization of Nature," *Journal of American History* 86, no. 3 (December 1999): 976–86.

6. These last two aspects are in some way addressed in this book; see Marco Armiero's essay about the Alps as a place for conflicting processes of nationalization and Marcus Hall's contribution about the Rockefeller Foundation eradicating mosquitoes in Sardinia.

7. As John McNeill wrote in his introduction to a group of essays on Pacific environmental history, we would like "to help establish a scholarly field rather than [edit] a book that seeks to describe a venerable one"; see "Introduction," in *Environmental History in the Pacific World,* ed. John McNeill (Aldershot, UK: Ashgate 2001), xiii.

8. On the grand tour, see Jeremy Black, *Italy and the Grand Tour* (New Haven, CT: Yale University Press, 2003).

9. Carlo Cattaneo, "Agricoltura e morale," in *Notizie naturali e civili su la Lombardia e altri scritti su l'agricoltura* (Milan: Edizioni Risorgimento, 1925), 104–5.

10. On George Perkins Marsh's Italian education, see David Lowenthal, *George Perkins Marsh: Prophet of Conservation* (Seattle: University of Washington Press, 2000); Marcus Hall, "The Provincial Nature of George Perkins Marsh," *Environment and History* 10, no. 2 (2004): 191–204; Caroline Marsh, *Una Americana alla corte dei Savoia: Il diario dell' ambasciatrice degli Stati Uniti in Italia dal 1861 al 1865,* ed. David Lowenthal, trans. Luisa Quartermaine (Turin: Umberto Allemandi, 2004).

11. See as an example of this kind of approach Dario Paccino, *L'imbroglio ecologico* (Turin: Einaudi, 1972). For a historical overview, see Giorgio Nebbia, "L'ecologia è una scienza borghese?" *Ecologia Politica CNS* 28, no. 1 (2000), http://www.ecologiapolitica.it/web/4/articoli/nebbia.htm (accessed 28 August 2008).

12. Laura Conti, biologist and member of the Communist Party, was probably the leading figure among these minority groups. For the relationship between the Communist Party and environmentalism, see Wilko Graf von Hardenberg, "Il rosso e il verde: PCI e questione ambientale 1972–1991" (Laurea thesis, University of Torino, 2000–2001). On Laura Conti, see Loredana Lucarini, ed., *Laura Conti: Dalla Resistenza, all'ambientalismo, al caso Seveso* (Milan: UNICOPLI, 1994), and "Il fondo Laura Conti," special issue, *Altronovecento* 8 (January 2004).

13. Stefania Barca, "Health, Labor, and Social Justice: Environmental Costs of the Italian Economic Growth, 1958–2000," in Agrarian Studies Colloquium,

Program in Agrarian Studies, Yale University, available at http://www.yale.edu/agrarianstudies/papers/26italiangrowth.pdf (accessed 5 May 2009).

14. To date, there is no comprehensive history about the PCI's attitudes toward nature. Obviously, the largest Communist Party of the West was long in trouble with any kind of discourses or politics that may have limited economic growth, that is, the key tool for redistribution and employment. Nevertheless, it would be unfair to dismiss PCI contributions to the development of a green culture in Italy. With so-called austerity, the Communists proposed to address the oil crisis in the 1970s by changing lifestyles and models of consuming, using typical green arguments. On PCI-environmentalism relationships, see Wilko Graf von Hardenberg and Paolo Pelizzari, "The Environmental Question, Employment, and Development in Italy's Left, 1945–1990," *Left History* 13, no. 1 (2008): 77–105.

15. On Italian environmental cultures and associations, see Luigi Piccioni, *Il volto amato della patria: Il primo movimento per la protezione della natura in Italia, 1880–1934* (Camerino: Università di Camerino, 1999); Edgar Meyer, *I pionieri dell'ambiente: L'avventura del movimento ecologista italiano—Cento anni di storia* (Milan: Carabà, 1995); Roberto Della Seta, *La difesa dell'ambiente in Italia: Storia e cultura del movimento ecologista* (Milan: Franco Angeli, 2000); James Sievert, *The Origins of Nature Conservation in Italy* (Bern: Peter Lang, 2000). See also Patrick Barron and Anna Re, *Italian Environmental Literature: An Anthology* (New York: Italica Press, 2003).

16. Emilio Sereni's *Storia del paesaggio agrario italiano* (Bari: Laterza, 1961), translated by Robert Burr Litchfield as *History of Italian Agrarian Landscape* (Princeton, NJ: Princeton University Press, 1997), is a precocious example of a broad, Braudelian approach to the history of agriculture coming from a Marxist tradition. On Italian environmental history and its relationships with other subfields, see Marco Armiero and Stefania Barca, *Storia dell'ambiente: Una introduzione* (Rome: Carocci, 2004), 49–55.

17. On the history of recent Italian environmentalism, see Andrea Poggio, *Ambientalismo* (Milan: Bibliografica, 1996); Roberto Della Seta, *La difesa dell'ambiente in Italia;* Donatella Della Porta and Mario Diani, *Movimenti senza protesta? L'ambientalismo in Italia* (Bologna: Il Mulino, 2004).

18. Marco Armiero, "Seeing Like a Protester: Nature, Power, and Environmental Struggles," *Left History* 13, no. 1 (2008): 59–76.

19. Donatella Della Porta and Gianni Piazza, *Voices of the Valley, Voices of the Straits: How Protest Creates Communities* (New York: Berghahn Books, 2008), esp. 57–78.

Foundations

CHAPTER 1

The Distinctive Character of Italian Environmental History

Piero Bevilacqua

A Complex Territory

THE PHYSICAL features and habitat of the Italian peninsula set it sharply apart from other European regions. Italy is almost entirely surrounded by the sea and joined to the rest of Europe by the Alps, a mountain chain of superb beauty and a major repository of zoological and botanical biodiversity (this, of course, is a natural feature that Italy shares with its border countries). The most original characteristic of the Italian landscape, which makes it unique in Europe, is the presence of four variously active volcanoes on the mainland and on islands just off the coast. These are Vesuvius near Naples, Etna in Sicily, and Stromboli and Vulcano on their namesake islands. With the exception of Iceland, no other European country still has active volcanoes. This disquieting presence bears witness to the comparative geological youth of the Italian peninsula, most of which emerged from the sea no earlier than a million years ago. At the same time, it draws attention to the instability of the Italian landscape through the ages. Wherever there are volcanoes, the crust of the earth is continuously shifting. Earthquakes, which are among the most terrible of natural catastrophes, frequently occur in volcanic areas. One statistical report indicates that out of 481 disastrous earthquakes that hit the Mediterranean basin between 1501 and 1929, 188 were located in Italy.[1] A list of major earthquakes in Italy from 461 BC to 1980 shows that every 100 years, an average of over 100 earthquakes with magnitudes between 5 and 6 occur in the Italian peninsula, as well as 5 to 10 with higher magnitudes.[2] This long and woeful history has left Italy with a diffusely unstable landscape. Today, about 2,960 municipalities, comprising 45 percent of the national territory and encompassing about 40 percent of the population, lie in seismic areas.[3]

Other natural features besides volcanoes and earthquakes have contributed to the historical instability of Italy's young landscape. Hundreds of torrents and rivers, for example, flow down both sides of the mountainous Apennines, which run through the Italian peninsula. These watercourses are powerful forces constantly remodeling the land.[4] By continuously carrying the products of erosion downstream, they have formed, and continue to form, a variety of habitats. The extensive coppices dotted with ponds and swamps that have long characterized the Italian coastal landscape are the result of rivers flowing down from the Apennines. Areas such as the Tuscan Maremma, the Pontine Marshes, and the southern Italian coastal lakes—among them Averno, Varano, and Salpi—are the historical result of this phenomenon. Venice's lagoon was also formed in the same way, although in its case, the rivers are fed from the Alps. The habitats that arose in these areas at the mouth of large rivers, such as the Po delta, are some of the most unusual in Italy and some of the richest in wild flora and fauna. Birds, in particular, which often stop there en route from Africa to Europe, are a real treasure of biodiversity.[5]

Apennine watercourses also produce negative effects; notably, erosion and hydrogeological instability. Italy is a landslide-prone country.[6] At the end of the last century, all of 3,671 municipalities, comprising over 45 percent of the national territory, were considered to be at high or very high hydrogeological risk.[7] Italian landslides have long been destroying houses, fields, farms, crops, and livestock, while claiming human lives.

The complex and contradictory biophysical picture I have briefly sketched would be seriously incomplete if I were to neglect a major and long-lasting environmental feature that affected much of the Italian peninsula for thousands of years, namely, malaria.[8] As late as the twentieth century, this dangerous and specifically environmental endemic disease, carried by mosquitoes of the genus *Anopheles,* was a major deterrent for human settlement in Italy. Official statistics show that until the end of the nineteenth century, malaria killed at least fifteen thousand people a year;[9] but this is an under-estimation because malaria often caused other diseases, resulting in deaths officially attributed to other causes. The spread of quinine treatment in the twentieth century sharply reduced malaria's mortality but not its diffusion, which continued for decades to discourage human settlement in the Italian plains and along the coast. *Anopheles* prospered in stagnant waters and mild temperatures, and hence thrived in coastal plains. Farmers continued to suffer from malaria during the main work seasons, that is, in early summer and autumn.

Land Reclamation and Habitat Modification

The preceding premise is necessary to an understanding of at least some of the distinctive features of the environmental transformations that have affected Italy for many centuries, especially in the contemporary age. For thousands of years, hydraulic instability forced local Italian populations to continually undertake land reclamation works. They drained swamps, repaired riverbanks, and dug canals. This kind of work was necessary both in the Po Valley and in the valleys and plains along the Apennine mountain range. In the Po Plain, the many rivers flowing down from the Alps caused floods and formed vast wetlands. In the Middle Ages, many areas in the lower plain were only reachable by boat.

Similarly across much of the plain, travel was difficult and stable settlement was quite challenging without land reclamation—a task that lasted for centuries. Even today, many areas in the plain are below sea level and must be kept dry by means of pumps.

Administrators, technicians, and local populations faced comparable and even greater difficulties in the plains and valleys of central and southern Italy. In those regions, draining land and protecting it from hydraulic instability were even harder tasks, mostly accomplished in the nineteenth and twentieth centuries. Many of the swamps posing an obstacle to human settlement were the result of the deforestation of the mountains. Flooding torrents that came down over their bared slopes carried stones and sand that eventually dammed the water flow and prevented it from reaching its natural outlet into the sea. Torrents thus formed swamps in the coastal plains, an ideal habitat for the malaria-carrying *Anopheles*. As a result, in central and southern Italy, land reclamation could not be limited, as in the Po Plain, to the draining of swamps; intervention upstream of the swamps was also called for. Woods needed to be replanted on slopes, and the upper courses of streams had to be shored up. The work was complicated by the fact that, historically, many people lived in the mountains, earning a living from agriculture and woodcutting. An important challenge was to break the vicious circle and find an agreement between the peoples of the plains and those of high hills and mountains.[10]

The War against Water

The abundance of water in Italy eventually resulted—especially in the nineteenth and twentieth centuries—in hostile relationships between populations and their surroundings, between people and nature. For at least a couple of centuries, water appeared to many Italians (especially engineers, doctors, and landowners) as an enemy to be combated. Malaria was another natural enemy.

In much of the Po Plain, the water of major rivers has been a source of prosperity from the Middle Ages down to the present day. It facilitated transportation and commerce between northern cities and allowed the rise of an irrigation agriculture that for a long time was one of the richest and most advanced in Europe. But things were different in the rest of Italy, particularly where water did not manifest itself as rivers that could be used as a source of mechanical power or to fill irrigation canals. Thus, in many areas, water came to be regarded as an obstacle to progress and, in some cases, an outright enemy, especially in the nineteenth century, when the expansion of capitalist agriculture began to transform the Italian countryside.

Possibly the most remarkable case in the history of environmental modifications in nineteenth-century Italy was the draining of Lake Fucino, in Abruzzo.[11] This body of water covering 155 square kilometers was the third-largest lake in Italy. Surrounded by a necklace of mountains, it was a place of exceptional beauty. Then between 1862 and 1875 a private citizen, Prince Alessandro Torlonia, had the lake completely drained to exploit its bed for agricultural purposes. The basin of the former lake is today the Fucino Plain, an industrial agriculture area. The draining of the lake meant the end of fishing and generations of fishermen and of the many plants and trees that used to prosper along its shores. The climate changed too: it is now colder in the winter and hotter and drier in the summer.

In both the north and south of Italy, the purpose of land reclamation works (or bonifica) was always to drain watercourses or divert them away from the countryside. In vast areas of the Po Plain—for example, in the Ferrara and Modena area—and in the delta, the draining frenzy grew so intense that even the engineers in charge of land reclamation operations must have realized the flaws of this approach.[12] Drained lands soon turned into drought-prone farmland parched by the sun in the summer and lacking water for irrigation.

In the Maremma, a marshy, coastal region in central-western Italy (especially in Tuscany), a crudely productivist mentality and the fear of malaria led to the indiscriminate draining of ponds, cutting down of bushes, and leveling of dunes. Habitats that had arisen spontaneously over thousands of years were thus transformed into agricultural land.[13] The most dramatic example of this strategy, which was to have a heavy impact on the natural habitats of the Italian peninsula, was certainly the reclaiming of the Pontine Marshes, southeast of Rome.[14] During the 1930s under the Fascist regime,[15] this vast and ancient forestland—dotted with lakes, springs, watercourses, and clearings and peopled with a variety of animals and plants—was almost completely drained and leveled, to be replaced with villages, roads, fields, and several new towns, such as Latina. The only surviving relics of this ancient wetland forest, known as "Selva di Terracina," are Circeo Lake and Circeo Park. Although much of this drained coastal area became valuable agricultural land, a rich biological heritage was lost forever.

Deforestation

Deforestation has been extensively practiced in all European countries. Throughout the modern age, as populations grew and grain prices rose, farmers increased cultivable surface by cutting down forests. This phenomenon intensified markedly in the late eighteenth and nineteenth centuries, when the European population grew considerably and the expansion of world markets caused a hike in grain prices. Deforestation affected all of Europe, but it had especially dramatic effects in Italy, where, as we have seen, the erosion of mountains had an immediate impact on the plains below.[16] Particularly in southern Italy, where the Apennines run very close to the coastal plains, the effects of erosion were aggravated by a lack of space for depositing the eroded material. As a consequence, settlements in the plains were hit by especially severe landslides and mudslides. Settlements on slopes were also affected. In the eighteenth and nineteenth centuries, whole villages crumbled downhill, sweeping away everything in their path. But erosion was not the only negative effect of deforestation. Besides protecting slopes from erosion, forests also turn mountains into water reservoirs. When it rains or snows, both the trees and the undergrowth soak up water like sponges. The water they absorb trickles deep into the mountain and runs along subterranean paths, to reemerge as springs farther downhill. When slopes lack vegetation, however, water flows downhill immediately and violently and is lost into the sea, without forming springs or watercourses that local people might harness. Tree cutting therefore destroyed land as well as water resources.

Deforestation had long-lasting effects on the settlements and econo-mies of the Po Plain. People living there had been exposed to disastrous floods for many years. Even the population of the Po Plain was not spared. In 1951, a memorable flood of the Po River claimed lives among the popu-lation of the Polesine Delta area and caused severe damages.[17] The Po has overflowed again twice in recent years (in 1994 and 2000). Equally memorable and disastrous was the flood of the Arno River that submerged much of Florence in 1966.[18] These inundations, however, had causes dif-ferent from those of southern Italy, which were often the result of human manipulation of mountain slopes. In these southern regions, many floods followed by landslides wreaked havoc among villages in Campania, Basili-cata, and Calabria, especially during the 1950s and 1960s.

To sum up, for over a century, deforestation was one of the main causes of the disruption of the environmental balance in the Italian pen-insula. This was because it impacted one of the historically most fragile parts of the Italian territory, the Apennine Mountains, which are affected by intense erosion and often stand very close to the plains below.

Over the last decades, in spite of the reforestation carried out in the second half of the twentieth century, floods and landslides have continued to cause damage and claim victims in the Italian peninsula. According to data supplied by the European Commission for Research, floods killed more people in Italy than in any other European country between 1980 and 2002: Italy accounted for 38 percent of the European total, followed by Spain (at 20 percent). Italy is also the country that suffered the most damage, on a par with Germany (at 11 billion euros).[19]

What accounts for this grim primacy? The answer lies partly in the history I have outlined so far. But there are other reasons as well. In recent decades, millions of Italian farmers have abandoned the hills of the interior. Through their presence and work, these farmers had guaranteed constant maintenance of the land. The many sharecroppers living in the countryside in the central strip of the peninsula acted as a sort of filter for intercepting the waters flowing from the Apennines down to the lowlands. These people rebuilt ditch and torrent banks, diverted dangerous watercourses, repaired walls, protected the vegetation, and planted trees and bushes. Today, those farmers are gone, and the vast hilly areas of the interior are depopulated. The population now is concentrated at the bottoms of valleys and along the coast, near the mouths of the innumerable rivers and torrents that crisscross the peninsula. Because of settlement expansion, houses now stand dangerously near to riverbanks. In a country plagued with illegal building, urban sprawl now extends even onto the floodplains of rivers. And "cementification" also robs the land of soil capable of absorbing water during heavy and prolonged rainfall. Thus, during storms—which have become increasingly frequent and violent in recent years—rainwater has little ground to soak into, and hence easily produces disastrous floods that sweep away people and materials.

Industrial Pollution

Italy did not suffer the shock of industrial and mining pollution that hit Great Britain, Germany, and Belgium in the nineteenth century. The peninsula lacked coal, an essential—but highly polluting—resource for industrial growth. Furthermore, Italy's industrialization was late and slow. Until World War I, the most important sector was silk manufacturing, a low-environmental-impact textile industry. Although we know little of the polluting effects of this industry and of health conditions in nineteenth-century Italian factories, there were certainly few polluting industrial centers back then, and their impact was restricted to a local scale. There were, however, polluting sulfur mines in Sicily and iron mines on the island of Elba. Later on, during the twentieth century, Sardinia suffered the polluting effects of mining lead and zinc in the Iglesiente and coal in the Sulcis. The ironworks and mechanical industries of Genoa and Naples, as well as the paper mills of Isola Liri, certainly had a major environmental impact even before the unification of Italy. Ironworks use a lot of water, and even today, paper production is a highly polluting industrial process. Ever since 1884, the main center of the Italian steel and iron industry has been the Società Altiforni Fonderie e Acciaierie in Terni.[20] Contemporary or later ironworks included those of Piombino, Savona, and the Bagnoli neighborhood in Naples. The history of the environmental transformation of those areas is yet to be written, as is that of environmental impacts of the early twentieth-century Italian chemical industry, mainly fertilizer and rubber plants, along with cement factories.

The environmental consequences of Italian industrial growth became especially dramatic in the second half of the twentieth century. The most affected area was the triangle between Milan, Turin, and Genoa, which is the historical core of Italian industry where most of the country's chemicals, steel, and iron are produced.[21] Historians have yet to reconstruct the effects of heavy industry on this area. In southern Italy, too, chemical industry and petroleum refineries—often located near fragile natural habitats, as in the case of the industrial areas of Taranto, Brindisi, Siracuse, and Sardinia's Porto Torres—have defaced long stretches of the coastline and polluted the sea. The tanning industry deserves separate mention. By the end of the twentieth century, Italy had about three thousand small tanning factories, mostly concentrated in Veneto, Tuscany, and Campania.[22] This small-scale production has had a major environmental impact, mainly in the form of chemical contamination of the water. This contamination, however, appears to have been reduced today thanks to the cooperative use of purification plants and greater public control of industrial waste.

It was the Seveso incident, in Lombardy, that first gave rise to a national awareness of the environmental impact of industrial production and the threat it posed to public health.[23] In July 1976, a vast toxic cloud rose above the roofs of Seveso, Meda, and other nearby small towns, originating from the ICMESA factory, owned by the Swiss company Hofmann La Roche, which officially produced perfumes and deodorants. But that cloud contained dioxin, a dangerous chemical agent. It was the first time that the Italian population had heard the name. After days of inertia and uncertainty following hundreds of domestic animal deaths in the Seveso area, the whole population was evacuated. Many people, especially children, contracted chloracne, an unusual skin disease, and there was an increase in spontaneous abortions. The incident put the spotlight not only on industrial risk but also on the deceit and intrigue whereby certain productive activities were kept secret from the population, violating national autonomy. What was dioxin doing in a perfume factory?[24]

In the early 1980s, public alarm was raised again when contaminated mud discharged by the Montedison factory of Porto Marghera in the Adriatic Sea caused an extensive proliferation of algae along the coast of Romagna.[25] This new environmental emergency drew attention to the vulnerability of the marine habitat to the uncontrolled industrial discharge of chemical waste, as well as the other forms of pollution discussed in the pages that follow. But the Montedison factory—a constant threat to the Venetian lagoon—was implicated in a much more serious pollution case. In the Enichem and Montedison plants, a chemical compound called polyvinyl chloride (PVC) contaminated both the sea (probably entering the food chain) and workers who were more directly exposed to the substance. An investigation started in the early 1990s proved that there was a connection between the spread of various diseases among workers and the polluting effects of PVC.[26] In 2001, in an important trial held at Mestre, 28 managers of the incriminated companies were absolved on the grounds that, at the time of contamination, negligence in PVC control was not a legal offense, in spite of the fact that 546 workers had suffered diseases, of whom some 200 had tumors. The appeal of 2004, however, reversed the sentence: the judges pronounced the managers guilty. Five were sentenced, but the rest were set free due to the lapse of time.

As with most industrial countries, Italy also has a tragic history of asbestos pollution.[27] It is a very dangerous type of pollution because it affects a very large area and continues to kill people even after its removal. In the second half of the twentieth century, asbestos rapidly found widespread application, especially for making the "asbestos concrete" used in roofs of industrial sheds, buildings, drop ceilings, and so on. It was eventually discovered that the dust produced by crumbling asbestos has devastating effects on the human respiratory system. To inhale even tiny quantities of asbestos dust is sufficient to bring on, even decades later, an incurable disease called asbestosis, which affects respiratory capacity. Workers in plants where asbestos was used also contracted a new type of tumor, mesothelioma, which attacks the pleura and inevitably leads to death. In places such as Casale Monferrato, where the Eternit factory was located, and Balangero, the site of the largest asbestos quarry in Europe, both in the Piedmont region, asbestos-related deaths have been reported down to this day, not just among former workers in these facilities but also among people who simply happened to live near the polluted sites. Today, many affected families are seeking reparations for the harm they suffered and for the deaths of their loved ones in several pending trials.

Asbestos was banned in 1992, but the large-scale decontamination operation started years ago is still not completed. At least fifty dangerous industrial sites still need to be cleaned up.[28] The story of asbestos in Italy carries a grim warning: many technological inventions only reveal their harmful potential over time and may eventually have disastrous effects on human health.

There is, of course, far more to the geography and history of industrial pollution in Italy than what I have outlined so far. It is important to stress that, as a reaction to these tragedies and thanks to the struggles of environmental organizations such as the Italian section of the WWF and Legambiente—and sometimes even labor unions—European legislation has increased and public control of pollution has become much stricter since the mid-1990s. Furthermore, technical advances now allow industry to employ smaller quantities of toxic substances, while limiting waste and disposing of refuse and emissions more efficiently. Still, industrial waste has been increasing steadily in Italy as well as in the rest of Europe. In 2002 alone, Italy produced over 92 million tons of industrial waste, 5 million of which were classified as hazardous (in 1997, it was 3.4 million tons of hazardous waste out of a total of just under 61 million tons).[29] And Italy still systematically lags behind when it comes to complying with European legislation, especially in regard to waste disposal, not to speak of cases where the law is eluded altogether.[30]

Seas, Rivers, and Water

The Italian peninsula extends right into the middle of the Mediterranean and is thus extraordinarily well positioned for access to the sea. Almost eight thousand kilometers of coastline, some of incomparable beauty, together with a temperate climate, mild water temperatures, and a rich marine biology, make Italy an enviable country. Besides fishing and aquaculture, Italian seas support a flourishing tourist industry. Still, over the centuries, the Italian ruling class and populations, far from safeguarding this priceless heritage, have actually launched an attack on it. The coast and sometimes even beaches have become the sites of vacation houses, villas, and hotels, mostly built in the second half of the twentieth century. The Versilia region is an especially eloquent example. As Antonio Cederna, a pioneer of Italian environmentalism, noted in 1975, over thirty kilometers of Italy's most beautiful coastlines had been transformed "into a squalid, continuous, linear, and shapeless town."[31] But the worst was yet to come. Along some of the most charming littorals of Sicily and Calabria, houses were built right on the rocks at the water's edge. Many coastal areas in Sardinia met the same fate. By 1985, according to a WWF investigation, only a thousand kilometers of the island's coastline were still preserved in their original state. All the rest had been modified or often completely destroyed.[32] With the exception of some developing countries, such as Lithuania and Slovenia, Italy witnessed a higher percentage of urban growth along its coastline from 1975 to 1990 (25.8 percent) than any other European country.

This disruption of the coastal environmental balance has had a heavy impact on the marine habitat. The increase in population has brought an increase in sewage, as well as the loss of beaches, dunes, and littorals. The replacement of beaches with buildings has exacerbated erosion, one of the most serious threats in the coastal environment. Erosion actually depends on other causes as well. One is the alteration of watercourses. In addition, the damming of rivers, the digging of their banks for sand, increased quarrying, and the cementification of banks have all reduced the quantity of silt that actually reaches the sea. Since less sand is washed onto beaches, coasts are less protected against marine erosion. By 2001, according to estimates of the "Eurosion" European investigation, about 2,349 kilometers of the Italian coastline were affected by erosive processes of varying degrees of intensity.[33]

As for Italian rivers, instead of bringing protection and life to seawater, they have been dumping poison into it for decades. First and foremost is Italy's largest watercourse, the Po, which runs through a highly industrialized area collecting the discharges of an uncontrolled intensive agriculture based on chemicals. The Po alone discharges into the Adriatic an estimated 40 percent of the waters of all the Italian territory. The phosphorus and nitrogen it dumps into the sea have led to extensive eutrophication, that is, the abnormal proliferation of algae that consume oxygen and cause the death of fish and flora.[34] The case of the Po stands out, but all Italian rivers, with the exception of the Tagliamento and a few others, are more or less polluted, and their natural basins have been modified, their floodbeds encroached upon by buildings, their urban stretches enclosed in concrete, and so forth.

The national government and European authorities have been trying to find legislative solutions to this state of things. In the late 1970s, EC Directive 78/659 imposed continuous monitoring of the quality of fresh water. The Italian administration, however, never applied the directive. A more systematic legislative effort was an Italian national law (Legge Merli) of 10 May 1976 (with later amendments).[35] The Merli Law provided for organic action in pollution prevention, discipline in waste disposal, and establishing a region-by-region "national plan for the sanitization of water." A later law (of 18 May 1989) on soil protection had the virtue of taking into consideration the full water cycle (collection, distribution, consumption, purification, recycling, and so on) and, even more important, of defining so-called hydrographic basins, that is, the areas where rivers across the national territory are formed and flow. Finally, EC Directive 2000/60 has provided an organic legislative framework for the protection of water, establishing the important principle that "water is not a commercial product like any other but, rather, a heritage to be protected, defended and treated as such."[36]

In spite of this rapid and fruitful legislative evolution, the freshwater situation in Italy is not ideal. Paradoxically, the country is rich in hydraulic resources, both superficial and subterranean. According to certain estimates late in 1990, the overall hydraulic balance is some 296 billion square meters a year, 44 percent of which is lost to evaporation.[37] In spite of this large quantity, a good deal of drinkable water destined for urban consumption is lost along the way for a number of reasons, including outdated aqueducts. And many towns and villages, especially in the south, suffer from water scarcity during the summer.

Towns and the Defacing of the Land

The distinctive characteristics of the Italian environment I have briefly outlined have not helped to spread the love of nature or environmental awareness among Italians. Threatened by earthquakes, volcanic eruptions, and malaria and exposed to floods and landslides, the people of the

Italian peninsula have traditionally seen the natural world more as a threat to humans than as being threatened by humans. Furthermore, unlike what happened in Germany and elsewhere, Italy's belated industrialization did not have a violent and sudden impact on its territory and environment and hence did not elicit protest and recrimination among the population, politicians, and intellectuals. Nor did the country's long history contribute to the rise of an appreciation of the natural world in its collective conscience.

Already in the late Middle Ages, if not before, Italian civilization was largely urban: although the majority of the population was (and would have long been) rural, Dante's land was an urban place when judged by nodes of power, diffusion of culture, and economic control of the countryside. The whole territory of the peninsula was dotted with towns. Landowners preferred to make their homes in the city, and they looked disparagingly at the countryside, which they regarded as an inferior social and environmental reality, to be exploited for its wealth but not worthy of inhabiting. Nature, even the domesticated nature of the countryside, was to bow to the needs of the owner and the requirements of the urban market. Rarely and only in certain limited contexts was nature experienced as a reality unto itself, to be protected against encroaching towns and urban economies.

This specificity of the Italian people's environmental awareness—or lack thereof—did not have noticeable effects on the environment at least until the early twentieth century. Thereafter, however, and especially in the second half of the century, Italy's lack of environmental awareness became one of the main causes for some the country's most serious environmental problems.[38] As the urbanist Antonio Cederna remarked, Italian heritage laws, such as the one of 29 June 1939, ignored nature and environmental protection.[39] Even the 1948 Constitution of the Italian Republic—one of the most politically and socially advanced constitutions in the world—does not mention the safeguarding of natural heritage as such. Unlike the constitutions of many other countries, from Germany to Portugal and from Switzerland to Czechoslovakia, the Italian constitution "protects the landscape and historical artistic heritage of the nation" (art. 9) but not nature as a living reality, as wild animals, plants, water, and woods.[40] In other words, it acknowledges the existence of nature and judges it worthy of protection only when it seems to be endowed with aesthetic worth, that is, when it takes the form of a landscape attractive to people. If this conception was the best that Italy's elite (who wrote the constitution) could come up with, one can easily imagine what attitudes toward nature the rest of Italians held.

What happened to the Italian environment after the 1950s is unparalleled in other European countries. In those years, especially during the so-called economic miracle, and until the 1980s, the Italian territory was subjected to the most dramatic and widespread period of modification in its long history. As I mentioned earlier, those years witnessed a new and more intensive industrialization process, generating demand for more factory sites, ports, and railroads. The automobile industry grew at an amazing rate, resulting in the construction of a network of highways extending across the peninsula, so that today, bridges, viaducts, and tunnels run through mountains and alongside Apennine villages, putting their mark on previously bucolic habitats.[41] Those years also saw an unprecedented demographic growth and internal migration. The northern regions, where industrial growth was more intensive, drew people from the south, as well as from the rural areas of every Italian region. The demand for houses and services kept growing from year to year. It was in this phase of Italian history that the country's territory—first and foremost in the cities—was subjected to unlimited and unregulated exploitation. Towns, where the demand for housing offered construction contractors a sure profit, were turned into immense building sites. The urban plans whereby municipalities tried to manage urban growth were approved only after inexcusable delays by the central administration, and systematically eluded or violated at the local level. The traditional urban fabric of some towns, including Rome and Naples—already compromised by the urban politics of the Fascist period—was seriously damaged, and vast urban green areas were destroyed. Huge suburbs sprang up practically overnight. They frequently lacked services, and buildings were often packed so close together that they robbed their tenants of sunlight. At the end of this building frenzy, Italian towns found themselves with one of the lowest ratios of urban green per capita in Europe. By the end of the 1970s, no town had more that 3 square meters of green per capita; nothing compared to the 30 to 40 square meters of Holland, Great Britain, and the Scandinavian countries. In Naples, the ratio was as low as 0.5 square meters per capita; in Palermo, it was even less: 0.3 square meters.[42]

Uncontrolled urban expansion was soon followed by a new phenomenon, that of illegal building. Private individuals began to erect houses without any authorization whatsoever in the most diverse locations—on beaches, along the banks of rivers, on hilltops, inside natural parks, and in historical centers. Irreparable damage was thus inflicted on Italy's landscape and urban heritage. Furthermore, this misuse of the territory has made the country increasingly vulnerable to floods.

Today, there is no urban planning strategy to protect or manage the growth of Italian cities, whose greatest current problem is automobile traffic. According to the Organization for Economic Cooperation and

Development (OECD) data from the end of the last century, Italy has one of the highest ratios of cars per capita in the world: 53 cars for every 100 inhabitants, as compared with 51 in Germany, 50 in Great Britain, 49 in the United States, 44 in France, and 37 in Japan.[43] Only a few small historical towns, such as Siena, Orvieto, Perugia, and Taormina, have succeeded in banning or limiting automobile traffic within their perimeters. All the others are choking on smog that keeps increasing, damaging people's health and architectural heritage, while traffic becomes slower and more chaotic every year and cars take over streets, plazas, and spaces that once belonged to human beings.

Notes

1. Data from Emanuela Guidoboni, "Un'antirisorsa del Sud: I disastri sismici nella sfida economica," in *Ambiente e risorse nel Mezzogiorno contemporaneo,* ed. Piero Bevilacqua and Gabriella Corona (Corigliano Calabro: Meridiana Libri, 2000), 245–61.

2. Emanuela Guidoboni, Graziano Ferrari, Dante Mariotti, Alberto Comastri, Gabriele Tarabusi, and Gianluca Valensise, *CFTI4 MED: Catalogue of Strong Earthquakes in Italy 461 BC–1997 and Mediterranean Area 760 BC–1500—An Advanced Laboratory of Historical Seismology,* 2007, Istituto Nazionale di Geofisica e Vulcanologia, available at http://storing.ingv.it/cfti4med/ (accessed 5 June 2009).

3. Emanuela Guidoboni focuses on earthquakes in her essay in this volume.

4. On the hydrography of Italy, see Piero Bevilacqua, "Le rivoluzioni dell'acqua: Irrigazioni e trasformazioni dell'agricoltura tra Sette e Novecento," in *Storia dell'agricoltura italiana in età contemporanea,* vol. 1, *Spazi e paesaggi,* ed. Piero Bevilacqua (Venice: Marsilio, 1989), 255–318.

5. On Italian wildlife, see Ministero dell'Ambiente e della Tutela del Territorio, *La fauna in Italia* (Milan: TCI, 2002); on birds in marsh environments, see particularly pp. 198–203.

6. Walter Palmieri discusses this issue more thoroughly in his essay.

7. Ministero dell'Ambiente, *Classificazione dei comuni italiani in base al livello di attenzione per il rischio idrogeologico* (Rome: Servizio per la difesa del territorio, 2000), 20, available at http://www2.minambiente.it/pdf_www2/pubblicazioni/monografie/rischio_idrogeologico.pdf (accessed 19 August 2009).

8. It is impossible to quote the impressive quantity of studies on Italian malaria. Among others, see Franco Bonelli, "La malaria nella storia demografica ed economica d'Italia: Primi lineamenti di una ricerca," *Studi Storici* 4, no. 4 (1966): 659–88; Paola Corti, "Malaria e società contadina nel Mezzogiorno," in *Storia d'Italia,* Annale 7, *Malattia e medicina,* ed. Franco Della Peruta (Turin: Einaudi,

1984), 635–78; Frank M. Snowden, *The Conquest of Malaria: Italy, 1900–1962* (New Haven, CT: Yale University Press, 2006). For a worldwide overview on malaria, see James L. A. Webb, Jr., *Humanity's Burden: A Global History of Malaria* (New York: Cambridge University Press, 2009). On malaria, see Marcus Hall's contribution to this volume.

9. Angelo Celli and John Eyre, *Malaria According to the New Researches* (New York: Longmans and Green, 1905), 17.

10. On land reclamation and deforestation in Southern Italy, I may refer to my book *Breve storia dell'Italia meridionale* (Rome: Donzelli, 1993), 32–38, 127–32.

11. Sergio Raimondo is the author of an excellent environmental history of Fucino Lake: *La risorsa che non c'è più: Il lago del Fucino dal XVI al XIX secolo* (Manduria: P. Lacaita, 2000).

12. On reclamation in the Po Plain, see Franco Cazzola, *Storia delle campagne padane dall'Ottocento a oggi* (Milan: Bruno Mondadori, 1996); Giorgio Porisini, *Bonifiche e agricoltura nella bassa Valle Padana* (Milan: Banca Commerciale Italiana, 1978).

13. Piero Bevilacqua and Manlio Rossi Doria, "Lineamenti per una storia delle bonifiche in Italia dal XVIII al XX secolo," in *Storia delle bonifiche in Italia dal '700 a oggi,* ed. Bevilacqua and Rossi Doria (Rome: Laterza, 1984), 17–28.

14. Ibid., 28–35; Snowden, *Conquest of Malaria,* 142–80; Salvatore Lupo, *Il Fascismo: La politica di un regime totalitario* (Rome: Donzelli, 2005), 349–58.

15. On the Fascist regime, see Wilko Graf von Hardenberg and Luigi Piccioni in this volume.

16. Forests and deforestation have been the main topics in Italian environmental historiography; therefore we have abundant studies on these issues. Among others are Mauro Agnoletti, "Osservazioni sulle dinamiche dei boschi e del paesaggio forestale italiano fra il 1862 e la fine del secolo XX," *Società e storia* 108 (2005); Marco Armiero, *Il territorio come risorsa: Comunità, economie e istituzioni nei boschi abruzzesi (1806–1860)* (Naples: Liguori, 1999); Antonio Lazzarini, ed., *Diboscamento montano e politiche territoriali: Alpi e Appennini dal Settecento al Duemila* (Milan: Franco Angeli, 2002); Pietro Tino, "La montagna meridionale: Boschi, uomini, economie tra Otto e Novecento," in *Storia dell'agricoltura italiana in età contemporanea,* vol. 1, *Spazi e paesaggi,* ed. Piero Bevilacqua (Venice: Marsilio, 1989), 677–754; Bruno Vecchio, *Il bosco negli scrittori italiani del Settecento e dell'età napoleonica* (Turin: Einaudi, 1974).

17. On the 1951 Polesine flood, see Gian Antonio Cibotto, *Cronache dell'alluvione: Polesine 1951* (Venice: Marsilio, 1998).

18. On the 1966 Florence flood there are several resources available online. Italian Public Television dedicated a documentary to it: (http://www.lastoriasiamonoi

.rai.it/puntata.aspx?id=248); other information is available at http://www.mega.it/
allu/ (accessed 19 August 2009). In English, see Franco Nencini, *Florence: The Days of the Flood* (London: Allen and Unwin, 1967).

19. European Commission, Research Directorate-General, Directorate I—Environment, "Floods: European Research for Better Predictions and Management Solutions, Dresden, 13 October 2003," available at http://ec.europa.eu/research/environment/pdf/ec_research_floods_dresden_en.pdf (accessed 19 August 2009).

20. On the Società Altiforni Fonderie e Acciaierie, see Augusto Ciuffetti, *Condizioni materiali di vita, sanità e malattie in un centro industriale: Terni 1880–1940* (Naples: Edizioni Scientifiche Italiane, 1996).

21. On the history of industrial pollution in Italy, see Salvatore Adorno and Simone Neri Serneri, eds., *Industria, ambiente e territorio: Per una storia ambientale delle aree industriali in Italia* (Bologna: Il Mulino, 2009); Bruno Dente and Pippo Ranci, eds. *L'industria e l'ambiente* (Bologna: Il Mulino, 1992).

22. Franco Foggi, ed., *Nel segno di Saturno: Origini e sviluppo dell'attività conciaria a Santa Croce sull'Arno,* vol. 1 (Pisa: Cassa di Risparmio di Pisa, 1985) and vol. 2 (Florence: Alinea, 1987); Roberto Pastena, *Strumenti di controllo operaio sulla novità ambientale e sulla salute nelle concerie di Solofra* (Naples: n.p., 1987).

23. The Seveso disaster is addressed by Laura Centemeri in this volume. On Seveso, see also Laura Conti, *Visto da Seveso: L'evento straordinario e l'ordinaria amministrazione* (Milan: Feltrinelli, 1977); and Laura Centemeri, *Ritorno a Seveso: Il danno ambientale, il suo riconoscimento, la sua riparazione* (Milan: Bruno Mondadori, 2006).

24. According to some investigators, the ICMESA chemicals were relayed through Switzerland to the United States, where they were used to produce the defoliant Agent Orange, employed by the American army to destroy large sections of Vietnam's forest during the 1960s. This hypothesis is supported in Daniele Biacchessi, *La fabbrica dei profumi: La verità su Seveso, l'ICMESA, la diossina* (Milan: Baldini & Castoldi, 1995). According to Laura Centemeri, this thesis has never been proven or disproven; see Centemeri, *Ritorno a Seveso,* 183.

25. Fabrizio Fabbri, *Porto Marghera e la laguna di Venezia* (Milan: Jaca Book, 2003), 95–97.

26. On Marghera and the trial, see Gianfranco Bettin and Maurizio Danese, *Petrolkiller* (Milan: Feltrinelli, 2002); Felice Casson, *La fabbrica dei veleni* (Milan: Sperling and Kupfer, 2007); Paolo Rabitti, *Cronache della chimica: Marghera e le altre* (Naples: Cuen, 1998).

27. On asbestos contamination in Italy, see Martino Maria Rizzo, *Ambiente e salute* (Trento: UNI service, 2008), 11–60; some information on asbestosis is

also in Saverio Luzzi, *Salute e sanità nell'Italia repubblicana* (Rome: Donzelli, 2004), 72.

28. Piero Bevilacqua, *La Terra è finita: Breve storia dell'ambiente* (Rome: Laterza, 2006), 181.

29. Data from Agenzia per la Protezione dell'Ambiente e dei Servizi Tecnici and Osservatorio Nazionale sui Rifiuti available at http://www.apat.gov. it/site/_contentfiles/00138200/138219_ComunicatoRapportoRifiuti_2004.pdf (accessed 19 August 2009).

30. Marina Castellaneta, "Italia maglia nera Ue per le infrazioni verdi," *Sole 24 Ore*, 14 August 2009, 22. A case study on the intervention of the European Union in Italian environmental policies is in Marco Armiero, "Seeing Like a Protester: Nature, Power, and Environmental Struggles," *Left History* 13, no. 1 (2008): 59–76.

31. Antonio Cederna, *La distruzione della natura in Italia* (Turin: Einaudi, 1975), 31.

32. Fulco Pratesi, *Storia della natura in Italia* (Rome: Editori Riuniti, 2001), 184.

33. Data from "Eurosion: A European Initiative for Sustainable Coastal Erosion Management" available at http://www.eurosion.org/index.html (accessed 4 April 2009). At the same Web site there is a concise explanation of the project: "EUROSION is a project commissioned by the General Directorate Environment of the European Commission, which was won by a consortium led by the National Institute for Coastal and Marine Management of the Dutch Ministry of Transport, Public Works and Water Management."

34. Bernard Kayser, "Il Mediterraneo: Geografia della frattura," in *Il Mediterraneo: Economia e sviluppo: Enciclopedia tematica aperta,* ed. Centro de Estudios Internacionales de Barcelona (Milan: Jaca Book, 2001), 25.

35. Francesco Mantelli and Giorgio Temporelli, *L'acqua nella storia* (Milan: Franco Angeli, 2008), 145; 205–8.

36. "Directive 2000/60/ EC of the European Parliament and of the Council of 23 October 2000 establishing a framework for Community action in the field of water policy," *Official Journal L 327,* 22 December 2000, art. 1, available at http://ec.europa.eu/environment/water/water-framework/index_en.html (accessed 19 August 2009).

37. Paolo De Castro, "La gestione in Italia delle risorse idriche," *Silvae* 6 (2006): 1. At that time the author was minister of agriculture.

38. On environmental movements, see Luigi Piccioni's essay in this volume.

39. Cederna, *La distruzione della natura,* 5.

40. For a comparison among constitutions in Europe see Domenico Amirante, ed., *Diritto ambientale e costituzione: Esperienze europee* (Milan: Franco Angeli, 2000).

41. On automobiles, see Federico Paolini, *Un paese a quattro ruote: Automobili e società in Italia* (Venice: Marsilio, 2005), and *Storia sociale dell'automobile in Italia* (Rome: Carocci, 2007).

42. Cederna, *La distruzione della natura,* 28.

43. Ministero dell'Ambiente, *Relazione sullo stato dell'ambiente* (Rome: Tipografia la Piramide, 2001), 205.

CHAPTER 2

Upside-Down Landscapes

Seismicity and Seismic Disasters in Italy

Emanuela Guidoboni

> La storia non è fatta da chi la pensa e neppure da chi la ignora.
>
> [History is made neither by those who think about it nor by those who ignore it.]
>
> —Eugenio Montale, *Satura I*

PROBLEMS LINKED to the environment are generally regarded as being visible or predictable: they concern the uses of the landscape, its transformations, the economic exploitation of the lands or waters, and even lifestyles and visions of economic development. But the environment is not only the result of what can be seen or planned. There are also hidden geological features, such as the ones that cause earthquakes and strongly influence the inhabited world. We have no direct perception of this underground landscape (located from a few to a dozen kilometers beneath the earth's crust); we have only indirect knowledge of it, and a distorted knowledge at that. Our knowledge of earthquakes is constructed partly by way of the effects that shape our inhabited surface world and partly by way of various types of instrumental data that reveal different aspects of the phenomenon. The earthquake landscape can be defined as *subterranean* and hence only partially perceived, not only because earthquakes originate underground but also because various social and cultural norms tend to ignore (or underestimate) them as ever-present features of the inhabited countryside.

Earthquakes are wholly natural, frequent phenomena of life on earth, at times turning into disasters that trigger economic and social crises or harm the lifestyles and livelihoods of the people affected by them. However, the relationship between earthquakes and disasters is equivocal, as multiple preexisting economic, social, and cultural factors combine to form a "disaster" as such. Because of their geographic diffusion, their frequency, and the sheer scope of the damage they cause, earthquakes represent one of the least understood aspects of Italy's environment in terms of the relationship between human society and the natural environment.

To date, Italian academic historiography has not turned earthquakes into a research topic, but over the past twenty years historical research has become an important component in the science of seismology. Interestingly, scientific questions were the motivation for bringing history into play in seismology. Earthquake science requires a record of events occurring over long periods in order to identify active seismic areas and to predict possible future magnitudes. The data now available for Italy date back some two thousand years (with sporadic information from earlier periods); their quality and frequency are rather variable, depending on the places and periods. Consequently, indirect information about earthquakes that historians have traditionally neglected is now being uncovered: descriptions of early building types, ruins, collapses, reconstructions, abandonments, social and economic trends, and administrative and political responses involving both local inhabitants and distant governments. Earthquakes have given rise to a new discipline, one that poses new questions arising from freshly unearthed archival information. Through such research, ancient and medieval seismic landscapes are emerging from obscurity. Today, we certainly have a much better understanding of earthquakes and their impact on human history, especially in Italy.

The Birth of a New Discipline: Historical Seismology

For centuries, scholars and literati have taken an interest in ancient and medieval earthquakes, and during the last two centuries, seismologists and geologists have also turned to earthquake history. But only since the late 1980s has this field emerged as a new discipline, now known as historical seismology, founded and developed on the ideas and research methodologies of historians today. Three factors have contributed to the development of this new field: (1) seismologists' demand for long-term earthquake data (instrumental data have registered only twenty or so mid- to large-sized earthquakes in Italy over the past few decades); (2) the systematic identification and cataloging of thousands of earthquakes in Italy, starting from the fifth century BC; and (3) the identification and availability of resources adequate for such research.

In the systematic historical study of past earthquakes, it is impossible to ignore the particular viewpoint of the earth sciences, just as it is impossible to use traditional historical methods (another reason for developing a new field). It has required the establishment of specialized research groups and the capacity to store and manage the data in specific databases. Scientific issues have also stimulated different uses of the historical sources, challenging the anthropocentric vision that characterizes a great deal of environmental history in Italy.

The goal of historical seismology is to retrieve, interpret, and assess, in various cultural and economic contexts, written sources attesting to the occurrence and the effects (at all levels) of the earthquakes of the past.[1] Through the analysis of qualitative data, it is possible to delineate areas affected by earthquakes even in the very remote past. Like the pieces of a mosaic, the territorial image of an earthquake is made up of a set of numerous descriptive elements: at some times, thousands of pieces of information contribute to our understanding, while at others, only a few disjointed data sources are available. Hence, the design of the mosaic may be quite detailed, or it may remain quite patchy. Yet preserving even a few traces of an earthquake, which otherwise would be lost, is nonetheless an important step forward.

The indispensable quantitative parameters are calculated on the basis of elaborated qualitative elements: the chronology of the event in universal time (an earthquake is nearly always a set of complex shock sequences) together with the intensity of the effects in various geo-referenced sites. Starting from this network of classified sites, the epicenters are localized by means of specific methods of calculation, and magnitude equivalent (Me) values can be assigned. The calculation procedures available today also localize the seismic event to a fault zone that probably generated it. Active faults in Italy are not usually visible from the surface. The parameters are critical because they allow us to classify and compare earthquakes across space and time, pinpoint active faults, and improve our knowledge of the ongoing seismogenetic processes.[2] This specialized seismic historical research has given rise to a new generation of earthquake catalogs[3] maintained on databases and managed by so-called geographical information systems (GISs), now available online.[4]

Sources and New Archival Pathways

Where do the thousands of pieces of information that underlie the numeric parameters of current earthquake catalogs come from? For the sake of simplicity, we can say that they stem from two great data sets: institutional sources (administrative, fiscal, and juridical, whether public, private, or ecclesiastical) and memorial sources (annals, chronicles, diaries, letters, and the like).[5] In fact, human memory and perception allow us to learn about earthquakes that occurred even in distant times and for which no other traceable source has survived. An abiding human desire to record and describe seismic events has provided valuable sources of information on the size and effects of earthquakes, their precursors, the duration of perceived shocks and long seismic sequences, the condition of buildings prior to the earthquake, the damage suffered, and many issues relating to human perception. Memorial sources also allow us to compare independent testimonies about the same event, corroborating other observations stemming from individual memory. These memorial sources are the hardest sources to use: as expressions of former times, they are for us moderns replete with puzzling or unfamiliar information that was recorded in very different cognitive and cultural contexts.

From the viewpoint of a historical seismologist, these earthquake testimonies can be considered a sort of "seismogram" to be decoded and understood. Since the 1980s, significant improvements have been made in our understanding of seismic effects, especially by resorting to "institutional memories" preserved in archives. Unlike sources produced by individuals, institutional sources record key elements of the economic impact of strong earthquakes on society in a relatively objective way. Such sources focus on administrative and financial activities, on communications between central and outlying administrations, and diplomatic correspondence between courts and their administrative centers across the territory. Ecclesiastical and monastic documents and annals are a particularly plentiful and thorough source of information.

The monastic annals are an irreplaceable source for learning about medieval earthquakes. Thanks to the extraordinary networks and exchanges that linked European Benedictine monks to Italy (the most important route to the Holy Land), European annals contain precious information about Italy's earthquakes. Moreover, records derived especially since the late Middle Ages reveal numerous administrative concerns that focus on reconstructing damaged monastic and ecclesiastical buildings with the help of tax exemptions and other incentives. From this broad range of records, direct and indirect information can be processed, interpreted, and then synthesized in subject-specific databases. Currently, over fifty thousand cataloged and archived historical sources provide a historical picture of Italy's seismicity, useful for both scholarly analysis and environmental protection.[6]

Earthquake history, when it talks with the earth sciences, has created a new disciplinary space. Combined with ongoing geological observations and instrument data, historical seismology has contributed to identifying seismic areas in Italy, to evaluating their potential magnitude, and to predicting the timing of future major quakes. Such contributions have had a real impact on the scientific world and on the demand for mitigating seismic hazards. This information can also offer new approaches to answering broader questions about human societies in relation to the natural world.

The Seismic Problem in Italy

How many earthquakes have indeed struck Italy? And where did they occur? According to our historical results, 257 strong seismic events have hit Italy since antiquity, with an intensity of at least VIII on the Mercalli-Cancani-Sieberg (MCS) scale, which is the level at which many buildings collapse, roughly equivalent to a magnitude of 5.5 or 6 on the Richter scale. Ninety-four of these quakes occurred before the seventeenth century. The relative scarcity of systematic information on seismic effects prior to the 1600s is due to both a loss of historical sources and a lack of usable sources. Interpreting the history of these medieval earthquakes also depends on the fact that their main chroniclers were monks and clergymen. As these observers focused on the ethical and religious aspects of human life, they showed a certain detachment from the concrete aftermath of an earthquake unless it had struck the monastery. Despite the ideological bias of the sources, however, many large medieval earthquakes have been reasonably well reconstructed, offering precious insight into historical seismicity, even when compared to the information available in such ancient civilizations such as China. Indeed, detailed records of China's earthquakes contained in the court annals can be used only after the thirteenth century.

To get a fairly realistic picture of earthquake frequency in Italy, we need only consider the last four centuries, the best-documented period in our records. The past four hundred years have recorded 162 strong earthquakes—an average of 41 per century, or one earthquake every two years. As the geological dynamics that determine seismic activity change only over millions of years, the earthquakes of the past few centuries are expressions of continuous seismic activity, meaning that this same activity can be expected in the future. The picture becomes more detailed if we consider the countrywide distribution of the effects, which is a way of outlining Italy's current earthquake geography. Earthquakes that have hit villages and cities are represented in maps according to classes of effects, starting from a "significant" level of damage (VII MCS degree). According

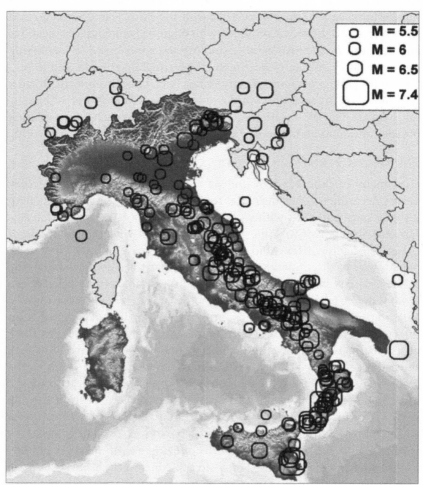

Map 2.1. Epicenters of strong earthquakes in Italy, AD 1000 to 2000, by class of magnitude. Some 238 events are known to be larger than Me 5.5. From Emanuela Guidoboni et al., *CFTI4 MED: Catalogue of Strong Earthquakes in Italy 461 B.C.–1997 and Mediterranean Area 760 B.C.–1500, An Advanced Laboratory of Historical Seismology*, http://storing.ingv.it/cfti4med/

to our research, there have been 5,975 seismic effects causing damage of the VII and VII–VIII degrees since antiquity, of which 4,174 were in towns and villages. Furthermore, 3,107 effects have been of the VIII and VIII–IX degrees, and 1,141 of the IX and X degrees. Up to 586 known seismic effects were of the most severe degrees, X and XI: so strong that they destroyed nearly every structure in the villages or cities affected at that level.

With regard to the number of the victims, there were around two hundred thousand in the twentieth century, more than eighty thousand of them caused by the 1908 earthquake and tsunami in the Messina Strait. In addition to the human fatalities and the destruction of buildings, one must also take into account migration, demographic decline, loss of productivity, and other unquantifiable factors, such as disrupted societies and the resulting loss of cultural identity; obliterated family and social ties; and widespread pain, distress, and upheaval.

Monetary costs incurred by Italy have been huge, and they are increasing. According to official Italian government statistics, from 1950 to the end of the twentieth century earthquake damage amounted to over 80 billion euros—about $100 billion, a figure not too far from the country's total gross national product (GNP) in those years. An additional problem has involved dealing with the management and distribution of relief funds.

Although Italy experiences more seismic events than just about any other Mediterranean country, most Italian earthquakes are of average to high intensity. Historically, those of Greece and Turkey have been more powerful. Nonetheless, Italy faces high seismic risk, as determined by the combination of seismic activity with economic and demographic factors. Italy's dense concentration of cultural and historical monuments heightens this risk, both because the ancient buildings themselves are extremely vulnerable and because an entire tourist economy revolves around them. Moreover, low-quality construction materials, shoddily reconstructed buildings, and limited economic means—combined with unstable ground—mean that earthquake effects are particularly dramatic in Italy.[7] These factors persist today and have in many ways increased. The recent phenomenon of coastal development, largely for tourism, exacerbates the threat from earthquakes and tsunamis.

However, the economic and social threats of earthquakes are not very visible and so are greatly underrated in most government measures and in the culture of the country. Gaps in perception are often linked to the individual's ignorance of the problem and to the mass media's failure to communicate the risk.

The low visibility of seismic threats among the population is not due to the hidden nature of deep tectonic plates or to a lack of evidence of the effects of earthquakes on buildings and cultural landscapes, be they ruins, unfinished construction projects, temporary dwellings turned into permanent structures, irreparably cracked or disfigured historical buildings, or dilapidated villages that look like film sets. Nor is there any shortage of earthquake witnesses, particularly in central and southern Italy. The problem is that seismic landscapes become enveloped by the cultural cloak of lengthy and intricate reconstruction processes, whereby seismic memories quickly fade. Earthquake planning should go beyond merely restoring buildings and should move toward preparing for future earthquakes, when a new generation inherits the legacy of earlier preparations.

Ruins, Reconstructions, Abandonment

Before addressing larger historical questions surrounding village reconstruction and abandonment following an earthquake, I would like to draw attention to the cultural and metaphoric uses of ruins, which have for centuries characterized the figurative arts in Italy and across Europe. Earthquake ruins were an image used as a metaphor of pagan society and religion, juxtaposed to the vitality of Christianity. Although there may be only weak links between real ruins and conceptualized ruins in paintings, I believe that Italy offers reasons to reappraise these links. Indeed, ruins were too common across Italy, too frequent, and too often associated with ancient and prestigious architecture to be envisioned as being wholly separate from earthquakes. Ruins became fashionable in the seventeenth century, sparking an artistic trend with the Neapolitan *rovinisti* (literally meaning "ruinists"). The seventeenth century witnessed some of Italy's great seismic disasters across the whole of the peninsula (in 1624, 1688, 1693, 1694, and 1695).[8] In the early eighteenth century, great Neapolitan landscape painters (such as Leonardo Coccorante, Gennaro Greco, and Gaetano Martoriello) embellished their paintings with elements foreshadowing romantic visions of nature, to include the ruined buildings that were so cherished by the rovinisti. In their grand tours, French and English artists continued this theme of ruins in their own works: suffice it to mention John Constable or the dramatic J. M. W. Turner. These elements were not wholly new in painting: as early as the mid-fifteenth century, traces of "real" seismic destruction seemed to arouse the interest of Andrea Mantegna, such as in his altarpiece *Polittico di San Zeno, Orazione nell'Orto,* painted after his stay in Naples from 1456 to 1459 (see figure 2.1). Art historians have not mentioned how the details of this painting can be linked to the great earthquake of 5 December 1456, which destroyed hundreds of villages in the Kingdom of Naples.[9] Mantegna added a third circle of walls to the imaginary city (Jerusalem), painting a damaged tower.

Each reconstruction that follows a seismic disaster is not just an administrative act. In the time taken for the work to be done, in the technical limits of rebuilding, in the social priorities that followed, and in the attention given to preparing for future seismic encounters, one can discover the socially accepted levels of safety, which are geographically, culturally,

Fig. 2.1. Andrea Mantegna (1431–1506), detail from Polittico di San Zeno, Orazione nell'Orto, painted between 1456 and 1459. Tours, Musée des Beaux-Arts

and historically dependent. Strabo (13.4.10), writing about the ancient city of Philadelphia (now Alasehir, in Turkey), expressed concern about the high risks accepted by inhabitants and their adaptations to them: "Philadelphia . . . [is] frequently hit by earthquakes. Indeed, the walls repeatedly crack and at times first one part and then the other part of the city undergo damage; hence, this is why few people inhabit the city, while everyone else lives in the countryside and cultivates the land; we may be surprised at how people remain in their village, even though they live in unsafe dwellings."

Landscapes with dilapidated houses that are half-abandoned or badly repaired are a characteristic of the Mediterranean. People are bonded to the land, which can help explain their resistance to adapting to extreme natural phenomena. Sixteenth-century Italian cities, built as magnificent court headquarters but then brought crashing to the ground by the trembling earth, represented an enormous loss of image and prestige for the prince. Royalty's swift response to the seismic damage, according to political convenience and urgency, seems to have been an attempt to deny the divine wrath that an earthquake represented (a case in point is the Ferrara earth-quake on 17 November 1570).[10] Until the end of the premodern era, it was rare to completely demolish damaged buildings because of the scarcity of construction materials and the need to recycle them or seal over damaged walls: complete demolition and reconstruction were uncommon. Though quick repairs saved human and economic resources in the short term, these hasty measures meant that future damage might be even worse. Yet after the 1600s, some central powers began to see seismic destruction as an op-portunity to build impressive new palaces and redesign urban spaces and the settlement networks of villages, leading some to be abandoned while new ones were built from scratch. Following eastern Sicily's two strong earth-quakes in January 1693, fabulous late Baroque architecture arose in Noto, Ragusa, Modica, Scicli, and other small Sicilian cities continuing to enthrall visitors and architectural historians.

At the same time, the forced abandonment of partially destroyed villages often went unacknowledged. Sometimes, local populations were obliged to live for years among ruins and rubble. Partially reconstructed or abandoned buildings marked parts of the Italian landscape, as can be seen in Calabria.

Earthquakes and Unstable Life: The Case of Calabria, Southern Italy

In spite of recent efforts to develop its tourist potential, the southern region of Calabria remains a poor region attached to a comparatively rich north. Its poverty has been variously explained by scarcely populated mountains, isolated villages, poor-quality roads, distance from economic centers, and lack of investment and market activity. But together with these factors, earthquakes have to be added to Calabria's economic and social difficulties. Indeed, the region's history is inseparable from the frequent earthquakes that have shaken it.

The Calabria-Apennine mountain chain frequently produces earthquakes of magnitudes above VI degree (MCS scale), and over the past three centu-ries, the region has experienced more strong earthquakes than all other Ital-ian regions. When intervals between destructive earthquakes are too short to allow for significant economic recovery, poverty rises, triggering emigration, which further impoverishes the economic and social fabric.[11] In Calabria, the reconstruction of buildings has almost always been carried out too superfi-cially and with too little attention paid to preparing for future earthquakes. With the possible exception of the 1908 quake and its aftermath, Calabria's residents have always rebuilt with a view to immediate survival.[12]

The year 1743 is remembered in southern Italy as a year of plague and earthquakes. While the plague was rolling across Sicily and attempts were

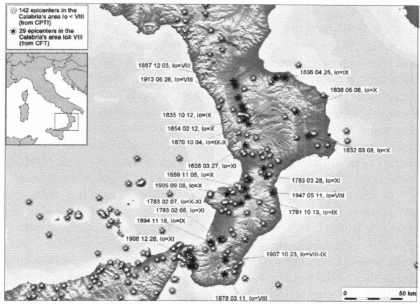

Map 2.2. Calabria (southern Italy), showing epicenters of known earthquakes from 1600 to 2000. Black stars show the most destructive events (VIII MCS and above).

made to create a cordon sanitaire to prevent its spread to Calabria, in December 1743 an earthquake struck the middle of the region, centering on the southern Sila massif within the "ball" of Italy's boot and destroying a number of villages there. Just three months later, another earthquake hit nearby Roccabernarda and Catanzaro.[13] On 14 July 1767, the Crati Valley north of Cosenza was hit. Then, in 1783, a long and devastating sequence of five earthquakes again struck the region (between 5 February and 28 March), ushering in a new economic, social, and cultural phase for Calabrians.[14] This last quake was the strongest since that of Lisbon in 1755, and both events caused a furor across Europe.

The cumulative picture of the damage is huge and serious: the destructive effects, accompanied by extensive landslides and interrupted river flows, affected a vast area of southern Calabria, from the isthmus of Marcellinara to the Strait of Messina and extending across to northeastern Sicily. Altogether, 182 Calabrian villages were almost completely destroyed; 33 of these were reconstructed in different sites. In the affected area, 35,000 out of 400,000 inhabitants died, that is, some 8 percent of the resident population. These seismic events, especially those of 1783, shook the social order to its core. General crisis and rampant epidemics, coupled with a fatalistic view of earthquakes, left a deep mark on society, being reflected in key political decisions at the turn of the eighteenth century.[15]

Spectacular side effects on the natural environment captured the attention of the day's scientists and naturalists: landslides, rock avalanches, and other collapses, along with new lakes and ground liquefaction phenomena, became the subjects of numerous surveys and illustrations. Hillsides sliding down into valleys carried houses and obstructed waterways, while forming new water diversions. Near Scilla and Torre Faro on the Tyrrhenian coast, an enormous landslide roared down Mount Campallà on 6 February 1783, giving rise to a deadly anomalous wave (akin to a tsunami) in the Strait of Messina that flooded inland for 350 to 1,000 meters, claiming 1,500 lives.[16]

In nearby Reggio Calabria and Catanzaro, the Bourbon government of Naples saw that seismic disaster as a chance to redistribute resources, especially landholdings. In June 1784, a complex process of expropriating church properties began in Calabria through the establishment of the Congregazione di Cassa Sacra, or Sacred Fund Congregation. By administering and selling ecclesiastical assets, the aim was to amass capital for reconstruction, while simultaneously initiating (through land redistribution) a new phase of development for this economically weak region. Yet by most measures, efforts to repair the damaged social fabric and absorb losses were largely ineffective, even though the main causes of Calabria's backwardness had been readily identified. Such causes included (1) the prevalence of a

Fig. 2.2. Calabria, 1783 earthquakes. Table III, showing the remains of the village of Pizzo Calabro, is drawn from the *Atlas of Pompeo Schiantarelli and Ignazio Stile* (1784), which catalogs effects on buildings and landscapes of Calabrian villages, as surveyed by the Naples Academy of Sciences.

feudal agricultural system (83 percent of the Calabrian countryside was owned by latifundia barons); (2) the large number of absentee landlords; (3) the declining quality of the pasture-, farm-, and woodland; (4) the burden of the central fiscal system; and lastly, (5) the relatively weak state as compared with baronial power. All of these factors did not change much during the lengthy reconstruction phase. Moreover, the exodus of the rural population toward urban areas continued unabated, accentuating the already serious lack of manpower in rural areas.

The disastrous effects on the economic and social life due to the 1783 earthquakes contributed to Calabria's relatively diminished demographic trend, at least until the mid-nineteenth century. In some centers, earthquakes contributed directly and indirectly to a strong economic crisis. In Palmi, wool and silk industries were crippled by an epidemic fever; in Pizzo, those who did not die under the rubble succumbed to the epidemic; that summer in Seminara, Oppido Mamertina, and Briatico, another epidemic caused nearly nineteen thousand deaths.

According to central government reports, reconstruction projects were designed to improve the urban layout and upgrade building materials. Indeed, in the first instance of sending engineers and academics to disaster zones, experts related damage effects to types of construction. The troubling characteristics of Calabrian buildings were excessive height, heavy decorative elements, excessive roof weights in relation to the scarce quality of the supporting rafters, and insufficient foundations, along with poor building materials (such as clay, mud, straw, unseasoned timber) and poor construction techniques. These elements were combined with Calabria's other village characteristics, including narrow roads, steep slopes, and a lack of open squares in inhabited areas. All of these elements made Calabria especially prone to the effects of earthquakes.

Thanks to the reports provided by the day's technicians and scientists, the Bourbon government decided to adopt new building regulations in the reconstruction phase. The goal was to comply with specific building techniques inspired by earthquake-resistant criteria. The plans of entire villages were redrawn, making inhabited areas proportional to the number of inhabitants. Furthermore, village plans were developed around an orthogonal reticulum so as to safeguard a regular pattern of urban design. Buildings were to comply to the *casa baraccata,* that is, a house consisting in a load-bearing wooden framework embedded in a brickwork structure. Tall buildings were forbidden, and were limited to just one inhabitable floor.

However, such innovative designs clashed with resource availabilities and local ideas and therefore remained in many cases merely paper projects.

Scarce timber in a large number of damaged areas meant that many construction projects could not rely on wood. Due to the chronic shortage and high price of materials, rubble was recycled; timber, iron, and stones were reused; and fallen buildings were pillaged. Prolonged reconstruction times and accompanying social conflicts contributed to depressing the economy. As years passed, government constraints were relaxed and compromises were adopted, until the rules were completely ignored. Subsequent earthquakes would prove the dramatic folly of disregarding the earlier government recommendations.

On 13 November 1791, a strong shock hit Calabria's mountain towns and villages, still rebuilding from the 1783 quake. Some thirty locations in central and southern areas registered complete collapses; even more places experienced cracks in walls and other damage. The archaic Calabrian economy, based on an agro-pastoral system, was unable to deal with these repeated emergencies. Most people lived in precarious hygienic conditions, sometimes housed in wooden sheds (although the latter situation probably helped to limit the number of victims in 1791). Government relief during this last earthquake was limited to distributing wooden planks to the homeless; it undertook repairs to damaged houses and constructed new sheds.

Calabria in the Nineteenth Century: Seven Earthquakes in a Period of Severe Economic Crisis

The next century saw continued strong earthquakes in Calabria. In the 1830s, the Bourbon kingdom confronted a serious political and economic crisis, which further diminished its capacity to provide earthquake relief. On 8 March 1832, the earth shook in northeastern Calabria above the present-day province of Catanzaro, seriously damaging a dozen or so villages, including Cutro, Mesoraca, and Rocca di Netro, which would need to be reconstructed on new sites. Buildings in another forty localities either collapsed or became uninhabitable, as at Catanzaro. According to the Calabrian *intendenza* (government authorities), most damage stemmed from the slipshod repair work that followed the 1783 earthquakes. A tsunami along thirty kilometers of marshy coastland between Steccato and Marina di Catanzaro contributed to the mayhem, as did stormy conditions.

Just three years later, on 12 October 1835, the upper valley of the river Crati northeast of Cosenza was hit. Numerous communities suffered serious damage, especially ones located on unstable alluvial deposits. The city of Cosenza itself, thanks to its urban layout and its greater economic potential, recovered more quickly than outlying villages. Just a few months later, on 25 April 1836, this area received another quake, with a heavy loss of human life and over half of the 1,538 buildings recording irreparable damage. This time, Cosenza escaped with only minor additional cracks. Remarkable for this quake was that it rocked a fertile agricultural zone and its associated warehouses, oil mills, depots, stables, and livestock. Public relief did not adequately compensate for the resulting agricultural losses, so the economy suffered from multiplier effects for over two decades.

A strong earthquake on 12 February 1854 caused additional problems across the Cosenza area. According to many reports, numerous cracks and fissures opened in the ground, contributing to slips and landslides, in areas already destabilized by intensive forest uses in previous decades. Heavy rain weighting down steep slopes made the situation even worse.[17] In those days, few roadways existed in Calabria, and many of these were just *mulattiere* (mule paths), with very few bridges over rivers, so people had to wade across the rivers. The lack of transport routes hampered relief programs.

Not surprisingly, another quake buckled the province of Cosenza, this time on 4 October 1870. Many buildings between the Crati and Savuto rivers were seriously damaged. In some cases, cracks that had formed during previous quakes had simply been filled with quicklime. This area was only moderately industrialized, the inhabitants practiced subsistence agriculture and had a poor road network. The new Kingdom of Italy, which had annexed Calabria along with the whole Bourbon Kingdom of Naples in 1860, allocated few economic resources to these seismic landscapes. Indeed, the north's more competitive, efficient, and specialized economy caused the south's weak industrial and agricultural sectors to fall into even deeper crisis. This economic backwardness was also manifested in the poor quality and maintenance of local buildings, making them even more vulnerable to the earthquakes.

The strong earthquake of 3 December 1887 in the Crati River valley reflected how tremors could follow class lines. In the village of Roggiano Gravina, for example, the poorer farmhands lived in small houses, one next to the other, with walls made of beaten earth or mixed with straw or interwoven wood and roofs made of clayey earth mixed with straw. In these dwellings there were few victims. But in the small buildings made of stones that housed low-to-middle-class villagers, there was extensive damage, with many victims. A large number of these stone houses were old and badly built, with heavy roofs and inadequate foundations, often only ten to fifteen centimeters deep.

After years of earthquakes in the central area, it was southern Calabria that was violently hit on 16 November 1894. About one hundred people died, and one thousand more were injured. In Reggio Calabria, nearly all of the buildings suffered extensive cracks to the walls. Besides causing material damage, this earthquake paralyzed most manufacturing and agricultural activities. In spite of the subsequent detailed scientific reports about the damage and ways to rebuild (the first such reports in contemporary Italy), no legislative and administrative measures were instituted to rehabilitate the disrupted social and economic life.

Calabria: The Disastrous Twentieth Century

But the worst was still to come. The twentieth century ushered another series of earthquakes into Calabria, culminating in the 1908 disaster along the Strait of Messina and then the quake of 1913. In that period the very existence of the villages and towns of Calabria, including its chief town, Reggio Calabria, was in jeopardy. In a very brief summary, here are the dramatic phases.

The earthquake on 8 September 1905 struck the Catanzaro area, seriously damaging 326 villages and killing 560 people. Only the better-constructed buildings withstood the impact, buildings that were owned by so-called

Fig. 2.3. Calabria, earthquake of 8 September 1905 (Me 6.7), showing the effects on the village of Stefanaconi (Vibo Valentia) in a photograph preserved in the archive of SGA (Bologna). The scene demonstrates how low-quality construction was more susceptible to damage in an earthquake.

americani, that is, well-to-do emigrants, built with suitable materials and complying with proper building rules. This earthquake struck during a strong economic depression when protectionist tariffs did not allow for productive development in Calabria. This economic context meant that the earthquake produced particularly devastating effects: within a year of the disaster, thousands of families were homeless and reduced to starvation. The great landholders quickly repaired their homes with the assistance of civil and military engineers or abandoned them. Smaller landowners did not have the means to repair their houses and lived with perhaps eight to ten people sharing a shabbily repaired room. Poor farmhands abandoned their villages. Those who remained repaired their houses with rubble extracted from the ruins, reinforcing the same dangerous building standards as before and extending the chain of Calabria's earthquake vulnerability. And then, just two years later, on 23 October 1907, a strong earthquake centering on the villages of Calabria's southern Ionian coast destroyed from 30 to 50 percent of all the buildings. Government records report that almost nine thousand houses became uninhabitable.

On 28 December 1908, a very strong seismic event occurred leaving an indelible mark not only in the destroyed areas along the Strait of Messina

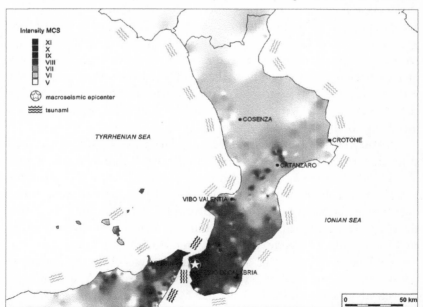

Map 2.3. Calabria and the area near the Strait of Messina, showing effects of the earthquake of 28 December 1908 (Me 7.1). Calabria was the area hardest hit by the earthquake and tsunami, as gauged by the number of villages with extensive damage.

Fig. 2.4. Messina, Sicily, showing the effects of the 1908 earthquake.

and as far as central Calabria but also in the conscience and historical memory of Italy and the whole of Europe.[18] This earthquake is among the strongest in Italian seismic history (XI MCS and magnitude 7.2), rippling across an area of six thousand square kilometers and causing serious damage (equivalent to degrees IX, X, and XI MCS). Many Calabrian localities witnessed dramatic destruction accumulating over several previous earthquakes. Reggio Calabria, a city of about thirty-two thousand inhabitants, was almost completely destroyed, with reconstruction commencing as long as ten years later in the midst of huge difficulties and dangerously precarious living conditions.

Across the strait in Sicily, at Messina, an active merchant city and strategic port, 42 percent of the inhabitants died (some 65,000 individuals). In Reggio Calabria, the numbers were 12,000 to 13,000. Overall, in the two regions, from 80,000 to 100,000 people died. A large tsunami rolled over Italian shores in eastern Sicily, from Messina to Catania, as well as the Calabrian coastline. Waves up to thirteen meters high swept away the rubble of buildings already collapsed, along with hundreds of people.

Looking at the economic damage, many analysts of the day compared this earthquake to a lost war and a great national emergency. The earthquake devastated a modern urbanized city like Messina, in Sicily, as well as poor villages and small towns situated in inland Calabria. In this latter, poorer context, the earthquake reduced already scarce opportunities for escaping isolation and economic backwardness. Certain industrial areas like Villa San

Giovanni, Cannitello, and Santa Caterina experienced relatively rapid recovery, in which silk workshops regained most of their productive output, then based mainly on female and child labor. But traditional farmworkers found that the earthquake obliged them to change to other activities.

Waves of emigration followed hard on the heels of this seismic destruction. Along with internal migration to the north, there was massive migration to other countries, especially Canada and the United States. Some destroyed villages became slowly repopulated because they offered job opportunities for desperate individuals from villages further inland. Widespread losses of cultural identity characterized these populations for decades. The cultural fabric of daily life, woven from human bonds and habits, became unraveled for decades or even, in the case of many Calabrians, forever.

Following the 1908 earthquake, the Italian government enforced various laws that outlined the normative framework for institutional responses to catastrophes. There was by this date no lack of resources for dealing with the aftermath of the quake, especially considering that Italian society was undergoing the transition toward a modern industrial economy, about one century behind northern Europe. The period from 1896 to 1908 was characterized by annual industrial growth rates of 6.7 percent, the highest in the 1881–1913 period. But even though fiscal incentives and special funds were created for reconstructing Calabria, the corruption that accompanied the enormous flow of public moneys sometimes aggravated Calabria's hardships.

A Legacy of Earthquakes and Ruins

The temporal gaps between Italy's numerous seismic disasters may give the illusion to a historian studying any single earthquake separately that a rational process for interventions actually existed. Particularly destructive earthquakes were usually followed by rules and regulations for proper construction, building constraints, and guidelines issued by a central government. But the passing of time served to cancel new norms. Subsequent seismic disasters (two or three generations later) hit people with short memories. The supposedly new regulations that followed a strong earthquake, which should have protected against subsequent destructive events, soon fell by the wayside. Prior or worse construction practices were reinstated, paving the way for a new round of seismic disasters. Italy's earthquake history, especially that of the center-south, is a repeating pattern in which each strong quake is followed by a long, drawn-out, and irresponsible aftermath. Only a synergy of disciplinary skills would be able to account for the many uses of the countryside, the relationships between peoples using it, and the necessary precautions required for safely dealing with seismicity.

The predictability of Italy's earthquakes, at least in certain regions, means that such disasters should be expected in the mid and long term.

Today, the ruins of villages damaged by the 1968 earthquake in western Sicily (Gibellina, Montefalco, Poggioreale, Santa Ninfa, and Santa Margherita Belice) are testimony to a rugged Mediterranean landscape of rare beauty. Not far from the rising new settlements are the ruins of old villages that testify to a story that cannot be forgotten. The old site of Gibellina, destroyed by the 1968 earthquake, has become the first earthquake monument in the Mediterranean: between 1985 and 1989, the sculptor Alberto Burri leveled out the remains of the village, (about one meter seventy centimeters in height) and then covered everything with white concrete, thereby preserving the original layout of ancient roads and medieval plan. This ghostly artistic creation (called *Cretto*), visible many kilometers away under blinding sun and moon-filled nights, provocatively jolts our conscience into perceiving an almost tangible earthquake, carved indelibly into that landscape.

Is there a legacy of ruins? Will this legacy ever disappear? Perhaps a Martian might consider this landscape of ruins and rubble to be appealing to earthly inhabitants, as humans have systematically and laboriously created

Fig. 2.5. Gibellina Vecchia (Valle del Belice, southwestern Sicily) was destroyed by the earthquake of 13 January 1968, which also left the villages of Salaparuta and Poggioreale abandoned. The remains of the village of Gibellina were turned into a sort of monument to the ruins by the sculptor Alberto Burri between 1985 and 1989. The new village rises in the plain, about ten kilometers away.

those ruins as the result of natural and human events, including wars. But without waiting for insights from aliens, perhaps a new historiographic approach that is more sensitive to such thematic points while incorporating carefully evaluated scientific data can foster a new culture of safety, making obsolete the notion of "acting only in an emergency" and other alibis for the mismanagement of events believed to be unforeseeable.

Notes

1. Currently, over fifty thousand cataloged and archived historical sources give a picture of Italy's historical seismicity, useful for scholarly analysis and environmental protection. See Emanuela Guidoboni, "Method of Investigation, Typology and Taxonomy of the Basic Data: Navigating between Seismic Effects and Historical Contexts," in "Catalogue of Strong Italian Earthquakes from 461 BC to 1997: Introductory Texts, with CD-ROM," special issue of *Annali di Geofisica* 43, no. 4 (2000): 621–66.

2. Emanuela Guidoboni and John E. Ebel, *Earthquakes and Tsunamis in the Past: A Guide to Techniques in Historical Seismology* (Cambridge and New York: Cambridge University Press, 2009).

3. Enzo Boschi, "A 'New Generation' Earthquake Catalogue," in "Catalogue of Strong Italian Earthquakes from 461 BC to 1997: Introductory Texts, with CD-ROM," special issue of *Annali di Geofisica* 43, no. 4 (2000): 609–20.

4. Emanuela Guidoboni, Graziano Ferrari, Dante Mariotti, Alberto Comastri, Gabriele Tarabusi, and Gianluca Valensise, *CFTI4 MED: Catalogue of Strong Earthquakes in Italy 461 BC–1997 and Mediterranean Area 760 BC–1500: An Advanced Laboratory of Historical Seismology,* 2007–, Istituto Nazionale di Geofisica e Vulcanologia, available at http://storing.ingv.it/cfti4med/ (accessed 5 June 2009).

5. Guidoboni, "Method of Investigation."

6. Ibid.

7. On landslides, see Walter Palmieri's essay in this volume.

8. See Guidoboni et al., *CFTI4 MED*, by year.

9. Bruno Figliuolo, *Il terremoto del 1456,* 2 vols. (Altavilla Silentina: Studi Storici Meridionali, 1988–89); Emanuela Guidoboni and Alberto Comastri, *Catalogue of Earthquakes and Tsunamis in the Mediterranean Area from the Eleventh to the Fifteenth Century* (Rome: INGV-SGA, 2005), 625–724.

10. Emanuela Guidoboni, "Riti di calamità: Terremoti a Ferrara nel 1570–74," *Quaderni Storici* 55, no. 1 (1984): 107–36; Guidoboni, ed., *Pirro Ligorio—Libro di diversi terremoti,* (Rome: De Luca Editori d'Arte, 2005); Stefano Breventano, *Trattato del terremoto,* ed. Paola Albini (Pavia, Italy: IUSS Press, 2007).

11. I have used the case of Calabria for a more general social and economic analysis in Emanuela Guidoboni and James Jackson, "Seismic Disasters and

Poverty: Some Data and Reflections on Past and Current Trends," in *The Causes of Poverty and the Fight Against It: A Multidisciplinary Approach to an Urgent Problem*, ed. Thomas Riis (Kiel, Germany: European Science Foundation, 2008), 153–84.

12. All the data used here are drawn from *Catalogue of Strong Earthquakes in Italy*, Guidoboni et al., *CFTI4 MED*, cit. See also James Jackson, "Fatal Attraction: Living with Earthquakes, the Growth of Villages into Megacities, and Earthquake Vulnerability in the Modern World," *Philosophical Transactions of the Royal Society of London* 364 (August 2006): 1911–25; and J. Jackson, "Surviving Natural Disasters," in *Survival, 2006 Darwin Lectures*, ed. Emily Shuckburgh (New York: Cambridge University Press, 2008), 123–45; Roger Bilham, "Earthquakes and Urban Development," *Nature* 336 (December 1988): 625–26; and R. Bilham, "Urban Earthquake Fatalities: A Safer World, or Worse to Come?" *Seismological Research Letters* 75, no. 1 (2004): 706–12.

13. This earthquake is analyzed in detail, with the bibliography of the archival sources, in Emanuela Guidoboni and Dante Mariotti, "Revisione e integrazione di ricerca riguardante il massimo terremoto storico della Puglia: 20 febbraio 1743," RPT SGA no. 272, October 2005, unpublished report, available from the central library of the Istituto Nazionale di Geofisica e Vulcanologia, Rome, and available from the Milan branch. See also *CFTI4 MED*.

14. The five strong earthquakes of 1783 are documented by countless sources of various types: administrative acts; treatises; and reports of scholars, literati, and scientists of the day. This vast production of writings is due to the very strong impact of earthquakes across the whole of southern society and in European culture. The historical events in eighteenth-century Calabria before this seismic disaster have also been studied by Italian historiography: fundamental are the studies of Augusto Placanica, who, besides studying the cultural reactions to the earthquake, also published a substantial amount of contemporary documentation. For the bibliography and the analysis of the sources, see *CFTI4 MED*, 2007.

15. See, in particular, the following works by Augusto Placanica: *L'Iliade funesta: Storia del terremoto calabro-messinese del 1783* (Rome: Casa del Libro, 1982), and *Il filosofo e la catastrofe: Un terremoto del Settecento* (Turin: Einaudi, 1985).

16. See Alberto Comastri and Dante Mariotti, "I terremoti e i maremoti dello Stretto di Messina dal mondo antico alla fine del XX secolo: Descrizioni e parametri," in *Il terremoto e il maremoto del 28 dicembre 1908: Analisi sismologica, impatto, prospettive*, ed. Guido Bertolaso, Enzo Boschi, Emanuela Guidoboni, and Gianluca Valensise (Rome: DPC–INGV, 2008), 215–54, esp. 231–34.

17. See Ferdinando Scaglione, "Cenno storico-filosofico sul tremuoto che nella notte del dì 12 venendo il 13 febbraio dell'anno 1854 ad un'ora meno un quarto scosse orrendamente la città di Cosenza e varii paesi vicini," *Atti della Reale Società Economica di Calabria Citra*, 1854, 41–109; see also *CFTI4 MED*, 2007.

18. See John Dickie, *Una catastrofe patriottica: 1908, il terremoto di Messina*, trans. Fabio Galimberti (Rome: Laterza, 2008).

CHAPTER 3

Moving Ground

Vesuvius and the Nola Mudslides of the Nineteenth Century

Walter Palmieri

Epilogue: Sarno, May 1998

In the wee hours between 5 and 6 May 1998, following two days of abundant rainfall, hundreds of thousands of cubic meters of mud and debris let loose on Mount Pizzo d'Alvano in the outskirts of Naples, sweeping down over the towns of Sarno, Quindici, Siano, and Bracigliano. The final toll listed 160 victims, hundreds of destroyed homes, whole areas completely devastated, and many millions of euros in damages.

In subsequent weeks and months, the most common opinion of this terrible disaster was that it had been easily foreseeable. For years, scholars, geologists, and environmentalists had been raising the alarm about Italy's hydrogeological risks, especially in Campania.[1] Now, thanks to the general public uprising in the aftermath of the catastrophe, these experts finally had the opportunity to reach a wide audience and discuss the probable causes for what had happened: first and foremost, they blamed the geological fragility of that area, which is largely covered with unstable volcanic deposits from the eruptions of Vesuvius; next, they pointed out the steepness of slopes and the heavy rainfall. But according to these experts, alongside these "natural" factors were other causes that had contributed, directly or indirectly, to making that event particularly disastrous: the presence of settlements in high-risk areas at the mountain base, unauthorized building and waste disposal, little or no land maintenance, poor management of forest resources, lack of high-altitude meteorologic stations, and lack of forecasting and prevention plans. All these factors, of course, are anthropic. They involve human beings and their interaction with natural resources.

One side effect of this tragedy's high public visibility was an unusually wide interest in what Italian experts call *franosità storica* (landslide proneness). Following the Sarno disaster, scholars began to investigate the area's landslides and general hydrogeological instability over previous decades and centuries. Interestingly, this theme attracted the interest not just of geologists but also of several historians. As a result, in recent years numerous historical essays have appeared providing a detailed overview of what has happened in these towns from the seventeenth century onward.[2] Until the appearance of these latest essays, however, Italian historians (and social scientists generally) rarely turned their attention to landslides, floods, or other hydrogeological disasters. Yet historical data has long been an important part of geological investigation. The presence of a rich record of landslides and floods provides an important means for predicting and preparing for future catastrophes of mud, water, and rock. One may hope that this new historical interest in landslide history will not prove ephemeral. Not only will this interest offer excellent opportunities for contributing to environmental history, it may also contribute to practical applications in the present.

Slides under the Volcano

Let us look deeper at the 1998 disaster. As mentioned previously, much of the area's instability has been traced to the volcanic material that Vesuvius—continental Europe's largest active volcano—spewed over gentle and rugged terrain east and northeast of Naples.

Ash, pumice, and stones emitted by Vesuvius in its many eruptions over thousands of years was sedimented into the plains and slopes of the Campanian Apennines, forming deposits that sometimes reached thicknesses of several tens of meters, depending on distance from the crater, winds, and other factors. Yet these deposits have represented something of a paradox: since before ancient times, volcanic materials made Campania's plains very fertile and favorable to human settlement, yet thick layers of these same materials on hills and slopes posed a major threat to inhabitants.

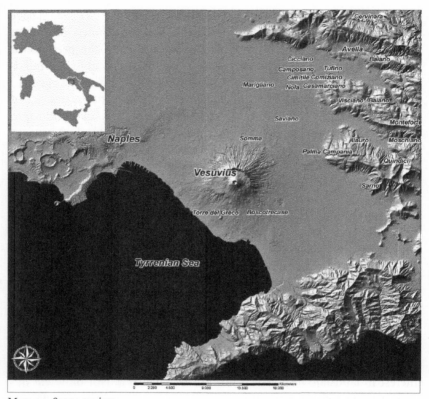

Map. 3.1. Sarno region

This threat stems from the high permeability of pyroclastic covers. Rainwater readily trickles down through these layers to the underlying rock, which is much less permeable. As a result, the sinking water encounters an underground barrier so that during heavy rainfall, the superficial layer becomes soaked with water and is then lubricated on its underside to allow the whole mass to begin sliding and crumbling downhill. The resulting rapid mud-debris flows are among the most dangerous of landslides because they can carry huge quantities of material suddenly and violently, like an avalanche of rock.

The high speed attained by these mudflows and the high kinetic energy they release require especially careful monitoring of areas where they are prone to occur. Disasters can only be avoided by preparing evacuation plans, as well as by preventing human land uses from jeopardizing already fragile environmental equilibria. Unfortunately, the Sarno disaster is a grim reminder that these obvious measures may be neglected, as they were again just twelve years earlier—on 22 February 1986, when another mudslide with very similar characteristics hit the nearby town of Palma Campania, devastating its territory and killing eight people.[3]

The disasters of Sarno and Palma Campania, however, are merely the latest in a long string of landslides and floods that have occurred in the Campania region. The first such events known to us date to prehistoric times. Archaeologists recently brought to light an early Bronze Age village at Croce di Papa, near the town of Nola, that had been destroyed by the so-called Avellino Pumice eruption occurring four thousand years ago. After being covered with pumice stones and ashes, this town was buried by a mudslide that flowed into and around the huts, serving to preserve them. This mudslide appears to have been a lahar, or a slide generated in pyroclastic soil that usually arises from a sliding mass during or immediately following the volcanic eruption. Such floods occur because violent eruptions often produce microclimatic alterations; specifically, huge quantities of vapor emitted during an eruption can generate violent rainstorms. The resulting torrential rains then sweep downhill some of the material issuing from the crater, with consequences that can be more catastrophic than the eruption itself.

These volcanic rainstorms therefore pose extra risk in Campania. Although areas near extinct volcanoes are always prone to a high risk of mudslides, they are no longer threatened by pyroclastic slides. But in areas near active volcanoes, the risk is considerably higher. Today, Vesuvius is quiescent, having last erupted in 1944, but its earlier eruptions were rather frequent and often destructive. The most famous eruption was undoubtedly that of AD 79. During the ash-spewing episode that covered Pompeii, there were also mudslides stemming from the great quantity of vapor that the volcano emitted, probably contributing to burying Herculaneum, not far from Pompeii. In more recent times, the most violent eruption occurred in 1631. On 17 December of that year, just a day after the onset of volcanic paroxysm, immense mudslides descended northeast over several towns of the Nola plain (including Cicciano, Marigliano, and Pomigliano), causing death and destruction.[4]

Vesuvius continued its outbursts in the following centuries, too. There were mudslides after the eruptions of July 1707, May 1737, and October 1767.[5] In the eruption of 1776, a bystander noted that "the pouring water mixed with the ash ejected by Vesuvius . . . ; this ash did worse damage than did the stones and lava in previous days."[6] Similar eruptions followed by floods were recorded in 1779 and 1794,[7] when destructive flows invaded settlements along the northern slopes of the volcano.[8] In the nineteenth century,

Vesuvius became even more active. There were over twenty eruptions in that century—ranging from small to major—and they deepened the pyroclastic layer of the surrounding area, further destabilizing the soil substrate.

But it was the eruptions of October and November 1822 that were Italy's most dramatic volcanic events in recent history. According to an anonymous article published shortly after these eruptions, "Wind blew the ash all the way to Calabria, where it fell in such abundance over some areas that it covered the leaves of trees."[9] Again, the worst damage was caused by lahars triggered by the copious rainfall induced by the eruption. On 28 October, just seven days after the first discharges of Vesuvius, "violent" mudslides swept over the Ottaviano area. On 9 and 10 November, an even more formidable mudslide filled houses in the Ottaviano neighborhoods of Terzigno, Torre del Greco, and Boscotrecase, in the latter case with "rocks and mud."[10] Mudslides did not just inundate towns at the foot of Vesuvius; for many years afterwards, they broiled through towns lying northeast of Vesuvius within what was once the Nola district.

Nola District: Engineers and Slides in the 1820s

Here, I will focus on the story of the 1822 eruptions, having pieced it together from documents at the State Archives in Naples.[11] It is an emblematic tale, since it bears witness to the hydrogeological fragility of the area and serves to shed light more generally on the relationships between culture and nature in that specific period. As we shall see, the archival documents do not merely report on these catastrophic events. They also provide eloquent evidence that human activities significantly increased the area's already high susceptibility to landslides. Such documents also contain revealing information about the means by which the authorities dealt with these disasters, as well as the difficulties they encountered.

On 22 December 1822, engineer Filippo Giuliani wrote a long report warning that recent volcanic activities had aggravated the hydrogeological danger in the Nola district. He explained that abundant, newly deposited Vesuvian ash had profoundly modified the earlier hydrographical system, seriously threatening the territorial balance. Giuliani went on to point out the principal streams that posed threats. Perhaps most threatening was the Gaudo, which drained the mountains of Monteforte. Following a fairly straight stretch, the Gaudo's streambed became quite sinuous, so that it readily flooded settlements and fields. These problems, Giuliani argued, depended on natural causes as well as on human factors: riverbank maintenance was insufficient, and, worse, farmers were extending their fields "into the stream's bed, thereby narrowing its section." These river encroachments, said Giuliani, were the main cause of floods resulting in "incalculable damage to inhabitants of the villages of Casamarciano, Tufino, Cumignano, Cimitile, Cicciano, and Camposano."[12]

Another problematic river mentioned by Giuliani issued from the mountains of Avella. The so-called Avella torrent once followed a fairly straight course and was used to drive mills in the local village. But problems appeared when villagers tried to build up its banks to contain minor floods. These embankments proved insufficient, soon collapsing and allowing larger floods. Downstream, this river joined the Gaudo River at the Cicciano Canal, which had been constructed three decades earlier; this canal frequently overflowed, inflicting "severe damage to the inhabitants of Cicciano and Camposano." Giuliani recommended that landowners along the river be obliged to plant poplars to reinforce the banks.

But the stream that had caused the most damage to the district was the one that flowed down from the Quindici mountains, gathering several tributaries as it ran down the Lauro Valley. Giuliani reported that its bed had filled with rocks and gravel in places. And as in the case of the Gaudo, farmers had narrowed the bed to increase cultivable area. These riverbed rearrangements had allowed "immense" areas to be inundated, including the towns of Quindici and Lauro. Giuliani completed his sketch of the Nola district's hydrology by mentioning two watercourses flowing directly from the volcanic complex of Somma-Vesuvius: the *lagni* of Marigliano and S. Martino. These slow-moving watercourses had silted up, resulting in significant flooding of the countryside and submerging of settlements.

To understand what lagni are, we need to take a step back in time. Some portions of the hydrographical network described earlier were actually the result of human activities during previous centuries. Because of repeated volcanic flows and related floods, swamps and marshes dominated the plains of the Nola district until the end of the sixteenth century. This was true of many other areas in southern Italy, but people living in regions north of Vesuvius were especially motivated to reclaim and drain swampy areas. Such areas were very fertile, and their proximity to the big city of Naples meant that they might supply some of the city's high demand for agricultural goods if the land could only be drained. Reclamation works carried out at the end of the sixteenth century and completed in the next led to the creation of *Regi Lagni,* complex drained areas dependent on a series of canals called lagni, which collected rain- and springwater over fifty kilometers to carry it to the sea.[13]

According to Giuliani's report, the best way to deal with hydrogeological emergencies centered on consolidating river courses and reinforcing riverbanks. But on 24 January 1823, even before work began, a flood struck several villages in the Nola district, as at Cimitile, where streets and houses filled up with silt and sand.[14] After the first measures were taken, mainly consisting of removing mud from houses and repairing the Regia Strada di Puglia, or Royal Road, the government sent engineers Bartolomeo Grasso and Giuseppe Giordano to the area. Their report of 5 March 1823, besides describing the event and its consequences, dwelled on the several-inch-thick layer of ash that had fallen on all the mountain slopes. As a result of this ash, "the torrential flow has increased . . . washing immense quantities of material down to the plains."

Some months later, on 18 October 1823, news of another disastrous flood proved that Grasso and Giordano's concerns had been fully justified. The Nola manager communicated the news to the *intendente,* or provincial governor, of the Terra di Lavoro district,[15] commenting that "everywhere you see flooded fields, destroyed roads, buried villages, collapsed homes, and corpses dragged through the streets." Practically all the townships in the area had been affected. Water and mud overran Saviano, Lauro, Palma, Marigliano, Quindici, and Nola. But the most serious damage was recorded in the triangle between the towns of Tufino, Camposano, and Cicciano. In the end, seven people died, with casualties adding up to thirty.[16]

The seriousness of the event was such that the central government immediately took action. Within a week, the King's Council of Ministers allocated thirteen thousand ducats for dealing with the emergency, eventually adding eight thousand more.[17] Correctional measures were entrusted to engineer Giuliani and carried out according to the guidelines he had laid down previously. The beds of the streams were deepened and widened, and their banks were reinforced. Work was completed in early February 1824. The inspector eagerly proclaimed his satisfaction with the job, assuring the Ministry of Interior that the townships of the district had been made safe for good. The general enthusiasm, however, was short-lived. On 3 November 1824, the same inspector reported that "in spite of significant expenditures," the October rains had caused new floods.[18] The central government responded by ordering an inspection on the work carried out to date, entrusting it to the Corpo di Ponti e Strade (the Bridge and Road Corps), which was founded during Naples's Napoleonic period and patterned after a similar French institution. The corps's director general, Carlo Afan de Rivera, wrote an extremely negative report, claiming that Giuliani's plan had been carried out employing erroneous and fraudulent methods. The report leveled serious accusations against the contractor, "who regarded the calamity as an opportunity to make a large profit rather than worrying about the solidity of the works." The banks of several watercourses, more-over, had been poorly reinforced with "sand and gravel taken from the bottom of the streams themselves" and reinforced with insubstantial wooden poles and fascines that were easily swept away by the currents.

But the central point of Afan de Rivera's criticism was that it was not possible to solve the problem of flooding in the Nola district merely by working on the lower courses of rivers. It was also necessary to take action upstream, on the mountain slopes. "All the works that one may carry out in the plain," wrote Afan de Rivera, "will have little or no effect unless one weakens the force of those formidable torrents up in the mountains." So, in addition to being poorly executed, Giuliani's plan was intrinsically flawed, he claimed, because it did not account for the principal cause of hydrogeo-logical instability, namely, the deforesting and tilling of the surrounding Nola plain.

Historians have studied the issue of Italy's deforestation in depth. As they all stress, deforestation was widespread across Italy. But in the Nea-politan surroundings, unprecedented demographic growth began in the second half of the eighteenth century, picking up speed in the nineteenth. The consequent demand for new agricultural land led to the dramatic reduction of forests and, as a consequence, increased the risk of hydrogeo-logical imbalances.[19] In the Nola district, moreover, this rapid deforestation combined with the instability of pyroclastic substrates to produce devastat-ing effects. "Today, one sees grapevines cultivated and crops planted on the steepest slopes," Afan de Rivera continued in his report. "Going through Monteforte Valley I noticed with amazement that crops and Indian corn are grown on slopes so steep that one wonders how anyone can climb up there at all. Going from Nola to Lauro, I observed the same problems on those mountain slopes. . . . It is no wonder that one sees the Gaudo and Quindici streams raging, which together with other smaller streams bring the to plains ruin."

As if to confirm Afan de Rivera's analysis, on 16 June 1825 several small mudslides again flooded fields in this region, affecting the town of Nola. Then another flood swept over the area seven days later, seriously damag-ing the hamlet of Vignola near Tufino as well as Camposano. The speed at which these alluvial events followed one another was such that the super-intendent wrote alarmingly, "The day will come, and it may come soon, when most of this district will be submerged." His pessimism was justified by the absence of a general mitigation plan for the area. Without such a plan, the intendente went on, "I shall not consider myself responsible for what will happen."

In the summer of 1825, engineer Grasso, who was charged with drawing up a new plan for coping with the situation, offered a stern critique of deforestation. The expansion of cropland to the detriment of woods and forests, he argued, was the main cause for the disastrous conditions prevailing in the district: "Already the inhabitants of Cotignano [in Cervinara township] have almost completely vacated their homes. Those of Camposano and Cicciano are under the constant threat of being submerged by water and mud. . . . Tufino is threatened with destruction by the rivers of Avella, Gaudo, and Visciano, which hem it in on two sides. . . . Many streams threaten the houses, plains, and fertile fields of Nola." Under such circumstances, Grasso stressed, placing a ban on tilling and logging, while obliging landowners to reforest steep slopes, was a prerequisite to any program for protecting the area. He also recommended building vertical steps in the streambed—check dams—to slow the speed of the streams' current, as well as deepening and widening other parts of their beds. In addition, Grasso opposed the notion of manipulating the hydrographical network in order to join several streams. He recommended, on the contrary, dividing up watercourses as much as possible to reduce their energy and, hence, the devastation they caused. Grasso's project, much of which was approved by the king a few weeks later, also included the building of two protective walls in the Gaudo Valley near Cicciano and Tufino.

By March 1826, work had not yet been completed, and engineer Grasso, though complaining about the project's slowness, was relieved to report there had been no flood in the Nola plain that winter, despite abundant rainfall. But this respite was short-lived. On 20 June 1826, the Gaudo stream overflowed, flooding the plain. According to Director Afan de Rivera, the failure to complete the work for lack of funds was not the only cause. There had been further deforestation and tilling: "In many hillside plots, hoeing has been forbidden, but in many others it has not."

In autumn 1826, new floods occurred. In September, Casamarciano was damaged by a flood from the mountains overlooking it. In November, the canal carrying waters of the Quindici Valley to the Regi Lagni overflowed. In spite of these events, work to maintain the canal did not proceed, since many landowners did not, or could not, pay their quotas.[20] There were further disasters. In May 1827, a "flood of immense proportions" submerged Cimitile, producing "incalculable damage." In June, several areas in the district were flooded. Heavy rainfall caused landslides and rivers to overflow in almost all the rivers in the district, killing two. In July, a flood in the Quindici Valley claimed two more lives. The intendente declared the situation to be desperate, dismissing as useless the "partial remedies adopted so far." His pessimism was reinforced by the fact that many of the district's landowners were unable to sustain more taxation to pay for new projects because they had already paid too much; others could not pay because they had suffered extensive losses from flooding.

Engineer Grasso's land maintenance plan was therefore hindered by financial difficulties. In August 1827, Grasso reported that in some cases, local landowners and tenants had themselves taken defensive actions to protect their plots.[21] He also stressed the huge gap between the sum still needed to complete the work and the approximately ten thousand ducats allocated to date. In another long report issued in October that year, Grasso requested an additional fifty thousand ducats. He again listed the works needed, and he itemized the recent floods in the district: a mudslide in early September "flooded fields and threatened several groups of houses"; another one later in the month washed abundant material across a vast area.

At the end of 1827 and in early 1828, new funds were granted, and work was finally resumed.[22] A large wall for protecting houses was completed in the Quindici Valley, and another one was built for shielding the hamlets of Bosagro and Beato, which were being submerged at every flood. The waters of the Quindici and Moschiano rivers were split into many different branches and were reuniting again near Nola, forming a canal that flowed into the Regi Lagni. A good deal of work was done on the watercourses near Lauro. A new bed was dug for the Casamarciano stream, as well as for a lagno leading from Croce di Cimitile to the Cicciano Bridge. Existing walls in the Gaudo and Avella valleys were also reinforced to protect the fields and houses of Cicciano and Camposano.

Still, the hydrogeological problems of the district were such that these new measures could hardly be the whole solution. In May 1829, especially abundant rains caused still more disasters. "About a thousand *moggia* [.33 hectares] of valuable plots of vineyards and cereals" were overrun with water and mud. At Palma Campania, water damaged several buildings, including the palazzo of the king's judge. Many places were devastated, including the fields between Baiano and Cumignano, on one side, and the Cimitile area, on the other. Projects carried out during previous months had certainly limited damages: "The embankments erected in the riverbeds of the Gaudo and Cicciano," wrote Grasso, "though still incomplete, helped to save several groups of houses." But according to the engineer, the real problem was that deforestation had continued incessantly, despite a new ban on logging mandated by the recent forest law.[23] Director Afan de Rivera agreed with Grasso, declaring that deforestation was the main issue needed to be confronted: "If we do not remove the causes of the great floods," he wrote in July of that year, "we will be deploying the tools of our craft in vain. The waters are carrying the crumbled mountains down to the plain."

Toward No Happy Ending

As these reports indicate, technicians of the Corpo di Ponti e Strade as well as the main district authorities were articulating clear connections between forests and hydrogeological balance. It is hard to say, of course, how widespread this awareness was at the time and, in particular, to what degree landowners and farmers were aware of the negative consequences of forest destruction. But whether they acted in ignorance or bad faith, it is clear that the benefits of the additional profits made by cutting trees and freeing land for crops surpassed the ongoing threats to land and life from capricious floods. This attitude was encouraged by lenient judicial authorities, as shown by a report that Afan de Rivera sent to the Ministry of Interior after yet another flood damaged the town of Cicciano and surrounding fields in November 1829. After again stressing that the cause of the disaster could be traced to the cutting of forests, Afan de Rivera noted that "orders for fines were issued, but most offenders were acquitted."

This report is the last document in the archival sequence. But the problems certainly continued. All indications suggest that the following decades witnessed events like those already described. Floods were reported in May 1833, again in February and October 1841, and then in October-November 1843.[24] As before, the authorities were unable to take the measures necessary for reestablishing the environmental balance. Despite concerted efforts in the following years, villagers living and working in the slide path had little choice but to rely on minor projects for protecting themselves from flood emergencies. A laissez-faire forest law issued in 1877 in the newly unified Italy aggravated the situation by allowing a further reduction of the area's forests.

Only in the early twentieth century did the forest quality and flood propensity near Naples begin to change. First, massive transoceanic emigration eased demographic pressure. In addition, government authorities were soon pushing novel reforestation policies. But the twentieth century also witnessed a violent eruption of Vesuvius in April 1906. In time-honored tradition, mudslides were again ravaging the towns that had suffered the same disasters in centuries past.[25] Today, although the historical and environmental contexts have changed completely, unstable pyroclastic soils still exist, further aggravated by the area's high demographic density and anthropogenic impact. The recent Sarno disaster stands as a harsh echo of Director Afan de Rivera's voice nearly two centuries ago: "Nature does not easily bow to the laws of men."[26]

Notes

1. A quite exhaustive overview of the vast technical and geological literature on the Sarno catastrophe is available in Antonio Vallario, ed., *Sarno sei anni dalla catastrofe* (Naples: Guida, 2004).

2. See, for example, Vincenzo Aversano and Guido Ruggiero, eds., *Montagna assassina o vittima? Per una storia del territorio e delle alluvioni di Bracigliano, Quindici, Sarno e Siano (1756–1997)* (Salerno: Laveglia, 2000). For a survey of all historical and sociological studies on the Sarno landslide, see Walter Palmieri, "La catastrofe di Sarno e la riflessione storiografica," *I Frutti di Demetra: Bollettino di Storia e Ambiente* 7 (2005): 5–10.

3. On this event, see Antonio Vallario, "La frana di Palma Campania del 1986," in *Frane e territorio: Le frane nella morfogenesi dei versanti e nell'uso del territorio* (Naples: Liguori, 1992), 335–50, with further references.

4. Information about this event can be found in Alfonso Corradi, *Annali delle epidemie occorse in Italia dalle prime memorie fino al 1850*, vol. 5 (Bologna: Gamberini and Parmeggiani, 1892), 376–77.

5. For further information, see Stefano Carlino, "Le alluvioni e le colate di fango successive alle eruzioni del Vesuvio: Storia e considerazioni sul rischio," in *Interventi di ingegneria naturalistica nel parco nazionale del Vesuvio*, ed. Carlo Bifulco (Naples: Ente Parco Nazionale del Vesuvio, 2001), 43–69.

6. Gaetano de Bottis, *Istoria di varj incendj del Monte Vesuvio* (Naples: Stamperia Reale, 1786), 229. All quotations in this essay have been translated from the Italian.

7. On that occasion, the most serious problems occurred "in areas northeast of the volcano. . . . There were 200,000 ducats worth of damages, mainly caused by the fall of pyroclastic fragments and mudslides." See "Tabella sintetica delle eruzioni del Vesuvio tra il 1631 e il 1944," Istituto Nazionale di Geofisica e Vulcanologia, available at http://www.ov.ingv.it/italiano/news/slideves/tabella_eruzioni.htm (accessed 5 June 2009).

8. See Carlino, "Le alluvioni," 61.

9. *Cenno storico dell'eruzione del Vesuvio avvenuta in ottobre dell'anno 1822* (Naples: Stamperia del Giornale del Regno delle Due Sicilie, 1822), 23–24. On this eruption, see also Teodoro Monticelli and Nicola Covelli, *Storia de' fenomeni del Vesuvio avvenuti negli anni 1821, 1822 e parte del 1823* (Naples: Gabinetto Bibliografico e Tipografico, 1823).

10. *Cenno storico dell'eruzione*, 22–25.

11. Ministero Interni, *Inventario II*, folders no. 4677–79, State Archives, Naples. All quotations in the text are from this group of documents.

12. Under a royal decree of 1909, the municipality of Cumignano changed its name to Comiziano, and this is the name designated in map 3.1.

13. On this subject, see Giuseppe Fiengo, *I Regi Lagni e la bonifica della Campania Felix durante il viceregno spagnolo* (Florence: Olschki, 1988).

14. On the same day, a disastrous flood with mudslides hit the Sorrentine peninsula, which lies south of Vesuvius and is affected by much the same problems as the Nola area. The worst damages were recorded in the municipality of Cetara, where eight people died.

15. From 1806 to the unification of Italy, the continental south was divided into fifteen provinces, each placed under the authority of an *intendente,* or provincial governor. Each province was in turn subdivided into districts, each headed by a *subintendente,* or district governor. The district of Nola was in the province of Terra di Lavoro, roughly corresponding to the present-day province of Caserta.

16. See Aversano and Ruggiero, *Montagna,* 32. Other information about this catastrophe can be found in Costanza D'Elia, *Bonifiche e Stato nel Mezzogiorno (1815–1860)* (Naples: ESI, 1994), esp. the chapter "Il distretto di Nola," 281–95.

17. Only a small part of this money came from provincial funds. Most of it came from *ratizzi,* or taxes on the landowners who benefited from the projects.

18. Up to then, wrote the intendente, a total of 11,547 ducats had been spent.

19. The abundant literature on the subject includes Piero Bevilacqua, "Uomini, terre, economie," in *Storia delle regioni dall'Unità ad oggi, La Calabria,* ed. Piero Bevilacqua and Augusto Placanica (Turin: Einaudi, 1985), 115–362; Pietro Tino, "La montagna meridionale: Boschi, uomini, economie tra Otto e Novecento," in *Storia dell'agricoltura italiana in età contemporanea,* vol. 1, *Spazi e paesaggi,* ed. Piero Bevilacqua (Venice: Marsilio, 1989), 677–754; Marco Armiero, *Il territorio come risorsa: Comunità, economie e istituzioni nei boschi abruzzesi (1806–1860)* (Naples: Liguori, 1999), 110–20; see also, Antonio Lazzarini, ed., *Diboscamento montano e politiche territoriali: Alpi e Appennini dal Settecento al Duemila* (Milan: Franco Angeli, 2002).

20. On the ratizzo system, see note 17.

21. "I observed," wrote Grasso, "several projects carried out by that subintendent in the Quindici valley, done partly with very limited means, partly without any expense at all to the public administration because it was the owners and tenants themselves who had undertaken to protect themselves from the floods. These projects concerned dividing and subdividing the waters running down this valley, and the widening and deepening of the streambeds to allow them to reach the Lagni."

22. On 2 April 1828, Afan de Rivera reported that 23,420 ducats had been spent so far.

23. Several laws against deforestation followed one another in the Kingdom of the Two Sicilies. One had been issued in 1811, another in 1819. A third one

was approved during the period considered here (on 21 August 1826). On this subject, see Walter Palmieri, "Il bosco nel Mezzogiorno preunitario tra legislazione e dibattito," in *Ambiente e risorse nel Mezzogiorno contemporaneo,* ed. Piero Bevilacqua and Gabriella Corona (Corigliano Calabro: Meridiana Libri, 2000), 27–62.

24. D'Elia, "Il distretto," 292–93.

25. On the eruption, see Carlino, "Le alluvioni," 62–63, and Francesco Aliperti, "L'eruzione del Vesuvio del 1906," in *Le pagine nere del XX secolo* (Marigliano: Anselmi, 2001), 15–39.

26. See note 11 for this quotation.

CHAPTER 4

Environmental Imperialism in Sardinia

Pesticides and Politics in the Struggle against Malaria

Marcus Hall

MALARIA IS second only to tuberculosis as the world's most deadly killer. Yet malaria is an environmental issue as well as a health concern. Because malaria parasites are transmitted by mosquito vectors, measures that kill mosquitoes, disrupt mosquito habitat, or prevent their contact with humans have been tested alongside a variety of drug treatments. Human efforts to control malaria mean that wetlands have been drained, rivers channeled, and pesticides sprayed, often through massively financed campaigns. The Rockefeller Foundation's Sardinian Project, lasting from 1946 to 1951, utilized thirty-two thousand DDT workers to spray ten thousand tons of DDT mixture over an area two-thirds the size of Switzerland, finally liberating the island of malaria. The environmental implications were enormous.

But even as Sardinia's ecosystems were being transformed during those postwar years, the political implications were also dramatic and far-reaching. In the days before the World Health Organization, the Rockefeller Foundation's International Health Division was the global leader in malaria control. If the foundation felt that something might be done to eliminate the malarial scourge, governments listened. The foundation explained to

Italian leaders that Sardinia was an ideal place to test not the insecticidal potency of DDT—for that potency had already been documented—but the combined abilities of powerful pesticides and extensive drainage projects to completely rid Sardinia of mosquitoes. The goal in Sardinia was not malaria eradication but mosquito eradication. Yet not all Sardinians were convinced that the Rockefeller Foundation was doing what was needed.[1]

The Sardinian Project may therefore be considered a health measure that was as political and ideological as it was chemical and environmental. And since this malarial campaign was directed from afar, it was also an imperial undertaking. Because Italians and Americans did not always agree on the best methods for combating malaria, Sardinians and the Sardinian environment were caught in the middle.

An Insecticide Proving Ground

Malaria, variously termed *ague* (in English), *paludisme* (in French), *le febbre* or *mal aria,* or bad air (in Italian), had been a seasonal scourge across much of Europe until well into the twentieth century. As cheap quinine, sturdy housing, and land drainage became more widespread across the continent, malaria receded southward to the Mediterranean.[2] Although some folk doctors had been blaming malaria on mosquitoes since at least the mid-nineteenth century—with the mosquito's role as a disease carrier given scientific proof in the 1890s—the difficulty of avoiding or killing this insect meant that until the 1920s, quinine pills were the treatment of choice, both for prevention and cure.[3] It was also observed that malaria often diminished as agriculture intensified, giving rise to the adage that "malaria fled the plow," which helped spur still more agricultural development. In Italy, thousands of hectares of marshlands were drained for the dual purpose of creating farmland and eradicating malaria.

Eradicating *mosquitoes* came into vogue as more powerful insecticides became available. But malariologists were generally skeptical about insecticides, at least initially. There had been reports of successful insect eradications, as when the Rockefeller Foundation's Fred Soper used arsenates and pyrethrum in the 1930s to rid northeast Brazil of *Anopheles gambiae,* an African mosquito that had found its way across the Atlantic. But other malariologists recognized the rather crude tactic of relying on insect poisons to improve human health. Even after the powerful insect-killing abilities of DDT were publicly demonstrated first in the Pacific theater in World War II and then in the 1944 louse epidemic of Naples, zoologist Marston Bates considered mosquito eradication to be "a sledge-hammer approach to malaria control."[4]

Malaria is a complicated disease. It arises not from a virus or bacteria but from a family of microscopic parasites (or plasmodium), individuals of which alternately thrive in blood cells or become dormant in the liver, being transferred between human hosts by certain kinds of mosquitoes. In theory, there would be a variety of ways to break the malaria cycle, such as killing the parasite, preventing human contact with mosquitoes, killing mosquitoes themselves, or disrupting mosquito habitat. The different life histories, behaviors, and habitats of different mosquito species mean that humans have relied on a range of antimalarial measures, from building tighter homes to draining swamps and covering wells, spraying pesticides, and administering medication. And some people are simply more susceptible to contracting the parasite or manifesting malarial symptoms. Lewis Hackett, one of the preeminent malariologists during the interwar period, likened his work to a game of chess: malaria, he said, "is played with a few pieces, but [it] is capable of an infinite variety of situations."[5]

DDT hardly targeted the parasite, then, but instead served to kill mosquitoes—at least most of them—while smashing plenty of other things that got in its path. By the early 1950s, malaria was disappearing across most Mediterranean lands as spray crews marched back and forth across its peninsulas and islands. Today, health experts note that DDT also served to eradicate malariology, a sophisticated science involving parasitology, entomology, epidemiology, ecology, and internal medicine.[6] At least for a time, DDT was the magic sledgehammer that ridded malaria from those areas fortunate enough to receive it quickly and massively before insect resistance to DDT set in. Or at least this is the usual story of DDT and malaria. In 2002, on the fiftieth anniversary of the Sardinian Project, elementary students in the village of Birori, Sardinia, proclaimed in their class project, "Today, thanks to DDT, malaria has disappeared from Sardinia and from temperate regions."[7]

Sardinia was always Italy's most malarious region. Statistics show that thirty-eight hundred Sardinians died of malaria in 1918, with around a hundred times that number (or about one-third of the one million residents) acting as carriers, many of them suffering but not dying from the disease. Sardinia in turn became a preferred target of governmental malaria control programs, such as those involving widespread quinine distribution. Sardinia was also a preferred target for experimental malariology. Hackett, a Rockefeller Foundation employee and codirector of Rome's Public Health Institute or ISS (also funded by the Rockefeller Foundation), carried out a number of malaria investigations in Sardinia. After reading about how the arsenic compound Paris Green was being used in the United States to kill mosquito larvae, Hackett and his colleagues tried it out in Sardinia in its first antimalarial use in Europe, some two decades before DDT was itself being sprayed across the island in unprecedented quantities. Whether or not Sardinians knew it, Sardinia was an insecticide proving ground.[8]

After 1946, the goal in Sardinia was to kill every last specimen of *Anopheles labranchiae* on an enormous and rugged island encompassing more than a million and a half separate springs, wells, swamps, and creeks—or wherever mosquitoes survived and bred—together with the inside walls of every human dwelling. Sardinia's mobilization of men, machines, and materials during this mosquito war rivaled the human war that had ended a year earlier. Nonetheless, scattered villagers maintained that malaria fevers really derived from pestilential waters, not from mosquitoes, and so they were reluctant to let sprayers into their homes, especially when houseflies quit dying (the most immediate benefit of spraying) by having acquired pesticide resistance. Some of Sardinia's own health experts, moreover, criticized "American" methods over tried-and-tested "Italian" methods, complaining that the project focused too much on mosquitoes and not enough on the disease. After the project's first director quit, secretly claiming that island-wide mosquito extermination was an impossible task, the next director orchestrated a final, all-out campaign before declaring malaria success while admitting mosquito defeat—and beating a hasty retreat out of Sardinia. Official reports concluded that the project came to within 99.936 percent of achieving success; that is, they missed a few mosquitoes. Although the Sardinian Project successfully rid the island of malaria, mosquitoes still persisted there. Some investigators deemed the project a failure.[9]

Although many Sardinians interviewed in the course of this research wondered about the long-term effects of DDT in their bloodstreams, few of them realize that their grandparents took part in an experiment. They are quick to say that absorbing DDT was the lesser evil compared to contracting malaria. But almost none of them know about the pre-DDT successes in controlling Sardinia's malaria with other remedies, including other pesticides, medical treatments, or land management practices. Before World War II, Italy's own disease control programs—which involved medication, drainage, and non-DDT pesticides—had cut malaria mortality in Sardinia by 90 percent, a statistic not often revealed in Rockefeller Foundation reports. With the disorganization brought on by the war and with a new malaria epidemic raging on the island by 1944, the disease needed to be controlled, and it certainly would have been in the absence of DDT and the Sardinian Project.[10] Judging from malaria defeats in other parts of Italy and the Mediterranean over the next three years, it was also

Fig. 4.1. DDT canisters being carried by donkeys as part of the Rockefeller Foundation's Sardinian Project, 1946–51. From John Logan, *The Sardinian Project: An Experiment in the Eradication of an Indigenous Malarious Vector* (Baltimore, MD: Johns Hopkins Press, 1953), 323

clear that *moderate* DDT spraying could have dramatically controlled malaria in Sardinia, without resorting to dousing. Just one year into the project, Rockefeller administrators were advising French malariologists on nearby Corsica—which was also afflicted with the disease—that they need use only one-third to one-fourth as much DDT as was being used in Sardinia if their goal was "merely" eradicating malaria instead of eradicating mosquitoes.[11]

Sardinian Project administrators may have questioned their DDT overkilling when faced with local reports that fish, honeybees, sheep—and maybe more—had succumbed to the effects of DDT poisoning. The fledgling World Health Organization had even issued cautions as early as 1947, saying that DDT, "especially when used from aeroplanes . . . may interfere with the normal biological cycles of the treated environment, [and] may upset the economy of the region, not only from the standpoint of animals but also of plants, both of crops and trees." Still, administrators felt that these problems would be outweighed by the enormous benefits gained. "The eyes of the world are on the Sardinian Project," declared the chief of the foundation's International Health Division when faced with on-site

Fig. 4.2. Fumigating a pond with DDT in Sardinia, 1949. From Logan, *The Sardinian Project*, 195

technical problems and frustrated personnel. Sardinia *was* the world's test site for the global eradication of malaria-carrying mosquitoes. If dangerous mosquitoes could just be eliminated from this island, they might be eliminated on a continental or even global scale. But the experimental nature of this project was not revealed in its full light until *after* project leaders went home and even then mostly in English, not Italian. Sardinians would have been the first to reap the expected benefits of prolonged DDT saturation, but they would also have been the first to deal with any negative side effects. Risk, real or unknown, was at the center of this transnational case of environmental justice.[12]

One suspects special treatment and special injustice when Sardinian courts absolved the Sardinian Project of all legal claims to DDT damages, especially when one realizes that Rockefeller Foundation officers were writing to each other about DDT's possible "contraindications," including fish kills and DDT-tainted cow milk. Perhaps lingering wartime hysteria and DDT's potential benefits justified lax pesticide precautions. Still, the Sardinian Project seems to have been an instance of technological hubris buttressed by hegemonic institutions that were more concerned about their own aspirations than the peoples their project was meant to benefit. In urging project leaders to continue spraying even when faced with the likelihood of failure, one officer mentioned that the foundation's "prestige as well as word is involved."[13]

"Give Thanks to DDT"

One indication of the wide gulf separating Sardinian villagers from Rockefeller personnel came to light during the fifty-year commemoration of the Sardinian Project. In school activities across the island, young children were asked to interview their grandparents about the last days of malaria, and some of the answers they collected reveal a number of surprises. Perhaps the biggest surprise centered on the range of assumptions about DDT's role in eradicating malaria. Though many rural Sardinians assumed DDT was a useful chemical, they often extended its use from insect killing to human healing: the wonder chemical sprayed in the corners of every human habitation was seen by many to have medicinal as well as insecticidal properties. It turns out that a good many villagers dusted this chemical directly on their skin or else sprayed it on themselves during those post–World War II years, fully assuming that it would eradicate disease as well as insects. Since DDT killed bugs, these Sardinians reasoned that it also killed malaria, and many of them took advantage of their ready access to this chemical by rubbing it generously on their bodies.

"Give Thanks to DDT," one second-grader titled her report of an interview with her grandmother. "Sards owe a lot to DDT," she explained; "thanks to this insecticide, malaria disappeared from the island." Other interviewers highlighted the extent to which Sardinians used this chemical for other than insecticidal purposes. After a conversation with his own eyewitness grandparents, a first-grader reported that "sometimes people took off their clothes and sprayed themselves with DDT." Eighty-year-old Zia Bonaria explained to her own young inquisitors that "from America they brought this medicine, and after using the medicine, there were no more mosquitoes." Conflating insecticide with medication was apparently quite common in rural Sardinia. One ex-sprayer explained to his grandnephews that "at the end of World War II, Americans understood this disease before we did, and so they distributed a medicine called DDT in order to kill mosquitoes that transmitted malaria; rivers, houses, and streets were disinfected." For these Sardinians, then as now, it did not really matter whether the remedy worked against the malaria parasite in the bloodstream or against the insect carrier of that parasite. The vital fact was that, whether as medicine or as insecticide, DDT wiped out malaria. It was unimportant whether Rockefeller Foundation experts and their hired spray crews were health workers or pest controllers, medical doctors or applied ecologists, as long as they successfully rolled back malaria.[14]

To many Sardinians, it made perfectly good sense: Americans had just liberated Sardinia and the rest of Italy of the Nazi nemesis, and following the war, Americans armed with boatloads of DDT began liberating the island of insects by land and air. DDT did wonderful things. It killed spiders, centipedes, and ants, and to the joy of all, it killed swarms of pesky houseflies buzzing about in every home. Its boosters nicknamed it D.D.T.—*Domani Dormiamo Tranquilli*—Tomorrow We'll Sleep Well. Of course, it also killed mosquitoes, whether in adult or larvae stages, and it certainly seemed that it would kill malaria if people would just rub a little bit on their skin.

Sardinia's reliance on medicinal DDT is best understood as stemming from at least two important precedents: the 1943–44 Naples typhus scare and Italy's ongoing quinine distribution program. At recently captured Naples, the Allied Command ordered the first widespread civilian use of DDT for controlling typhus by killing the body lice that transmitted the typhus-producing bacteria. Each week, spray nozzles were pushed under the armpits and into the crotches of hundreds of thousands of men and women, infants and elderly. Over a six-month period, Neapolitans received some three million separate DDT dustings. Noted one eyewitness, "The sight of persons on the street with powdered hair and clothing was too common to cause comment." Because the conceivable toxic aftermath of a scantily tested pesticide apparently never occurred to people, it made good sense for nearby Sardinians to apply DDT to their own bodies for curtailing their own epidemic.[15]

But typhus is not malaria. Even though many of the symptoms—headache combined with intermittent fever and chills—are common to both diseases, typhus relies on lice to transmit virulent bacteria; malaria relies on mosquitoes to transmit plasmodium parasites into the bloodstream. Although DDT kills *both* of these arthropods, lice live on human skin, whereas mosquitoes live in swamps. Sardinians threatened by malaria were not being good ecologists when they applied DDT to their skin.

At the same time, Sardinians were used to receiving cheap or free medication in their struggle against malaria. Since 1900, the Italian government had subsidized the widespread distribution of quinine, long the drug of choice for helping prevent the disease or treat it if contracted. Although quinine (usually given in pills) was far from being a certain cure, Italian malariologists recommended medicating everyone in their country's malarious regions, so that the persistent malaria chain—from person to mosquito to person—might be broken. After Turin's state-operated quinine factory began operation, Italians started downing their quinine pills daily.

A number of challenges hindered the quinine program. Sometimes, private pharmacies sought profits by reselling state-distributed quinine; sometimes, villagers refused to take their pills—or neglected to do so. When malaria levels declined, Italians were especially prone to forgetting their pills, which brought discomforting side effects such as nausea and even temporary blindness in some individuals. Malaria expansion during the war years brought heightened drugging campaigns, including distribution of the synthetic antimalarials such as atabrine. By the end of World War II, the Allies were distributing atabrine to soldiers and villagers alike to ward off malaria. Sardinians had become accustomed to getting free malaria remedies, and when DDT arrived, this insecticide seemed (and was often treated like) just another medication requiring frequent dosages.

Italy's malaria medication campaign went by the name of *bonifica umana*. Translated literally, this program of "human improvement" was a branch of Italy's larger *bonifica* movement, aimed at improving the land for human benefit. Bonifica projects focused on reforesting, fertilizing, diking, irrigating, and especially draining the land. The drainage of marshes offered the double benefit of producing arable farmland and eliminating malarial habitat, and it was one of Benito Mussolini's pet projects. Bonifica umana was special because it did not affect the land but acted on the public's bloodstream. Malariologists reasoned that if quinine could be maintained in high levels across the populace, malaria parasites would be eliminated. Yet by labeling medication programs bonifica, Italians were directly linking land use to public health. Improving the land seemed to improve human health. Or as Mussolini preached in parades across the country, "Redeem the land, and with the land the men, and with the men the race."

Bonifica umana—as widescale human drugging—also paralleled the ongoing effort to improve the race through good breeding, or eugenics. Rational, scientific management of human bloodlines was not very distant from medicating the masses to defend them from human pathogens. Each effort required central planning, with experts deciding on the best strategies for improving the public's well-being.

From the perspective of human improvement, then, there is little wonder that a good many Sardinians who struggled against malaria interchanged drugs and pesticides, as both kinds of chemicals were being used to eliminate malaria—and it did not matter much that one acted on the body and the other on the land. Because elements of the body and land flowed into one another, using powerful chemicals to improve either made good sense. Healthy lands promoted healthy bodies. Remedies overlapped, and one might enhance human health by rubbing in a little DDT.

The complication, of course, was that DDT did such an efficient job at killing everything else it touched. From insects to fish to birds and possibly to sheep and cattle, DDT was a systemic killer, and Sardinians observed the aftermath of islandwide poisoning. As noted earlier, fish farmers operating in estuaries complained of dead fish after airplanes dusted these marshy areas. Beekeepers filed suit against the DDT sprayers. Some shepherds blamed their sickly herds on the spraying. How could the spray that apparently made the land sick possibly benefit human health?

DDT's dangers were not as obvious as they might appear. For one thing, Rockefeller Foundation experts assured everyone that there were no dangers. The handbill tacked on public spaces a day or two before house-spraying squads arrived made it clear that there was very little to worry about. Small children, said the handbill, should not be allowed to stay in rooms being sprayed "because petroleum mist coming into eye contact may cause a little burning." It added, "Food and water containers must be covered so that they don't take on the smell of petroleum." In bold letters it concluded: "ONE MUST KEEP IN MIND THAT IN THE QUANTITIES USED, THESE SPRAYS ARE ABSOLUTELY HARMLESS."[16]

In response to accusations that DDT poisoned sheep, the Rockefeller Foundation sponsored investigations for measuring this chemical's possible toxicity. Sardinia's own Zootechnical Institute, located in Sassari, carried out the tests by inducing farm animals over several weeks to ingest various quantities of DDT. The results shut up at least some of the skeptics when three of the four animals *gained* instead of *lost* weight. The widely publicized results suggested that intestinal parasites had succumbed to heavy DDT doses, thereby fattening up the animals. Surely for animal husbandry, here was another medicinal benefit of DDT. According to the voice of authority, if the land seemed unhealthy, DDT should be seen as remedy, not as poison. Although I did not find any records of skinny Sards eating DDT biscuits for snacks, there are reports of dedicated DDT sprayers who aimed to prove the chemical's safety to skeptics by ingesting small quantities of it in front of them. For unsuspecting bystanders, the Rockefeller Foundation—staffed and directed by physicians—was injecting DDT as an antibiotic into an infected landscape.[17]

At times, DDT's medicinal powers seemed even more important than its insecticidal powers because it required such a leap to connect malaria with mosquitoes. Although painstaking British and Italian researchers fifty years earlier had revealed the role of *Anopheles* mosquitoes in transmitting the debilitating parasites, most Sards still considered the disease as emanating from *place,* not *insect.* Mal-aria (bad air) is how Italians labeled this disease, and those who could afford the leisure time took their children to the sea in the summer to breathe good airs and good sea breezes: "The sea is good for children," the saying goes even today. Others were convinced that a person could contract malaria through stagnant water; in fact, during the Sardinian Project's spray operations, some sprayers quit their jobs upon learning that they were required to wade through water in order to spray less accessible areas. More than one folk doctor suggested that malaria attached itself to submerged ankles like leeches in a pond. Besides, if mosquitoes were the source of malaria, how was it that some years were nearly malaria-free even though plenty of mosquitoes buzzed? Or how was it that malarious individuals sometimes suffered feverish relapses when no mosquitoes flew, as in the fall and winter? Malaria was a quintessential environmental disease. DDT certainly decimated bugs, but malaria emanated from sources aerial, ethereal, smelly, soggy, putrid, and pestilential—but not necessarily arthropodal. The fact that DDT killed big bugs suggested that it would certainly kill microscopic ones, and so Sards lathered and powdered it on.

Sardinia's malaria plot thickens when we learn that villagers sometimes avoided taking their real malaria medicine. Atabrine, handed out by the government and the military in the 1940s, came as little yellow pills to be taken daily. Unfortunately, like quinine, atabrine offered up the usual array of unpleasant side effects, in addition to tinting the frequent consumer's skin yellow. With the pill's striking yellow color, it did not take long for villagers to consider alternative uses for their free handouts, especially as malaria levels receded. More than one schoolchild told of how his or her grandmother (or grandaunt) ground up her free atabrine doses, mixed the powder with water, and then dyed white blouses and white skirts to beautiful shades of yellow.

Yellow was particularly fashionable at village dances in those final malaria years. One realizes that even as insecticides became drugs, drugs became dyes. Poisons became remedies, and remedies became embellishments.

The Rockefeller Foundation finally went home after deciding that every last mosquito in Sardinia could not be exterminated. Despite extra crews and extra insecticide applied in 1949 and 1950, so-called insect scouts, who passed through an area a few days behind the spray crews, continued to find odd mosquitoes still alive and buzzing. *Anopheles* eradication across a large Mediterranean island had failed. Worse for the Rockefeller Foundation, mainland Italy had easily been scoured of malaria with only light DDT spraying, so that the "experimental" nature of the Sardinian Project was becoming more obvious to local officials and villagers alike. Sardinians saw fewer benefits of DDT and more of its suspected problems, such as fish, bird, and livestock poisoning. Through a diplomatic courtesy, the Rockefeller Foundation narrowly avoided having to face a wave of lawsuits filed by disgruntled fish farmers, beekeepers, and animal breeders.[18]

A new, smaller insect control service was established in the wake of the American departure. But as the Rockefeller Foundation exited, it seemed that so did the power of DDT. Villagers complained that Sardinia's own spray crews, who marched into their houses and across their backyards, were minimally effective because Italian DDT was not as powerful as its American counterpart. With flies and mosquitoes returning in the mid-1950s, many villagers were unwilling to believe excuses about the onset of insecticide resistance. Moreover, with malaria gone, there was no more need for *medicinal* DDT—and now *insecticidal* DDT seemed to be creating more problems than it solved, especially with the irritating solvents that it required; a weakened DDT seemed to hurt, rather than help, human physiology. One seventy-eight-year-old women recounted her change of mind. "Yes, I remember the anti-malarial campaign," she told her seventh-grade interviewer. "They went into people's homes saying that [the spray] was not poisonous! And now see what they say! Well, they did it anyway because it was such a serious epidemic." With malaria gone, DDT became toxic instead of curative, a poison instead of a medicine. Powerful chemicals, be they drugs or pesticides, still circulated between body and place, but no longer could Sardinians ignore the harmful side effects. They were finally viewing DDT as had their Rockefeller Foundation liberators decades earlier.[19]

Combating Malaria, Shaping Landscape

Sardinia's history linking DDT and malaria presents us with a good opportunity to think about how imperial forces produced ecological changes.

Carlo Contini, one of Sardinia's leading entomologists who was involved in the Sardinian Project and who helped supervise subsequent insect control operations there, offers evidence from his own meticulously ordered insect collections to declare that Sardinia's insect fauna was forever transformed by postwar DDT spraying. Contini believes that if periodic species inventories of Sardinia existed, they would show changes in floral and faunal composition over the last half century, with powerful insecticides causing some of these changes.[20]

Malaria modifies not only human health but also environmental health through the human techniques employed in combating the disease. DDT's tendency to kill not just mosquitoes but also fish and birds and desirable insects is just one illustration of how malaria modifies the environment, with humans wielding spray guns as the agent of environmental change. Before the arrival of DDT, the even cruder and probably more dangerous Paris Green also altered ecosystems in ways besides merely killing the mosquito larvae that were its target.

In setting out to eradicate their malaria nemesis, then, humans did much more than introduce laboratory-synthesized toxins into the environment. Draining, damming, diking, and canaling were all carried out in the hopes that malaria would disappear forever. Eucalyptus was imported from Australia and planted by the linear kilometer in hopes of drying up marshland and sanitizing surroundings. Gambusia fish were brought in from Florida's Everglades to slurp up mosquito larvae, with concomitant effects on the aquatic food chain. The resulting reclamation projects are one large reason why Sardinia's current countryside can hardly be recognized in the black-and-white photographs taken of the same scenes sixty years earlier. These paired images demonstrate that malaria has been a potent factor in inducing humans to set environmental changes in motion.

Just as one can argue over precise distal and proximal causes of environmental change, by pointing to either humans or human disease as a powerful force in modifying Sardinia's landscape, biologists can argue over whether such changes were good or bad. Canaling riparian areas and draining coastal estuaries certainly diminished biodiversity. Spreading invasive exotics such as eucalyptus and gambusia likewise modified an already transformed ecosystem. I would be very surprised if many conservation biologists would celebrate the ecosystemic changes that arose from humans struggling to rid themselves of malaria.

But before condemning human efforts to fight malaria as having ruined the nature of Sardinia, environmentalists would be pleased to learn, for example, that Sardinia's highlands are no longer overgrazed. Because sheepherders traditionally migrated up and away from lowlands by summer—fleeing malaria-infested areas—the upper pastures and meadows saw intensive sheep use. Americans working on the Sardinian Project commented on the poor state of Sardinia's upland pastures. After malaria disappeared, herders could graze their animals more judiciously, balancing grazing between high and low pastures and thereby avoiding overuse in both. The flora and fauna across Sardinia's Mount Gennargentu, now a national park, are probably richer and healthier because humans struggled against malaria and won the battle. Whether these physical and biological footprints represent harm or benefit, there is little question that malaria and humans working in tandem helped remodel the face of Sardinia. When joining the social and political ramifications stemming from malaria's demise, one would have to agree with historian Denis Mack Smith's suggestion that malaria eradication may be "the most important single fact in the whole of modern Italian history."[21] Kings and queens, invading armies, agricultural inventions, networks of trade, and brilliant ideas all compose the rich fabric of Italy's past, but human disease—with malaria as a prime example—has served all along as agent, nemesis, and rationale for helping motivate kings and queens, farmers and planners, inventors and thinkers.

DDT Legacies

Today, Sardinia has became a favorite place for testing long-term DDT toxicity. Death rates and causes, cancer rates and types, and pesticide exposure and kinds are carefully tabulated, both for former DDT sprayers and for the larger Sardinian population. And to date, there is no study that concludes Sardinians suffered disproportionately from DDT-caused health problems. A battery of other tests beyond Sardinia that investigate links between DDT and human health suggest that the chemical really is not very dangerous to humans—with possible, discrete exceptions for small children and lactating mothers. Other studies, however, demonstrate that small creatures, from insects to fish and birds, are acutely affected by DDT. Opponents of the pesticide may therefore have more grounds to focus on disruptions to ecosystems than on disruptions to human health.[22]

It should also be clear that the Sardinian Project teaches us to be doubly cautious of any health or environmental measure imposed from afar. A case in point is the UN's recently ratified Stockholm Convention on Persistent Organic Pollutants (or POPs treaty), which restricts or bans twelve long-lasting chemicals, DDT among them. After several years of debate, the treaty was amended in 2004 to allow countries to continue using DDT under emergency circumstances if they follow strictly monitored procedures of registration, manufacture, and application. And though such DDT stipulations suggest long-term gains for everyone, the fact remains that any restriction on this pesticide—legal or bureaucratic—means that it will not be as available as it might have been. The UN's recent declaration "that no one will die of malaria because of the Stockholm Convention" may be true, but others may well have lived longer, healthier lives if this treaty had never been ratified. POPs is a restrictive measure, a measure that will continue to be more popular in the malaria-free north than in the malaria-plagued south.[23]

We can realize that DDT did (and does) help control malaria around the world, thereby saving lives. But we can also conclude that the Rockefeller Foundation did submit Sardinians and their environment to DDT levels that were much higher than was necessary for extinguishing malaria. The foundation had eradicated mosquitoes elsewhere, and it might have eradicated them on this island. But one must consider whether that risk was worth it, or whether Sardinians were aware of these risks or of the real nature of the project. One must also wonder why other islands lying closer to foundation headquarters, such as Long Island, were not chosen as the experimental site for eradicating a native mosquito.

Notes

1. The Rockefeller Foundation's International Health Division usually relied on establishing pilot health projects that it hoped would be emulated by the host country, but its Sardinian Project of mosquito eradication maintained a distinct experimental focus, thereby contributing to the controversial nature of this project. See John Farley, *To Cast Out Disease: A History of the International Health Division of the Rockefeller Foundation (1913–1951)* (New York: Oxford University Press, 2004).

2. For survey histories of malaria, see Gilberto Corbellini and Lorenza Merzagora, *La Malaria: Tra passato e presente* (Rome: University of Rome—Miligraf, 1998); Mark Honigsbaum, *The Fever Trail: In Search of the Cure for Malaria* (New York: Farrar, Straus and Giroux, 2001); James L. A. Webb Jr., *Humanity's Burden: A Global History of Malaria* (New York: Cambridge University Press, 2008).

3. The story of the link between mosquitoes and malaria, which culminates in the 1897 and 1898 observations of Ronald Ross and Giovanni Grassi, respectively, is nicely covered in Robert Desowitz, *The Malaria Capers: Tales of Parasites and People* (New York: Norton, 1991), 174–98.

4. Marston Bates, "Preface," in John Logan, *The Sardinian Project: An Experiment in the Eradication of an Indigenous Malarious Vector* (Baltimore, MD:

Johns Hopkins University Press, 1953), x. See also Malcom Gladwell, "The Mosquito Killer," *New Yorker*, 2 July 2002, 42–51.

5. Lewis W. Hackett, *Malaria in Europe: An Ecological Study* (London: Oxford, 1937), 266.

6. Robert Desowitz, "Testimony for Neglected Diseases in East Asia: Are Public Health Programs Working?" Senate Foreign Relations Committee, 6 October 2004, U.S. Senate Committee on Foreign Relations, available at http://foreign.senate.gov/testimony/2004/DesowitzTestimony041006.pdf (accessed 5 May 2009).

7. See http://www.macomer.net/scuolabirori/presentazione.html (accessed 1 September 2003).

8. Hackett, *Malaria in Europe*, 17.

9. Logan, *Sardinian Project*, 73, 104; *The Sardinian Project* (1948), Shell Film, 35 min. On the military ramifications of the project, see Marcus Hall, "World War II and the Axis of Disease," in *War and the Environment: Military Destruction in the Modern Age*, ed. Charles Closmann (College Station: Texas A&M University Press, 2009). An excellent survey of modern Italian malaria is given in Frank Snowden, *The Conquest of Malaria: Italy, 1900–1962* (New Haven, CT: Yale University Press, 2006).

10. See Marcus Hall, "Today Sardinia, Tomorrow the World: Killing Mosquitoes," *BardPolitik* 5 (Fall 2004): 21–28, also available at Bard Globalization and International Affairs Program, http://www.bard.edu/bgia/bardpolitik/vol5/21–28.pdf (accessed 5 May 2009).

11. John Logan to Leach, 16 June 1947, Rockefeller Archives Center, Pocantino Hills, New York (hereafter RAC), 1.1 / 502 / 1 / 2.

12. WHO Expert Committee on Malaria: Report on the First Session, Geneva, 22–25 April 1947, 15, WHO Archives, Geneva, Switzerland; D. B. Wilson to George Strode, 23 February 1947, RAC 1.2 / 700 / 12 / 106.

13. Fred Soper to George Strode, 8 July 1946; George Strode to Fred Soper, 12 July 1946, in RAC 1.2 / 700 / 12 / 104; D. B. Wilson to George Strode, 23 February 1947, RAC 1.2 / 700 / 12 / 106.

14. Pierluigi Cocco Collection, "Oral History Project of 'Maledetta Malaria,'" Medicina del Lavoro, University of Cagliari School of Public Health, Italy, 2004.

15. F. L. Soper, W. A. Davis, F. S. Markham, and L. A. Riehl, "Typhus Fever in Italy, 1943–1945, and Its Control with Louse Powder," *American Journal of Hygiene* 45, no. 3 (May 1947): 317, 320.

16. ERLAAS handbill, RAC 1.2 / 700 / 12 / 104.

17. See *Annali dell'Istituto Zootecnico*, Sassari, 1952. I would add that one of my informants confided to me he once tried massaging a mixture of DDT into

his hair to control dandruff after a friend remarked on how well this chemical seemed to resolve his own flaking problem.

18. See Logan, *Sardinian Project.*

19. The Rockefeller Foundation spray service (called Ente Regionale per la Lotta Anti-Anofelica in Sardegna, or ERLAAS) was converted into the locally run Centro Regionale Anti-Insetti (CRAI). See Pierluigi Cocco Collection, "Oral History Project of 'Maledetta Malaria.'"

20. Interview with Carlo Contini in Cagliari, 20 October 2003. Gianmario Prosperi, "Legislazione fitosanitaria italiana," *Regione dell'Umbria, Giunta Regionale,* I Dipartimento Agricoltura, 1981. The classic statement about environments transformed from afar is Alfred Crosby, *Ecological Imperialism: The Biological Expansion of Europe* (New York: Cambridge University Press, 1986).

21. Denis Mack Smith, *Italy: A Modern History* (Ann Arbor: University of Michigan Press, 1959), 494.

22. See, for example, Pierluigi Cocco, "Cancer Mortality among Men Occupationally Exposed to DDT," *Cancer Research* 65 (October 2005): 9588–94.

23. See "10 Things You Need to Know about DDT Use under the Stockholm Convention," World Health Organization, available at http://www.who.int/malaria/docs/10thingsonDDT.pdf (accessed 5 May 2009). See also United Nations Environment Programme (UNEP), News Release 2004/09, quoted on the GRID-Arental Web site, available at http://www.grida.no/news/press/1603.aspx (accessed 27 August 2009).

Commons and Forests

CHAPTER 5

The Decline of the Commons and the Environmental Balance in Early Modern Italy

Gabriella Corona

Common Possession between Backwardness and Sustainability

Does it still make sense today to look at forms of the collective use of natural resources—especially land—from the perspective of the great Marxist-inspired historiographical tradition? Is it best to regard collective resource use as a barbaric leftover from bygone times that hinders the spread of full and absolute property rights and prevents market forces from working at their full potential?

A very rich scholarly tradition, rooted in the works of eighteenth-century reformers, nineteenth-century economic and legal thought, and Marxist agricultural historiography,[1] has indeed viewed the evolution of the commons as part of the process of transforming the structure of property, one of the key aspects of the transition from feudalism to capitalism. This tradition has interpreted the struggle for agrarian individualism as a dialectic clash between the forces of progress inspired by a modern and individualistic conception of landownership that guaranteed higher productivity and those of conservation that hindered the productive use of the land.

More recent studies, however, seem to have distanced themselves from this approach. Notably, many case studies in different historiographical domains (especially social and legal history) have approached collective property from a different angle, especially one relating to environmental questions. Studies on common possession have gained new analytic vitality in the wide debate on how land management impacts the environment. Participants in this debate see different legally defined systems as alternative ways of using natural resources. Common property seems to have held out against the zeal of nineteenth- and twentieth-century legislators critical of feudalism mainly because it was founded on well-established premodern systems based on trust, village and group identity, and reciprocity. Thus, common property persisted in the regulatory mechanisms of the market, which were increasingly founded on individual interest and on nonlocal or impersonal economic relations.[2] Because of its importance for environmental preservation, the commons system is alive and well across large areas of Italy, in spite of the decline of the traditional values that used to go with it.[3]

Lately, Italian historians studying the issue of the commons have been asking themselves a number of questions. How, for example, did a commons system founded on economic mechanisms disconnected from the market manage to control unabated resource use? How has this regulatory mechanism evolved in modern times? What allowed the commons to survive up to the present? And how did forms of common property vary across the Italian peninsula?

In the late eighteenth and early nineteenth centuries, various forms of collective property still existed in vast areas of north-central Italy. Communities were organized in such a way as to manage common resources and put limitations on their use. Although towns had their own properties, most collectively managed resources were controlled by groups of families, parish organizations, and neighborhood networks. Thus, in these regions, collective property was managed by communities that only occasionally coincided with a municipality. The administration of these resources was a complex affair and implied that communal life was accepted as a fundamental value. "Collective property," writes legal historian Paolo Grossi," is never merely a legal instrument, or merely an economic one. It needs to draw on a whole world of values, to be rooted in a certain way of feeling, conceiving, and enacting community life and the relationship between man and cosmic nature."[4] We are looking at a society that is the very reverse of capitalism: solidarity versus individualism, self-sustainability versus boundless growth, community versus every man for himself.[5]

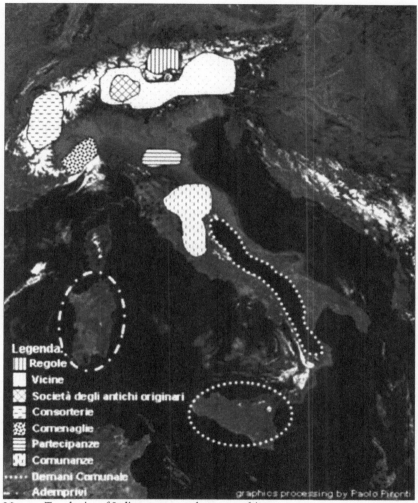

Map 5.1. Typologies of Italian commons by geographic areas

Organizations such as the *vicinie*, which are especially widespread in the east-central Alps, the *comunaglie* of Liguria, and the *comunanze* of the Apennines of Umbria and Le Marche included all or part of the inhabitants of a municipality. Only heads of families participated in the assemblies where decisions about commons were taken and their revenues distributed. In some cases, the community was made up of a network of families inhabiting the same neighborhood or parish or frequenting the same church. In parish communities, church representatives also took part in the assembly, and the community was referred to as the "men of the parish" (*uomini della parrocchia*).[6]

In other cases, such as that of the *regole*, organizations mainly found in the Cadore region of alpine Veneto, communities were made up of a group of coheirs descending from the same progenitor. This group administered a territory that it had inherited collectively. *Regola* was the name given to the assembly of coheirs.[7] Thus, *regole* were family organizations whose property belonged not to the citizens of a municipality but to members of the same family.[8] There were similar organizations elsewhere in Veneto and Lombardy, called *società degli originari*. In these organizations, also derived from the *vicinie*, only members of the families of the *originari* (the most eminent, wealthy, and old families)[9] presided over the parceling out of the revenues from the commons.[10] In the *partecipanze* of the Bolognese plain, south of the Po River, the prerequisite for the assignment of a plot of land was either citizenship in the municipality or *originarietà* (membership in an old, eminent family) or sometimes both. In this last case, one needed to be a permanent resident, the head of a family, *and* a descendant from a family of *partecipanti*.[11]

In other cases, the right to the use and possession of commons was reserved for a specific category of people defined by their productive activities. The *società della malga* (society of alpine hut), which existed in almost every village of the central Alps,[12] brought together all livestock owners. Similar organizations called *università agrarie* (rural communities) existed in Lazio. There, only the owner of at least two plow oxen could use the land in the territory of the *università*. This land was divided into three parts: pasture, fallow land, and cropland. Every year, lots were drawn to distribute fallow land among livestock owners.[13]

Far from being uniform and immutable, these organizations witnessed major changes in modern times. The changes were mainly brought about by the introduction of the typical regulatory mechanisms of the land and commodity market. Various dynamics of private appropriation of land took effect during this period. Besides illegal seizure of land, there were quite a few cases in which municipal land was incorporated by large private estates or capital-intensive farms.

Despite their sharing of common values and a system of relations based on reciprocity and trust, blood ties, and village identity, these communities were far from idyllic or conflict-free. Recent studies in social history have revealed highly conflictive situations marked by bitter internal struggles not necessarily connected to the simple dynamics of the push toward agrarian individualism.[14] Yet even with frequent social conflicts arising over resource possession, these cooperative communities managed to safeguard the environmental balance of their territories and protect them from devastation.

Based on kinship and/or common residence, the cooperative communities also formed power groups and bowed to rigid social hierarchies. Such communities were not free economic and social operators but were enmeshed in a close-knit web of ties, bonds, and obligations. At the same time, reciprocal trust, group spirit, and self-regulation often guaranteed the environmental success of the common property system. Various forms of common property provided for the safeguarding of resources and the guaranteeing of their reproduction. The code of one rural community near Brescia mentioned (in 1915) that written regulations had become necessary because "the grazing that should normally be available for all animals [was] extremely impoverished."[15] Livestock not belonging to a community was allowed onto the community's pastures in early spring but not during the winter, when the grazing was scarce.[16] As to freshwater fishing rights, there were sometimes bans on resource-depleting techniques such as using dragnets.[17] And at times, access to resources was restricted in order to protect the community as a whole from environmental depletion. Some assemblies fixed a threshold for per family firewood consumption, which usually depended on the productivity of woodland.[18] In many forests, local communities exacted a tax on woodcutting proportional to the quantity and quality of the wood.[19] Some forests belonging to *regole,* called *gazi,* were reserved for the exclusive use of the community. They provided lumber in case a house burned down or served as a hydrogeological barrier.[20] One was only allowed to cut as much lumber as was necessary, and the administrators' formal permission was required. In some areas, only coppice trees could be cut for firewood; indeed, sometimes there were rules requiring the planting of new trees in forests.[21] It was also forbidden to graze livestock on seeded or natural fields before these areas had been harvested, just as it was forbidden to graze coppiced areas after cutting, in order to protect saplings from being trampled or eaten by cattle.[22] There were also rules requiring putting rings in pigs' noses to keep them from tearing up pastures.[23]

Norms regulating land use and management often reflected the need to maintain the balance between the population and resources. Rigid bans against foreigners and neighboring communities, though confirming the oligarchic character of community interests, were meant to prevent demographic increases that might jeopardize this balance. In the case of the *società della malga,* statutory norms rigidly regulated access to pastures according to season, distinguishing between large and small livestock and between community members and foreigners.[24] Some scholars trace the very origin of commons to environmental concerns. Sandro Tiberini, for one, argues that the institution called *comunanza,* based on the parceling out of common pastures, arose to prevent demographic growth and the consequent extension of agricultural land by depleting forests.[25] The *partecipanze* of Emilia were formed to continue managing land collectively at a time when the population was growing and new settlers were coming in. When the need arose for drainage projects that required capital investment (as in the wetlands of the Bologna plain), there was a transition from simple communal rights to a rotating system of rights. The motive for this transition was to prevent private individuals from carrying out drainage (or *bonifica*) on their own and so appropriate common land. This new system involved the concession of a plot for a certain number of years. Such concessions were regulated by *ad meliorandum* emphyteutic contracts, that is, contracts that allowed one to use land if one kept it productive.[26]

The principle of the indivisibility of collective resources—that is, that such resources could not be divided, sold, or privatized—was upheld on the grounds that using resources collectively was more advantageous to individuals than using them privately. The system of privately owned land would have been insufficient for providing resources such as wood for fuel or building purposes; for winter or summertime grazing of domestic or wild animals; for fallow or crop fields; for land to grow trees; for water for livestock, fish, irrigation, or home uses; and so on. In Sardinia, the spatial organization of the commons left its special imprint on the landscape. In vast areas of the island, these common areas (called *ademprivi*) occupied distinct zones extending in concentric circles around a village. The first zone, the one immediately surrounding the village, housed, fenced, or delimited privately owned plots devoted to intensive agriculture.[27] Around it extended fields called *pardu* or *minda,* where work animals were grazed. Beyond these areas was a third zone called *aidazzoni,* used for fallow grain agriculture. At the end of the agricultural year, the cropland was used for grazing (*peberili*), and the aidazzoni was established elsewhere for one or more years. The pardu and the aidazzoni, which together formed the ademprivi, were owned by the village, and their use was carefully regulated. Grazing rights applied, instead, to areas such as forests, woods, bushy pastureland, and unproductive land. In these areas, sowing was forbidden except by special concession.[28]

The benefits that the community derived from its access to a variety of different resources often became evident when village commons were parceled

out. In many cases, the privatization of a section of these common resources seriously jeopardized the social equilibrium. "The plots assigned
to the users," wrote a late nineteenth-century jurist, "are almost never sufficient for the needs of these exuberant and growing populations, especially
with regards to pastureland and the gathering of firewood; in the plateaus,
privatization harms peasant families who make a living from woodcutting
and shepherding; in the farmlands, privatization does not appear to be
producing the hoped-for higher yields from tenants and share-croppers,
who utilize lands that were once tilled with better results."[29] Common
management was sometimes dictated by the very character of a natural resource. As pointed out earlier, most common areas were in the mountains,
comprising land naturally suited for woodland or pasture. In Italy's Alpine
areas, resources were used in the same way, independent from their legal
status. One observer noted in 1915 that "even where Alpine land is privately
owned by several partners, its enjoyment is nevertheless common . . .
because from an economic and legal standpoint Alpine land is indivisible.
It cannot be possessed in any other way."[30]

Thus, establishing commons, far from being an irrational or backward
practice, was simply inspired by a different rationale than that of industrial or capitalist societies founded on the triumph of individual property
rights.[31] The modes of production and resource exploitation of these village
societies appear to have been informed by a worldview in which nature and
society were intimately connected. The fundamental principle inspiring
these various ways of sharing resources (however different they were from
one another) was the maintaining of social equality through mechanisms
of redistribution. In the case of many comunanze, produce was divided
among families every year.[32] In the società della malga, milk was divided
among community members according to the number of milk animals
owned by each.[33] Agricultural land was divided into plots and underwent a
uniform compulsory rotation, which could last for a short or long span of
time, from five to ninety-nine years.[34] In Liguria, every family had the right
(subject to payment of a small tax) to a plot of land measuring 1,272 square
meters. Each plot was separated from the others by ditches and grassy embankments.[35] Working methods and times were also regulated by a body
of common rules.[36] The plots were assigned by the representatives of the
community and, depending on statutes, had to be adequate to the needs of
the designated family. No family could be assigned the same plot for two
years in a row. In the case of the comunanze, for example, if a family was
assigned a plot of land yielding more produce than it needed, the assembly
of representatives could oblige the family to give it up.[37]

Commons in Southern Italy

Collective ownership in southern Italy took a completely different form than in central and northern Italy. In the south, the history of the commons from the 1850s to the early 1900s was intertwined with the crisis and disintegration of feudal estates. The feudal system hinged on a complex allocation of land resources characterized by extremely flexible relationships between the *allodio* and the *demanio,* that is, between the feudal estate and permanent public land that was subjected to various norms, including covenants for local populations. Legal literature from the eighteenth century to the twentieth distinguished four different types of public land. The oldest were allegedly the royal public lands, arising directly from the king;[38] the next were the universal or communal public lands answering to the principle of *universitas,* popularized by the spread of the French administrative system. The third and fourth types were the feudal and ecclesiastical public lands, believed to have formed at a later date through the concession of portions of royal public land to lay or ecclesiastical feudal lords.

Rights of commons, however, were not restricted to public land.[39] They could also be exercised on private properties, lay or ecclesiastical feuds, or land owned by a village.[40] Although the universal public land was for the exclusive use of the commoners, rights of commons applied to the whole feud, as prescribed by the old principle *ubi feoda ibi demania* (literally: where feudal property is, there is also common property); in other words, local inhabitants maintained prefeudal rights to feudal properties. It is the widespread application of this principle that binds the history of commons in southern Italy with the dismantling of the feudal system, a gradual process that continued for decades even after the abolition of feudalism. Part of the southern Italian juridical tradition had always formulated the commons in terms of "legality," and this orientation prevailed for many years in public administration. Jurists censored barons' attempts to appropriate feudal land for their own private use and upheld the legitimacy of common rights in the southern Italian kingdom. Only by applying the law could the state curb the arrogance of the barons and protect itself from their abuses. This tradition of the commons remained strong even after the French Revolution and the consequent affirmation in Europe of the principle of full and exclusive private property.

Following the 1806 law on the abolition of feudalism,[41] southern Italians quickly realized that the country's agricultural economy would not benefit by destroying pastureland and abolishing all forms of collective landownership. The decree of 3 December 1808 was a first step toward limiting the application of the abolition law. This decree allowed the parceling out of municipal land that could be classified as "fields and grasses," that is, as cultivable land, but forbade the parceling out of forests, pastures, floodplains, and uncultivable mountain land. Another law, approved on 12 December 1816, stipulated that all public land subject to rights of the commons should remain reserved for that use. The decree of 3 July 1861 placed further restrictions on the selling of municipal property and ordered an investigation for determining whether parceling out public land had affected the people's ability to provide for their essential needs, be these for pasture or firewood.[42]

From the standpoint of economic management, municipal public land did not differ much from municipal property. The main difference was that municipal land could be sold, whereas public land was inalienable, the assumption being that it belonged to the population of the village from time immemorial. Although public lands could not be sold, a village had a certain degree of control over these resources. It could grant their free use or impose a tax called *fida*, it could grant concessions under emphytheutic contracts for a certain number of years, or it could rent them out.

In the early nineteenth century, according to contemporary sources, the most extensive municipal lands of southern Italy stood on the slopes of the Apennines in Abruzzo, Campania, and Lucania, mainly above 500 meters.[43] At the end of the nineteenth century, there were some 658,000 hectares of municipal land in southern Italy, along with 60,000 hectares of municipal land in Sicily. About 90 percent of this land was located in the hills and mountains.[44]

The main issue to focus on here is the comparison between the historical uses of the municipal lands of southern Italy and those of the commons in central and northern Italy. Did the south's municipal lands play a role in maintaining an environmental balance? Were they a means for redistributing wealth and striving for social equity? In attempting to answer these difficult questions, one can conclude that the gradual privatization of southern Italy's public land corresponded with the increase of hydrogeological instability characteristic of the nineteenth century, with important antecedents in the second half of the eighteenth century. In one way or another, all authors of the *Inchiesta sulle condizioni dei contadini nelle provincie meridionali e nella Sicilia* (Investigation on Peasants' Conditions in the Southern Provinces and Sicily) see a relationship between the distribution of public land and the increase of hydrogeological instability. Some authors even consider Italy's heightening emigration of the late nineteenth century as a further consequence of the disintegration of the commons. The agricultural expansion on the slopes of the Apennines, in order to keep up with demographic pressure and increasing commercialization of agricultural products, was a strong incentive for parceling out public land. However, the privatization of pastures and forestland provoked a crisis in the livestock industry, as fewer and fewer areas were available for grazing: "The animals are starving and the prairies are turning into fields of thistle and *scopilli.*"[45] The shrinking of common land led to the depletion and destruction of natural resources. Pastures became impoverished as livestock ate the best grass and left the worst behind to propagate even faster. With lighter grazing, soil nutrients were no longer reintegrated, resulting in an increasingly sterile soil. And as pastures deteriorated, forests were cut down to provide new pasture.[46]

The case of Sicily is emblematic of environmental degradation brought on by the loosening of communal ties. The island's current problem with droughts and water scarcity has its roots in the parceling out of the commons, which, along with population growth and extensive wheat cultivation, was one reason why forests disappeared from mountain slopes. The privatizing of former collectively owned woodland modified the Sicilian environmental balance: gushing rivers turned into irregularly flowing creeks, landslides threatened crops and houses, springs dried up, and rainfall patterns changed. The now-barren ground no longer absorbed water as it used to; large-scale, monocultural agriculture took the place of intensive, irrigation agriculture.[47]

The Decline of Common Properties

Royal Decree no. 751 of 22 May 1924, entitled *Riordinamento degli usi civici nel Regno* (General Law on Common Property Uses, later incorporated into Law no. 1766 of 16 June 1927), definitively abolished—although with important exceptions—all forms of the collective use of land. The 1927 law was the end result of an institutional trend going back to the last decades of the eighteenth century. This trend displayed such continuity that it can be regarded as a single historical phase during which legislators sought to transform natural resources from collective and complex assets subject to a variety of user rights into alienable and divisible privately owned assets. Until the unification of Italy, different legislative approaches were adopted to keep up with the evolution of the commons. Specifically, this phase witnessed two alternating political trends, one striving for the total abolition of all forms of collective use, another advocating the granting of compensation for the suppression of common rights.

The selling of the commons deserves separate treatment. In the late eighteenth and early nineteenth centuries, a number of possessions formerly subjected to various restrictions were put up for sale, by public decree, in the Regno Italico (Cisalpine Republic and Piedmont), the Repubblica Romana (notably in its central regions), Tuscany, and the Kingdom of Naples, where the sales targeted church possessions and village land. Further decrees were issued after the unification of Italy, in 1866 and 1867, to put onto the market large extensions of former church land.

The compensation-for-suppression approach was applied in Sardinia in 1865, when ademprivio rights were abolished and all ademprivio land was assigned to the villages. In Tuscany, after a long string of decrees allowing landowners to declare their lands free from common rights (in 1833, 1840, 1845, 1860, and 1862), the law of 15 August 1867 abolished common rights in the former principate of Piombino. The land was divided into *preselle* (little plots of land) assigned to the former commoners as compensation for the loss of common rights.[48] In Veneto, the law of 2 April 1882 abolished rights of pasture and herbage in the provinces of Vicenza, Belluno, and Udine but provided for compensation for the poorest users.

Most nineteenth-century legislators sought to do away with commons in all their forms. Most of the century was dominated by an individualist conception of property: "Property," writes Paolo Grossi, "was conceived in all its unlimited freedom of circulation, and hence necessarily as individual property, the only form of property that can aspire to such absolute mobility."[49] Most Italian jurists saw the commons as an anomaly. Commons undermined not only juridical and economic order by robbing commerce of vast lands but also moral order and public peace.[50] Nineteenth-century politics and legislation for the upholding of property rights, however, were incongruous. Some legislators recognized the social and environmental rationale advising against the total abolition of commons. The law of 1 November 1875 abolished rights of the commons in state-owned forests, while at the same time providing for compensation to the locals in the form of emphyteutic contracts or full property ownership of portions of these forests. The law was inspired by the principle that existing rights of the commons should be maintained if they were totally or partially indispensable for the livelihood of a population, a principle that was later reasserted by the forest law of 20 June 1877.[51] But the full reversal of the earlier, more radical trend came about when laws were issued in 1888 and 1891 to abolish pasture rights, the selling of herbs, wood gathering, and the imposing of pasture taxes in the former Papal States. These laws affirmed, at the same time, the principle that common rights should be maintained in areas that, owing to their altitude or nature, were not susceptible to agricultural improvement. Yet they stipulated that in cases where it was judged necessary to allow local communities to continue to exercise their common rights, the abolition of such rights could only be allowed if the owner rented out all or part of the land to commoners.[52] Another law issued in 1894 stated that assets deriving from the abolition of common rights should be managed by former commoners. Collective properties were thus formed again and gained legal status.[53] Similar provisions were taken for the università agrarie. A whole different phase had begun, at least as far as the status of collective property was concerned. The 1880s and 1890s were therefore a period of renewed sensitivity in regard to the commons, a renewal marked by harsh criticism of the French privatizing model. This approach is reflected in the writings of Giuseppe Salvioli, Carlo Calisse, Giovanni Tamassia, and Pasquale Del Giudice and especially those of Francesco Schumpfer. This author criticized the Roman conception of the natural right to private property and sought to demonstrate instead that individual property rights had historical origins of evolutionary character. Schumpfer maintained that private property of land was a recent phenomenon in human history; he emphasized the German tradition and drew on it for arguing that collective property was the original form of land appropriation.[54]

Legal treatises published in those years stressed previously uninvestigated aspects of collective property and their social function. The 1877–84 *Atti dell'Inchiesta Jacini* (Proceedings of the Jacini Investigation) were already highlighting historical forms of communal landownership and land management. Such was the case, for example, for Ghino Valenti's report on Le Marche region. This respected scholar showed that the very character of this mountainous area, along with its pastoral and forest economy, required property structures compatible with rotating land uses. It was not a matter of denying ownership rights as formulated in the Roman tradition but of allowing multiple ownership and adapting ownership rights to the exigencies of production and redistribution.[55] Collective property, far from hindering progress, served to promote cooperative forms of land management. "The principle on which collective property is founded," Valenti wrote, "is not antagonistic to the principle underlying cooperation for the simple reason that collective property is nothing but a special aspect of communal and agrarian cooperation, which live on today. Collective property is a true form of cooperative association; indeed, it is the perfect cooperative association."[56]

The 1920s witnessed the adoption of laws giving definitive consolidation on the national level to the question of the commons. These laws incorporated some of the corrections to the French model adopted over the previous decades. Thus, land naturally suited for pasture and forests was excluded from privatization,[57] even though a proposal to maintain collective ownership on lands better suited for agriculture was rejected.[58]

The evolution of Italian law on the commons from the late eighteenth century to the 1950s can be interpreted (with some significant exceptions) as an attempt to apply a dichotomous view: private versus public, market versus state. Today's jurists are questioning this approach on social and environmental grounds. The decline of Italy's mountain agriculture after 1950 has resulted in worsening hydrogeological instability, as manifested by floods, landslides, and erosion. The commons are now being seen as a socioeconomic system capable of accounting for economy and ecology, production and maintenance.[59]

As to the socioeconomic results of the stepwise disappearance of Italian commons after the late eighteenth century, some scholars argue that the main result has been the expansion of small farmsteads. Giuseppe Medici speaks of "innumerable cases whereby parceling out has given rise to flourishing farming businesses."[60] Especially in southern Italy, the parceled-out commons were mainly orange, lemon, olive, and almond groves as well as vineyards located in areas of Salerno, Abruzzo, Puglia's Murge, Capitanata, Catanzaro, Cosenza, and Siracuse.[61] In northern and central Italy, small farmers benefited from the sale of commons, especially in the Alps and Apennines, hilly regions, and parts of the Po Valley, to include lands near Rovigo, Novara, Vercelli, and areas of Liguria, Le Marche, Grosseto, and the Roman hinterland.[62]

In spite of these results, the overall expansion of municipal land was rather modest. By the end of 1927, common rights had been reasserted on some 711,000 hectares, of which only 19,000 were municipally owned plots.[63] Thus, considerable commons were maintained. On the eve of World War II, it was estimated that about a tenth of the Italian territory was owned collectively in one way or another. In the Alpine region, 1,364 out of 2,607 municipalities owned communal land, which included 804,000 hectares of forests and pastures, and 5,700 hectares of farmland. In southern Italy, 728 out of 1,591 municipalities owned communal land, which included 272,000 hectares of forests and pastures, and 11,800 of farmland.[64]

In conclusion, a consideration of environmental issues has sparked a new historical interest in the commons. Collective property ownership produced real and tangible consequences for the management of natural resources. Although there were important differences from one area to another, the commons favored the regeneration and sustainability of resources. Traditional ways of using nature within a framework of community relations based on trust, reciprocity, and group identity functioned as forms of environmental protection. This new perspective sheds light on the environmental implications of the nineteenth- and twentieth-century diffusion of the French model of private landownership across Europe.[65] Many scholars believe that as capitalism took hold in European rural areas, communal bonds slackened, thereby removing a sort of protective armor that had long been in place. As for Italy, in spite of a resurging late nineteenth-century interest in the commons, the legal trends that abolished feudal ownership practices ushered in profoundly destructive processes, especially in lands whose natural features and altitudes had always called for collective forms of natural resource use.

Notes

1. On this debate, see Gabriella Corona, "Stato, proprietà privata e possesso collettivo: Un dibattito secolare," in *Lo stato e l'economia tra restaurazione e rivoluzione,* vol. 1, *L'agricoltura (1815–1848),* ed. Ilaria Zilli (Naples: ESI, 1997), 43–63. From among many Marxist historians, I will limit myself to mentioning Emilio Sereni, *Il capitalismo nelle campagne (1860–1900)* (Turin: Einaudi, 1968); Pasquale Villani, "Signoria rurale, feudalità, capitalismo nelle campagne," *Quaderni Storici* 19, no. 1 (1972): 5–26; Giorgio Giorgetti, *Contadini e proprietari nell'Italia moderna* (Turin: Einaudi, 1974).

2. In spite of its ambiguity and analytic weakness, this concept seems to evoke major scientific and cultural issues. See Arnaldo Bagnasco, "Comunità: Definizione," *Parolechiave* 1 (1993): 11–30.

3. For example, in Umbria, a tenth of the region's territory is still municipally or collectively owned; see Ente sviluppo agricolo in Umbria, *Le comunanze agrarie dell'Umbria* (Perugia: Benucci, 1983). In comparatively recent times, commons were still quite extensive in the Marche region, too; see "Sulle comunanze agrarie e le terre comuni," in *Atti del convegno nazionale sulle comunanze agrarie e le terre comuni* (Macerata: Camera di Commercio Industria Artigianato e Agricoltura, 1970).

4. Paolo Grossi, "Il problema storico-giuridico della proprietà collettiva in Italia," in *Demani civici e risorse ambientali,* ed. Franco Carletti (Naples: Jovene, 1993), 7.

5. Ibid., 23–28.

6. This was the case of the Comunaglie of Murta, near Genova. See Gian Franco Croce, "Risorse collettive e conflitti locali: Il Bosco Ramasso (Genova), 1790–1930," *Quaderni Storici* 81, no. 3 (1992): 783–84.

7. Silvio Pace, *Usi civici, associazioni agrarie e comunioni familiari nella regione Trentino Alto Adige* (Trento: ICA, 1975), 93–94.

8. Ibid., 22–23.

9. Ibid. Law no. 1102 of 3 December 1971 included the Regole of Cortina d'Ampezzo and Complico, the Società di Antichi Originari of Lombardy, and the *Servitù* (easement or servitude) of Val Canale among family communes not subjected to the norms regulating rights of common.

10. Pace, *Usi civici*, 95–96. Membership of the originari was often the bone of contention in long-lasting internal conflicts, which the government sometimes settled. On 7 September 1764, the Senate ordered the inscription in a new book of vicinie all originarie families in the province of Brescia, as well as those who had resided there for at least fifty years paying contributions and taxes. But conflicts did not arise only over the admission of outsiders among the originari. There were also struggles between old and new originari over the division of common property.

11. Cf. Elisabetta Arioti, "Proprietà collettiva e riparto periodico dei terreni in una comunità della pianura bolognese: S. Giovanni in Persicelo (secoli XVI–XVIII)," *Quaderni Storici* 81, no. 3 (1992): 714. Similar restrictions apply even today, although with some differences. Today, plots are assigned to all members of partecipanti families at Nonantola; to the head of the partecipante family at S. Agata; to the legitimate descendants from male individuals at S. Giovanni in Persiceto; to adult descendants of a partecipante at Villa Fontana; and to male descendants of *partecipanti* families at Cento and Pieve di Cento. See Stefano Torresani, "Il territorio delle partecipanze agrarie emiliane: Un archivio storico 'a cielo aperto,'" in *I demani civici e le proprietà collettive: Un diverso modo di possedere—Un diverso modo di gestire,* ed. Pietro Nervi (Padua: CEDAM, 1998), 181.

12. This was especially true in the provinces of Bergamo, Brescia, Como, and Sondrio.

13. Alberto Cencelli-Perti, *La proprietà collettiva in Italia: Le origini, gli avanzi, l'avvenire* (Rome: A. Manzoni, 1890), 27.

14. These studies are mostly microhistorical in character. They include Marina Caffiero, *L'erba dei poveri: Comunità rurale e soppressione degli usi collettivi nel Lazio (secoli XVIII–XIX)* (Rome: Edizioni dell'Ateneo, 1983); Renata Ago, "Conflitti e politica del feudo: Le campagne romane del Settecento," *Quaderni Storici* 63, no. 3 (1986): 847–74; Edoardo Grendi, "La pratica dei confini: Moglia e Sassello, 1715–1745," *Quaderni Storici* 63, no. 3 (1986): 811–46; Bernardino Farolfi, *L'uso e il mercimonio: Comunità e beni comunali nella montagna bolognese del Settecento* (Bologna: CLUEB, 1987); Osvaldo Raggio, "Forme e politiche di appropriazione delle risorse: Casi di usurpazione delle comunaglie in Liguria," *Quaderni Storici* 79, no. 2 (1992): 135–70; Marina Caffiero, "Terre comuni, fortune private: Pratiche conflitti internobiliari per il controllo delle risorse collettive nel Lazio (XVIII–XIX)," *Quaderni Storici* 81, no. 3 (1992):

759–82; Massimo Vallerani, "Le comunanze di Perugia nel Chiurgi: Storia di un possesso cittadino tra XII e XIV secolo," *Quaderni Storici* 81, no. 3 (1992): 625–52.

15. See Giovanni Raffaglio, *Diritti promiscui, demani comunali, usi civici* (Milan: Società Editrice Libraria, 1915), 313.

16. There is a vast literature on this subject. I will limit myself to citing the following: Giovanni Curis, *Usi civici, proprietà collettive e latifondo nell'Italia centrale e nell'Emilia con riferimento ai demani comunali del Mezzogiorno* (Naples: Jovene, 1917); Curis, *L'evoluzione degli usi civici delle ex-provincie pontificie* (Rome: Civelli, 1908); Francesco Lauria, *Demani e feudi nell'Italia meridionale* (Naples: Tipografia degli Artigianelli, 1923); Manfredi Palumbo, *I comuni meridionali prima e dopo le leggi eversive della feudalità* (Cerignola: Montercorvino Rovella, 1910–16); Romualdo Trifone, *Gli usi civici* (Milan: Giuffrè, 1963); Trifone, *Feudi e demani: Eversione della feudalità nelle provincie meridionali—Dottrina, storia, legislazione e giurisprudenza* (Milan: Società Editrice Libraria, 1909).

17. See Andrea Zagli, "Pratiche e forme d'uso delle risorse collettive in un ambiente palustre: Il bacino di Bientina in Toscana," *Quaderni Storici* 81, no. 3 (1992): 809–10.

18. Cencelli-Perti, *La proprietà collettiva in Italia,* 39.

19. As in the case of the università of twelve families from Chiaserna, in the province of Pesaro, discussed in ibid., 20.

20. Fabio Giacomoni, "Le carte di Regola nel Trentino," in *Comunità di villaggio e proprietà collettive in Italia e in Europa,* ed. Gian Candido De Martin (Padua: CEDAM, 1990), 116.

21. Cencelli-Perti, *La proprietà collettiva in Italia,* 23.

22. Ibid., 21–25, and Raffaglio, *Diritti promiscui,* 245.

23. Cencelli-Perti, *La proprietà collettiva in Italia,* 21–22.

24. On this subject, cf. the statute of Berzo in Raffaglio, *Diritti promiscui,* 313–18.

25. Sandro Tiberini, "Le comunanze del Castello di Gaiche nel Contado perugino di Porta Santa Susanna: Dalle origini al secolo XIV," special issue of *Quaderni Regione dell'Umbria* 1 (1990).

26. On the organization of *partecipanze,* see "Terre e comunità nell'Italia Padana: Il caso delle Partecipanze agrarie emiliane—Da beni comunali a beni collettivi," special issue of *Cheiron: Materiali e Strumenti di Aggiornamento Storiografico* 14 and 15 (1990–91).

27. Antonio Ghiani, *Le leggi speciali per la Sardegna* (Cagliari: Editrice Sarda, 1954), 14–15. Gian Giacomo Ortu calls it *bidazzone,* a term originally designating the two-field system in the Sardinian language that later came to indicate

cultivated fields as opposed to fallow land, called *paberilis* (land of the poor). See, by the same author, "Economia e società rurale in Sardegna," in *Storia dell'agricoltura italiana in età contemporanea*, vol. 2, *Uomini e classi*, ed. Piero Bevilacqua (Venice: Marsilio, 1990): 325–29.

28. The term *cussorgia* designated the granting to an individual or a family of an area of exclusive use of an area singled out from the *ademprivi* to provide more secure grazing for livestock or improve the breed. More rarely, the concession was granted for cultivation. Cussorgia land generally became privately owned as a result of a long and peaceful process and through legal recognition.

29. Raffaglio, *Diritti promiscui*, 5.

30. Ibid., 294.

31. On the existence of economies historically characterized by a rationality founded on a nondissipative relationship with nature, see Piero Bevilacqua, *Demetra e Clio: Uomini e ambiente nella storia* (Rome: Donzelli, 2001), esp. 3–24.

32. Cencelli-Perti, *La proprietà collettiva in Italia*, 21.

33. Ibid., 313–18.

34. Ibid., 21–25.

35. Ibid., 45.

36. Ibid.

37. Ibid., 22–23. Such was the case for the "consortium of *originarie* families" of Terra sant'Abbondio, in the province of Pesaro.

38. In southern Italy, the two largest crown lands were on the Tavoliere plateau in Puglia and the Sila mountain range in Calabria. Rights of use over these areas were abolished, respectively, with the law of 25 February 1865 and that of 25 May 1876. On the effects of this abolition, see Girolamo Savoia, *I demani comunali* (Benevento: Stab. Tipografico di Gennaro, 1880). On the history of these areas, see Pasquale Di Cicco, "Censuazione ed affrancazione del Tavoliere di Puglia (1789–1865)," *Quaderni della Rassegna degli Archivi di Stato* (Rome: n.p., 1964); Pasquale Barletta, *Verificazione dei demani silani fatta dal 1849 al 1852 in virtù di rescritti del 27 marzo 1849, 18 marzo 1850 e 30 aprile 1851* (Cosenza: Tip. di G. Migliaccio, 1854); Giuseppe Zurlo, *Storia della Regia Sila e descrizione dei Regii Demani e delle camere chiuse* (Naples: Stamperia Reale, 1862).

39. There have been various legal interpretations of the origin of common rights. Although most scholars believe they arose in the Middle Ages at the same time as the municipalities (or *commune*), some claim their spread was simultaneous with that of the feudal system, and still others trace their origins all the way back to the crisis of the Roman Empire. Some scholars have an even more radical position. They argue that common rights are founded on natural rights and hence go all the way back to the very beginning of human settlement. Finally, there are those who argue for multiple origins of common

rights, tracing them partly to ancient Roman municipal statutes, partly to the new concept of barbaric property, and partly to privileges.

40. Guido Cervati, "Usi civici: Disciplina attuale e riforma," in *Atti del convegno nazionale sulle comunanze agrarie*, 49.

41. On this law, see also Stefania Barca's essay in this volume.

42. Raffaglio, *Diritti promiscui*, 104–5.

43. On this subject, see Commissione Reale per i demani comunali nelle provincie del Mezzogiorno, *Atti della Commissione Reale pei demani comunali nelle provincie del Mezzogiorno istituita con R. Decreto 4 maggio 1884* (Rome: Tipografia Nazionale di Giovanni Bertero, 1902), esp. 167.

44. Ibid., 70–71.

45. Oreste Bordiga, "Relazione," in *Inchiesta parlamentare sulle condizioni dei contadini nelle provincie meridionali e nella Sicilia*, vol. 4, *Campania* (Rome: Tipografia Nazionale di Giovanni Bertero, 1909), 85.

46. Ibid., 84–85. In Alees Del Toro and Alessandro Trotter's work, cited by Bordiga, one reads: "A single hectare of those summer pastures may sustain from six to eight sheep from 15 April to 30 November, whereas under normal circumstances it would be barely sufficient for two or three, as is the case in Abruzzo. Pastures for large animals, which are the best, from 5 June to 3 November—that is, for 150 days—feed up to two large animals per hectare, which the good fields of the Alps could barely support."

47. "Schema della relazione," in *Inchiesta parlamentare sulle condizioni dei contadini nelle provincie meridionali e nella Sicilia* (Rome: Tipografia Nazionale di Giovanni Bertero, 1911), 144. This investigation also points to other factors, such as the war against brigandage; the very nature of Sicilian soil, which allows cereal agriculture up to twelve hundred meters; and the demand for crossties (sleepers; pieces of wood between the rails) for Italian railway lines.

48. Ibid., 113–15.

49. Cf. Grossi, "Il problema storico-giuridico della proprietà," 8–9.

50. Ibid., 10.

51. Raffaglio, *Diritti promiscui*, 116. This law had been preceded by another issued on 20 June 1871, which had declared the inalienability of certain forests on public land.

52. Ibid., 120–23. These principles were confirmed by a 1902 law about the land and castle of Tatti in the province of Massa and Carrara.

53. Ibid., 121.

54. Cf. Paolo Grossi, *Un altro modo di possedere: L'emersione di forme alternative di proprietà alla coscienza giuridica post-unitaria* (Milan: Giuffrè: 1977), 39–51.

55. See *Atti della Giunta per la Inchiesta agraria e sulle condizioni della classe agricola*, vol. 9/2, for the provinces of Perugia, Ascoli Piceno, Ancona, Macerata, and Pesaro.

56. Ghino Valenti, "Cooperazione e proprietà collettiva," *Nuova Antologia di Scienze Lettere ed Arti* 118 (16 July 1891): 322.

57. Romualdo Trifone, *La questione demaniale nel Mezzogiorno d'Italia* (Rome: n.p., 1924), 30.

58. Ibid., 26.

59. Franco Carletti, "Il ruolo della proprietà collettiva per la tutela del territorio," in *Comunità di villaggio e proprietà collettive*, 297–99.

60. Giuseppe Medici, *La distribuzione della proprietà fondiaria in Italia: Relazione generale* (Rome: n.p., 1948), 72–73.

61. Cf. Piero Bevilacqua, "Terre comuni e usi civici in Calabria tra fascismo e dopoguerra," in *Trasformazioni delle società rurali nei paesi dell'Europa occidentale e Mediterranea*, ed. Pasquale Villani (Naples: Guida, 1986), 389–414; Salvatore Lupo, "I proprietari terrieri nel Mezzogiorno," in *Storia dell'agricoltura italiana in età contemporanea*, vol. 2, *Uomini e classi*, ed. Piero Bevilacqua (Venice: Marsilio, 1990), 105–49; Vincenzo Ricchioni, "Le leggi eversive della feudalità," in Cassa per il Mezzogiorno, *Problemi dell'agricoltura meridionale* (Naples: Istituto Editoriale del Mezzogiorno, 1953).

62. On the results of the parceling out of public land in Italy, see also Gino Massullo, "Contadini: La piccola proprietà coltivatrice nell'Italia contemporanea," in *Storia dell'agricoltura italiana*, 2:5–23.

63. Medici, *La distribuzione della proprietà fondiaria in Italia*.

64. Giuseppe Medici, "Proprietà collettive, demani, usi civici," *Rivista di Economia Agraria* 3 (1949): esp. 308.

65. Marie-Danielle Demelas and Nadine Vivier, eds., *Les propriétés collectives face aux attaques libérales (1750–1914)* (Rennes: Presses Universitaires de Rennes, 2003).

CHAPTER 6

Forest Visions in Early Modern Italy

Bruno Vecchio

The Eighteenth-Century Turning Point

Links between forest conditions and various physical-environmental processes (such as soil erosion, landslides, floods, and loss of soil fertility) were given special scientific treatment in the Italian literature during the eighteenth century and the Napoleonic age. To be sure, earlier centuries also saw attention paid to forests and their role, especially in Venetia and Tuscany, but the eighteenth century ushered in a special interest in forests and their effects, both in Italy and indeed across much of Europe.[1]

The reasons for this new concern over forests are understandable. In Italy and in most parts of Europe before the eighteenth century, the slow but steady pace of economic growth and the moderate human impact on forested areas created an environment that was becoming quite distant from what agricultural historian Emilio Sereni has termed the "silvan reaction" (or forest relapse) of the High Middle Ages. The landscape was nonetheless still rather wooded and quite distinct from the one we have today. Forested areas were still ubiquitous and their resources vast or at least sufficient for human needs. From this description, we can conclude that deforestation was considered to be a positive operation for centuries, until evidence began to accumulate to the contrary.[2]

Prior to the eighteenth century, deforestation was most often pursued to open up lands useful for subsistence cultivation. Beginning in the eighteenth century, however, the assaults on forest areas were carried out for an additional reason. As Sereni explains: "The problem is no longer about the poorer peasants who till the land in order to obtain a quantity of grain sufficient for their own consumption. . . . [It] is rather the pursuit of capitalistic profit which becomes the engine and decisive regulator of the rhythm of tillage. While tillage undoubtedly accelerated in the second half of the 1700s, it does not account for the heightening rate at which deforestation took place."[3]

Sereni continues by emphasizing that what needs to be taken into account are the effects of commerce and industry, for they allowed deforestation "to proceed at a rhythm independent from tillage, and much faster." Although it has been argued that some consequences of deforestation were well understood before these times, such effects were becoming known to a wider public due to the occurrence of macroscopic changes in the soil and water, along with more receptive attitudes toward such changes.

Deforestation occurred more rapidly in marginal agricultural areas, but the effects of deforestation were beginning to be perceived more generally.[4] As damage from deforestation increased, the willingness to explain these damages as stemming from other sources decreased. The accumulating body of knowledge about deforestation contributed to the assertion that this practice was "a deplorable operation until evidence is found to the contrary." By the beginning of the 1800s, authors who partially or wholly denied that deforestation caused damage were in the minority.[5]

The following discussion on how the public reacted to deforestation does not address the real conditions of various Italian forests in that period. It also does not address the social and economic questions of deforestation, which are treated elsewhere.[6] Instead, I focus here on three issues: the professional quality of forest observers, the interpretation of identified problems, and the interpretation of proposed policies.

Characteristics of Forest Observers

Let us begin by explaining the professional quality of those who studied the forests. Before the eighteenth century, most observers of forests and their effects were experts in hydraulic sciences. Having received strong impetus during the Galilean period, hydrology continued to develop due to the challenges of controlling water in the Venetian lagoons, the lower Po River, and the Adige River basins. Beginning with a study of these and other, smaller watercourses, a handful of experts found some systems to exhibit floodlike episodes (or torrents) that carried large amounts of sediment.[7]

Next, agricultural science writers must also be mentioned. A large number of them were present in certain preunified states, but they could be found almost anywhere. They generally viewed deforestation in terms of the problems it caused to landowners. Such problems included the washing—or eroding—of fields that had once been forested; the lack of wood for domestic or agricultural use; the lack of feed for livestock that formerly fed on forest underbrush; and the lack of leaves, formerly used as food or bedding.

Lastly, reformers of the Enlightenment also offered their views of deforestation. In the 1700s, agricultural problems challenged not only farmers and their interests but also politics and the state. Such was also the case for forest problems, which were expanding to become problems for many sectors, except that these problems were heavily dependent on public institutions for finding solutions. When political reformers recognized that forest areas were shrinking, many of them did not hesitate to nominate "political causes," while offering possible remedies and warnings about the eventual consequences of continued deforestation.[8] At the beginning of the nineteenth century, the ideas of the reformers tended to converge with those of the statistical reports (or *statistiche*), which were widespread during the Napoleonic era. The most important statistical forestry reports were those compiled by Melchiorre Gioia for northern Italy along with monographs published in the *Annali d'agricoltura del Regno d'Italia* (Agricultural Annals of the Italian Kingdom, 1809–14). Statistical forestry reports in southern Italy were less elaborate and so were not published until the twentieth century.[9]

The Problems Identified

In the late eighteenth and early nineteenth centuries, three practices or conditions were identified as being harmful to Italian forests: clear-cutting followed by cultivation, forest decay, and clear-cutting but not for cultivation.

Clear-Cutting Followed by Cultivation

Population growth in Italy in the 1700s was paralleled by the increasing area of cultivated land. The western Po Plain of Piedmont and Lombardy was the only area of significant size where agricultural productivity had strongly increased, usually through considerable investment. Farmers from other regions, from Venetia to Tuscany and Sicily, sought to increase their own production just by increasing tilled areas, often concentrating on grains.[10] Large and small estates converted forested areas into agricultural production, motivated by rising crop prices. As more and more land on these estates was put into crops, common and state land was also being converted into crop production, often without official permission.[11]

These agricultural trends were generally criticized because they did not increase production at levels that could justify the harm they were inflicting. This harm included the diminishing fertility of tilled land,[12] the dangers of torrential flooding,[13] the difficulties in maintaining wood supplies for essential use,[14] and the diminished ability to raise livestock.[15] Many Venetian authors concerned with the forest issue began their analysis with the problem of the scarcity of meat and other animal products; this problem was also highlighted by government authorities.[16]

Forest Decay

In reducing the areas of fields and woods used for cattle grazing, tillage not only hindered cattle production—which was a crucial activity in some regions—but also forced existing livestock into the remaining forests. Thus, not only did the area of forestlands diminish; so too did their quality. If to this we add the damaging effect that dense animal populations such as goats have on trees, together with the rising demands for wood for fuel and construction, heightened by rising human populations, one can understand why many wooded areas were shrinking and thinning. This happened chiefly to the village woods (which were common property), even though private woods and state-reserved woods were also seeing the effects of the high forest demands.[17] Some sort of forest "reform" appeared necessary, especially in common property woods.

Clear-Cutting but Not for Cultivation

Much attention was given to the problem of deforestation that was not motivated by farming. By all accounts, this practice was on the increase in the late eighteenth century. For example, much of the deforestation in Tuscany that followed Pietro Leopoldo's measures for liberalized clear-cuttings (1776–80) was due to opportunities that arose for encouraging wood trade. The consequences of these measures were noted by Luigi Tramontani, Pietro Ferroni, and Matteo Biffi-Tolomei at the beginning of the 1800s.[18] But voices beyond Tuscany were also raised in deploring this phenomenon. Giammarie Piccone held that wood exportation for speculative enterprise was the main reason for the reduction of Ligurian woods.[19] Giovanni Battista Giovio focused on the sizable clear-cuttings that followed the sale of common woods in the Como region of Lombardy.[20] During the Napoleonic era, it was the sale of large amounts of national goods that brought about an increase in clear-cutting. The best-known testimonies of clear-cutting are Carlo Perotti's and Melchiorre Gioia's accounts in Piedmont and Nicola Maria Nicolai's in the Papal States.[21]

But even before (or without) these sales, overexploitation of woods was traditionally connected to common ownership, which formerly assured forest preservation but now served the demands of *mercimonio* (illicit trade). These illicit forest uses were vigorously pointed out by several authors, particularly for the economically advanced north.[22] Common forests were therefore harnessed to meet strong market demands for providing more and more wood and charcoal for manufacturing and urban uses.[23]

When there was scarce social and institutional control of "sustainable" forest use, road construction itself was enough to cause the disappearance of forests in areas near the roadways, even if the forests were already poorly managed due to their inaccessibility. The consequence of road construction and lax control of common forests was a reversal in the wood trade, which happened in a relatively short amount of time. In Piccone's opinion, Liguria was so quickly impoverished by wood exportation that it soon turned to importing it.[24] This was also the case along the northern coast of Abruzzo.[25]

The Proposals

What follows are the main remedies that were proposed for addressing the deteriorated conditions of the forest.

- Intensify agriculture in spaces already cultivated. The importance of agricultural intensification, which was the core of the agronomical revolution, was the subject of a recurring argument that various authors proposed for dealing with the forest problem.[26] Some of them made the connection between the two problems quite explicit: if we limit ourselves to the eighteenth century, we could name Giuseppe Antonio Donadio and Jean-Baptiste Constans de Castellet's recommendations in the Kingdom of Sardinia,[27] as well as Bernardino Conte's suggestions for the Venetian Republic.[28]

- Substitute other combustible materials for wood. Such proposals were limited largely to the north and regarded lignite and especially peat.[29]

- Implement reforestation. Just as some authors judged deforestation excessive, others (often the same ones) recommended generic reforestation. Others did not offer details of how reforestation should be done, but they did give more carefully considered advice: they offered lists of tree species that, in their opinion, were better adapted, or else they named locations where reforestation would be effective.[30] Usually such locations were found in rugged mountains or in extremely sandy or clayey soil,[31] as well as along riverbanks and on the edges of roads and fields.[32] These suggestions may seem amateurish or of little relevance if we choose to ignore the very high consumption of wood that occurs in what Lewis Mumford called the "eotechnic age."[33] Planting trees in fields was the usual advice for Sicily and Sardinia,[34] as well as for Tavoliere in northern Apulia.[35] In general, these were not considered temporary solutions. With the placement of trees in fields, the intention was to domesticate, so to speak, these areas and allow them to evolve toward a more intensive crop production and toward general agronomic progress (sometimes by calling attention to advanced agricultural models being implemented elsewhere).[36] Trees were seen here not only as sources of wood but also as sources of fodder (from leaves), fruits (due to a favorable climate), shade, moisture, and natural fertilizers for other crops.

- Apply elaborate soil practices. When problems related to deforestation were considered largely in geohydraulic terms (excessive soil erosion, destructive floods), a call for reforestation could be substituted with a call for intensive hill plantings done *a traverso,* or perpendicular to the slope, along with various types of hand-built structures, including *ciglionamenti* (turf-covered terraces) and *terrazzamenti* (stone terraces). These methods were a common proposal of Tuscany's agrarian theorists.[37]

- Monitor grazing. Proposals that limited or carefully managed grazing were promoted by those who considered unrestrained livestock grazing as the main cause of woodland overexploitation. This perspective, promoted by certain creative thinkers,[38] required grazing interests to adopt very strict practices, such as banning goats or following other, more methodical practices.[39]

- Reform practices in common forests along with other projects
  advocated by "the reformers." Projects to limit grazing could be
  confused with projects meant to reform common properties, in
  which grazing (and a few other activities) was the main use of the
  land. Debates over common goods and civic uses were occurring
  across Europe, and as noted before, they were a critical aspect
  of the agricultural revolution. The same was true in Italy, where
  land reformers recommended privatizing common property and
  liquidating civic uses, even though such recommendations were
  somewhat cavalier and permeated with social concern. What
  follows are a few specific examples.

  Filippo Andreucci, for example, passionately wished to
  "distribute" Tuscan common forests with the aim of eliminating
  their "unhealthiness"; before long, he was satisfied.[40] Vittorio Giera
  intended to parcel out village common land as compensation to
  Venetian landowners who were forced to reforest their steeper
  terrain.[41] Other Venetian authors proposed distributing this
  common land for free among the villagers.[42]

  For Valsassina (Lake Como, Lombardy), Cesare Beccaria
  proposed that the town council set aside part of the common
  woods for its inhabitants so that each family got 150 bundles of
  wood per year; the rest of the wood was to be sold under strict
  regulations.[43] Still other authors suggested the town council rent
  out the land to wealthy families who already lived there but on the
  condition that they be kept as woodland.[44] Others recommended
  temporarily closing sections of the common forests to public
  use.[45] In Venetia, Giovanni Scola analyzed the commons from a
  clearly social dimension: these lands, he said, had been "*rapite
  alle tribù rustiche*" (stolen from the village), which had led to the
  proletarianization of peasants by forcing them to cultivate areas
  previously used for grazing, resulting in a negative series of events
  that joined grazing to cultivation.[46]

- Acknowledge that forests required a special policy. The wisest
  expressions on the forest issue, which included several examples
  that dealt with the forest commons, were due not only to their
  authors' technical understanding but also and especially to their
  social understanding. These authors demonstrated a concern
  for conservation and for forestry regulations based on principles
  that were different than those for other crops, as well as an

ability to plan coordinated forestry programs attuned to current and future institutions. In this category, one could mention the proposals of G. B. Vasco and, later, M. Gioia on the unsuitability of timber forests (*boschi ad alto fusto*) for private owners,[47] as well as criticisms made by G. F. Delfico,[48] R. Pepe,[49] and others about forest legislation in the Bourbon Kingdom of Naples, legislation they considered to be formalistic and irrelevant. Also praiseworthy are Napoleonic era proposals, such as those of Piedmont's Carretti,[50] Trentino's Giovanni Serafini,[51] and especially Vincenzo Cuoco,[52] who outlined the need for forestry management boards (or *direzioni*). These boards were considered advisable for providing the unity and autonomy required for looking out for public interests in this particular enterprise.

BETWEEN THE END of the 1700s and the beginning of the 1800s, the forest question in Italy offered no easy solutions. Expanding populations, rising crop production, and ongoing liquidation of common properties had all contributed to the forest problem, and none of these threats were going away.

Two parallel processes were necessary in order to implement an appropriate policy of forest conservation. On the one hand, arborists and other natural scientists had to improve their understanding of the nature and function of forests,[53] and then they had to spread this knowledge, as was already happening in Germany and France. On the other hand, political economists had to account for, within their own disciplinary parameters, the many resources provided by the forest. This interaction of points of view was incomplete and remained uncertain for a long time; even a position such as that expressed by Scola on common property was too rigid, although it did help to shed light on the social dimension of the issue.

In 1829, Salvatore Scuderi, botanist and professor at the University of Catania in Sicily, suggested completely abolishing all public forest uses on the slopes of Mount Etna in order to guarantee improved tree conservation there.[54] In reaction to this proposal, the economist and jurist Gian Domenico Romagnosi pointed out that under its provisions the farmers would suffer and that "this argument could not be detached from considerations of agrarian reforms across Sicily."[55] Romagnosi went on to outline a synthetic view of the agroforest question that was, for the most part, still to be developed, even by the most qualified public servants. Whether deforestation depended on the "hunger for land" (which itself depended on other causes), on population growth plain and simple, on land speculation, or on industrial development, the final solution to the forest problem would need to be found in "agrarian reforms"—reforms that relied on agrarian politics applying forest regulations that were technically correct along with management practices appropriate for each location.

Such interventions could have taken many forms: the creation of more agricultural space (through drainage and other forms of reclamation, transformation of large estates such as latifundia, and general agricultural intensification), the prevention of speculative clear-cutting through various restrictive measures, the enactment of economic measures to benefit rural populations, and acquisition of badly damaged areas with public moneys so that key forestlands could recover. And all of these measures could occur only with strong political will reinforced by the knowledge and experience referred to previously.

Certain forest policies were already clear, and though they were somewhat generic, they were widely applicable and could function on various levels under different circumstances. Such policies were articulated by Francesco Mengotti, Giuseppe Gautieri, and Melchiorre Gioia, whose essential points included prohibitions on speculative cutting and warnings about forest management based exclusively on individual profit. But such recommendations were largely unheeded or ignored, so that progress in Italian forest policy was not what it might have been had it been based on ideas and recommendations articulated in the eighteenth and early nineteenth centuries.[56]

Illustrations

The following illustrations are taken from *Atlante Illustrativo,* published in 1845 by Tuscan geographer Attilio Zuccagni Orlandini. Although these illustrations are not from the exact period I have analyzed in this essay, they still provide a description of Italian forests at the beginning of the nineteenth century. In the first three images, the vegetation appears to be luxuriant thanks to favorable precipitation (in Como and Lucca) or soil fertility (the volcanic deposits near Naples). The fourth image illustrates typical conditions of interior and southern Sicily, conditions that were similar to large areas of Italy's mainland south. There, the Mediterranean climate was unfavorable to the reproduction of forest vegetation, advancing an agriculture that did not alternate crops with trees. The *Atlante Illustrativo* does not include images showing the intensive cultivation of steep slopes mentioned by so many observers. Such intensive agricultural practices continued until the mid-twentieth century, when massive emigration from the interior mountains erased most memories of it while allowing forests to regenerate and fields to fill with spontaneous regrowth.

Fig. 6.1. Villa d'Este (Como). From Attilio Zuccagni-Orlandini, *Atlante illustrativo ossia raccolta dei principali monumenti italiani antichi, del Medioevo e moderni e di alcune vedute pittoriche per servire di corredo alla Corografia fisica storica e statistica dell'Italia,* vol. 1 (Florence: n.p., 1845), tav. 3 ved. 2

Fig. 6.2. Bagni Caldi (Lucca). From Zuccagni-Orlandini, *Atlante illustrativo,* vol. 1, tav. 1 ved. 1

Fig. 6.3. Agnano (Naples). From Zuccagni-Orlandini, *Atlante illustrativo,* vol. 3, tav. 7 ved. 1

Fig. 6.4. Girgenti, Sicily. From Zuccagni-Orlandini, *Atlante illustrativo,* vol. 3, tav. 7 ved. 1

Notes

Editors' Note: This essay updates and expands on issues highlighted in Bruno Vecchio, *Il bosco negli scrittori italiani del Settecento e dell'età napoleonica* (Turin: Einaudi, 1974).

1. On the effects of deforestation on floodwaters and sediment transportation of the Bacchiglione (the river near Padua), see Cristoforo Sabbadin, "Discorsi sopra la laguna di Venetia," [1543] in *Antichi scrittori d'idraulica veneta,* ed. Roberto Cessi, vol. 2, pt. 1 (Venice: Ufficio Idrografico del Magistrato

alle Acque, 1930), 37–38; for information on the floods of Piave in 1317 and 1512, refer to Giorgio Piloni, *Historia [. . .] della Città di Belluno* (Venice: Rampazetto, 1607), 83; on floods and sediment transport of many Venetian rivers, refer to Carlo Antonio Bertelli, *Discorso sopra l'origine delle alterazioni della Laguna Veneta Antica, e Moderna* (Venice: Bosio, 1676), 9; on floods and sediment transport of the Arno, see Vincenzo Viviani, *Discorso [. . .] intorno al difendersi da' Riempimenti e dalle Corrosioni de' Fiumi applicato ad Arno in vicinanza della Città di Firenze* (Florence: Matini, 1688), 28.

2. For more on Emilio Sereni's sylvan reaction, see Bruno Andreolli, "L'uso del bosco e degli incolti," in *Storia dell'agricoltura italiana,* vol. 2, ed. Giuliano Pinto, Carlo Poni, and Ugo Tucci (Florence: Accademia dei Georgofili-Polistampa, 2001–2), 116–28, 137–41.

3. Emilio Sereni, *Storia del paesaggio agrario italiano* (Bari: Laterza, 1972 [1961]), 306–7, translated by Robert Burr Litchfield as *History of the Italian Agricultural Landscape* (Princeton, NJ: Princeton University Press, 1997).

4. See Filippo Re, *Saggio storico sullo stato e le vicende dell'agricoltura antica dei paesi fra l'Adriatico, l'Alpe e l'Appennino fino al Tronto* (Milan: Silvestri, 1817). Filippo Re, botanist, lecturer on agriculture at the University of Bologna, was the founder and the director of *Annali d'Agricoltura del Regno d'Italia* (Milan, 1809–14).

5. For a discussion of deforestation in northern Italy, see Jacopo Filiasi, "Sopra il diboscamento dei monti," *Memorie Scientifiche e Letterarie dell'Ateneo di Treviso* 2 (1819): 32–70. With regard to Tuscany, see Giovanni Fabbroni, "Ragionamento sugli effetti della libertà e del vincolo sui boschi alpini," [1806] in Fabbroni, *Scritti di pubblica economia,* vol. 2 (Florence: Niccolai, 1848). Fabbroni was completely in favor of the free cutting of trees and against any restraint.

6. Some of these issues are taken up in Marco Armiero, Pietro Piussi, and Bruno Vecchio, "L'uso del bosco e degli incolti," in *Storia dell'agricoltura italiana,* 3:129–216. One can also consult this text regarding recent contributions to the history of social elements of Italian forests; space considerations preclude mentioning these contributions here.

7. See, for example, Sabbadin, *Discorsi;* Viviani, *Discorso;* and for Lombardy, Antonio Lecchi, *Piano per la separazione, inalveazione, e sfogo de' tre torrenti, di Tradate, del Gardaluso, e del Bozzente* (Milan: n.p., n.d. [but 1762]), 17. For Venetia, see Giovanni Poleni, *Delle lagune venete* [1717] (Venice: Alvisopoli, 1817), 12–13. For Tuscany, see Guido Grandi, "Esame della scrittura pubblicata dal sig. dottore Geminiano Rondelli nella causa del mulino dell'Era," [1714] in *Raccolta d'autori che trattano del moto dell'acque,* vol. 2 (Florence: Tartini and Franchi, 1723), 633. For Umbria, refer to Tommaso Perelli, "Parere sulla Marroggia," in *Raccolta d'autori che trattano del moto dell'acque,* 2nd ed., vol. 9

(Florence: Stamperia di Sua Altezza Reale, 1774). Francesco Mengotti's work *Idraulica fisica e sperimentale ossia Saggio sull'acque correnti* (Venice: Andreola, 1816), about the relation between deforestation and hydraulics in northern Italy, was heavily documented and widely cited. Mengotti was highly esteemed by George Perkins Marsh, who directed readers of *Man and Nature* to Mengotti's *Idraulica fisica e sperimentale*: "No writer known to me has so well illustrated this function of forest vegetation as Mengotti." See the first Italian edition: George P. Marsh, *L'uomo e la natura ossia la superficie terrestre modificata per opera dell'uomo* (Florence: Barbera, 1870), 238. See also Marcus Hall, "The Provincial Nature of George Perkins Marsh," *Environment and History* 10, no. 2 (May 2004): 191–204.

8. See, for example, the detailed considerations about the causes of forest decay in Liguria made anonymously [by Agostino Bianchi] in *Osservazioni sul clima, sul territorio e sulle acque della Liguria marittima di un coltivatore di Diano*, vol. 1 (Genoa: De Grossi, 1817–18), 116–80.

9. For a detailed analysis about how forest issues are treated in those collections, see Vecchio, *Il bosco*, 194–214, 239–69.

10. A not exclusively regional viewpoint is, for example, that of Tuscan scholar Giovanni Targioni Tozzetti, *Relazioni di alcuni viaggi fatti in diverse parti della Toscana*, vol. 5 (Florence: Cambiagi, 1768–9), 390–91.

11. For Molise and northern Apulia (province of Capitanata, now province of Foggia), see: Francesco Longano, *Viaggio per la Capitanata* (Naples: Sangiacomo, 1790), 79, 118, 235; and Giuseppe Maria Galanti, *Della descrizione geografica e politica delle Sicilie*, ed. Franca Assante and Domenico Demarco, vol. 2 (Naples: ESI, 1969), 136, 389–90, 425 (originally edited in 1786–90).

12. Targioni Tozzetti, *Relazioni*, 3:197.

13. Besides what is mentioned in note 9, see for southern Calabria *Piano intorno la rustica economia, le arti ed il commercio dell'Ulteriore Calabria* (Naples: Stamperia Regale, 1792), 4–5, which is attributed to Domenico Grimaldi, reformer and government official.

14. For Tuscany, see *Saggi di agricoltura di un parroco samminiatese* (Florence: Cambiagi, 1775), 230–35 (this anonymous work was done by agrarian scholar Giovan Battista Landeschi); for eastern Sicily, see Paolo Balsamo, *Giornale del viaggio fatto in Sicilia e particolarmente nella contea di Modica* (Palermo: Reale Stamperia, 1809), 95. The best estimation of wood requirements made in eighteenth-century Italy was probably carried out by Giammaria Ortes, "Della economia nazionale libri sei," in *Scrittori classici italiani di economia politica*, modern ser., vol. 21 (Milan: Destefanis, 1804), 137, 146–47. Ortes calculated the yearly requirement for the Republic of Venice (at the present time Venetia, Friuli, middle and eastern Lombardy, Istria, and Dalmatia) at 18 million *carra*

(wagons), being the equivalent of 189 million cubic meters (see Vecchio, *Il bosco*, 68n36, for the equivalence).

15. It is possible to find lively and detailed discussions about each of these inconveniences in southern Italy at the beginning of the nineteenth century in Teodoro Monticelli, "Su l'economia delle acque da ristabilirsi nel Regno di Napoli," in Monticelli, *Opere*, vol. 1 (Naples: Stab. Tipogr. dell'Aquila, 1841 [1809]), 11–13.

16. See, for example, Pietro Arduino, "Memoria [. . .] relativamente all'accrescimento dei bestiami," *Giornale d'Italia Spettante alla Scienza Naturale e Principalmente all'Agricoltura, alle Arti ed al Commercio*, 5 (1768): 145–65. Pietro Arduino was a botanist and lecturer of agriculture at the University of Padua. See Vecchio, *Il bosco*, 35–36, for similar points of view among other authors.

17. For a different interpretation of the condition of common woodlands in the eighteenth century, see Gabriella Corona's essay in this volume. Regarding the frequent rotations for clear-cutting common forests of Acqui (Piedmont), see Vincenzo Malacarne, "Corografia georgico-jatrica d'Aqui," *Memorie della Società Agraria* [Torino] 3 (1788): 291. Concerning the excess in the performance of common uses of forests in southern Calabria, see Domenico Grimaldi, *Saggio di economia campestre per la Calabria Ultra* (Naples: Orsini, 1770), 124–26, 257. For a discussion of this phenomenon in Lombardy during the Napoleonic age, see Melchiorre Gioia, *Sul dipartimento del Lario* (Milan: Pirotta and Maspero, 1804), 82.

18. Luigi Tramontani, *Istoria naturale del Casentino*, vol. 2 (Florence: Stamperia della Carità, 1800–1802), 19–22. Pietro Ferroni, "Sul taglio delle macchie alpine," *Atti dell'Accademia dei Georgofili* 8 (1817): 249–63; the text was read at the academy in 1807. Also see Matteo Biffi-Tolomei, *Saggio d'agricoltura pratica toscana e specialmente del contado fiorentino* (Florence: Tofani, 1804), 63–68. Some of these eighteenth-century forest voices were put in archives and published only in the twentieth century; for Piedmont and Lombardy, see Vecchio, *Il bosco*, 10–11 and 18–21.

19. Giammaria Piccone, *Memoria sul ristabilimento e coltura de' boschi del Genovesato* (Genoa: Eredi Scionico, 1796), 3–5.

20. Giovanni Battista Giovio, *Como e il Lario: Commentario di Poliante lariano* (Como: Ostinelli, 1795), 202–3.

21. Carlo Perotti, *Delle cagioni fisiche e politiche della grande estirpazione de' boschi in Piemonte da alcuni anni a questa parte* (Carmagnola: Barbie, 1811), 6–8; on Melchiorre Gioia, see Vecchio, *Il bosco*, 251. Also see Nicola Maria Nicolai, *Memorie leggi ed osservazioni sulle campagne e l'annona di Roma*, vol. 3 (Rome: Pagliarini, 1803), 277.

22. The phenomenon came later, but it was not less destructive for south-central Italy: see Pietro Tino, "La montagna meridionale: Boschi, uomini,

economie tra Otto e Novecento," in *Storia dell'agricoltura italiana in età contemporanea*, vol. 1, *Spazi e paesaggi*, ed. Piero Bevilacqua (Venice: Marsilio, 1989), 719–27; for the important case of Abruzzo, see Marco Armiero, *Il territorio come risorsa: Comunità, economie e istituzioni nei boschi abruzzesi (1806–1860)* (Naples: Liguori, 1999), 125–201.

23. For the Bologna Apennines, the process is well outlined by Bernardino Farolfi, *L'uso e il mercimonio: Comunità e beni comunali nella montagna bolognese del Settecento* (Bologna: Clueb, 1987). Among the authors of the day who were more aware of this process, see Lombardy's government official Odescalchi during 1773 and 1774 (see Vecchio, *Il bosco*, 19–21). In the nineteenth century, the documents about the role played by urban and industrial consumption in the Novara region (Piedmont) and in Lombardy were given full particulars by Melchiorre Gioia (see Vecchio, *Il bosco*, 246–47).

24. Piccone, *Memoria*, 3.

25. Gian Filippo Delfico, "Memoria per la conservazione e riproduzione dei boschi nella Provincia di Teramo," *Commercio Scientifico d'Europa col Regno delle Due Sicilie* 1 (November–December 1792). Reprinted in Vincenzo Comi, *Opere complete* (Teramo: Fabbri, 1908), 662–63.

26. Refer, for example, to the livestock husbandry question in Venetia; see note 19.

27. Bernardino Conte, "Saggio di agraria che versa sopra le cause della decadenza de' boschi," in *Raccolta di memorie delle Pubbliche Accademie di agricoltura, arti e commercio dello Stato Veneto*, vol. 18 (Venice: Perlini, 1797), 65–69.

28. Giuseppe Antonio Donadio, *Trattato dell'agricoltura* (Turin: Avondo, 1779), 150–51; Jean-Baptiste Constans de Castellet, *Discours sur cette question: Est-il plus important de défricher les terres incultes; ou est-il plus utile de cultiver avec plus de soins, et de s'occuper d'améliorer celles, qu'on a déjà mises en nature de rapport?* (Turin: Reycends, 1780).

29. See Marco Fantuzzi's proposal to use lignite in Sogliano, Romagna (see Vecchio, *Il bosco*, 125n25). The characteristics of pit coal at Acqui on the Bormida River are not specified; the use of pit coal is proposed by Malacarne, "Corografia," 288–89.

30. See Vecchio, *Il bosco*, 47–49, for a discussion about the possible uses of peat in Venetia. This problem was occasionally confronted in other regions, such as Tuscany and Abruzzo; see Vecchio, *Il bosco*, 102 and 157.

31. For Liguria, see Piccone, *Memoria*, 8–15.

32. For Abruzzo, grounds with slope greater than 45 percent are indicated; see Delfico, "Memoria," 678–80. In reference to the proposals for improving, by arboreal plantations, the less fertile soils of the Po Valley, such as the Lombard moors or similar soils (*baragge* in Piedmont, *magredi* in Friuli), see Vecchio, *Il bosco*, 74–78.

33. See note 17. On the eotechnic age, see Lewis Mumford, *Technics and Civilization* (New York: Harcourt, Brace, 1934), 107–42.

34. For Sicily, see Paolo Balsamo, *Memorie inedite di pubblica economia ed agricoltura*, vol. 1 (Palermo: Muratori, 1845), 70–75; for Sardinia, see Francesco Gemelli, *Rifiorimento della Sardegna proposto nel miglioramento di sua agricoltura* (Turin: Briolo, 1770), 76, 106, 193–205. Balsamo's *Memorie* is a reissue of his 1799–1800 lectures, in part already published in 1816.

35. See Vecchio's review, in *Il bosco*, 162–63.

36. Balsamo, *Memorie*, 79.

37. Vecchio, *Il bosco*, 106–8.

38. Among these authors, those worth mentioning are Giuseppe Gautieri, general forestry inspector for the Napoleonic Kingdom of Northern Italy, and Albertino Bellenghi, Camaldolese Abbot, the later belonging to an order that has long been linked with forest concerns. See Gautieri, "Quando e come abbiasi a permettere il pascolo ne' boschi sì resinosi che da fronda, sì d'alto fusto che cedui," *Annali d'Agricoltura del Regno d'Italia* 19 (July–September 1813): 97–145; Bellenghi, *Articoli sulla coltivazione dei boschi nel Piceno e nell'Umbria, e sull'utilità degli alberi indigeni* (Rome: Bourlie, 1816), 63–67.

39. For example, see Marco Lastri, *Corso d'agricoltura pratica ossia ristampa dei lunarj pei contadini della Toscana*, vol. 3 (Florence: Pagani, 1788), 320; *Saggi di agricoltura di un parroco*, 245–46; Antonio Bianchi, "Sui danni che arrecano le capre ai boschi," in *Commentarii dell'Accademia di scienze, lettere, agricoltura e arti del Dipartimento del Mella per l'anno MDCCCX* (Brescia: Bettoni, 1811), 76–80.

40. Filippo Andreucci and Luigi Tramontani, *La moltiplicazione del bestiame toscano esposta in due dissertazioni del signor dottore Filippo Andreucci e del signor dottore Luigi Tramontani* (Florence: Stecchi and Pagani, 1773), 6–7. The suggestion that forests were unhealthy was made especially in reference to parts of Tuscany and Latium, particularly in their coastal marshy and malarial regions. Concerning this debate in the eighteenth century, see Vecchio, *Il bosco*, 108–11, 120–23, 136–42. Concerning the dispute over clear-cutting of Cisterna woodland (southern Latium), which is characteristic of eighteenth-century debates, see M. Petrucci, "Alberi e venti: La vertenza di Cisterna e Sermoneta nel secolo XVIII," in Fondazione Lelio e Lisli Basso-Issoco, *L'ambiente nella storia d'Italia, Studi e immagini* (Venice: Marsilio, 1989): 115–29.

41. Vittore Giera, "Memoria [. . .] concernente i modi di aumentare le materie combustibili," *Nuovo Giornale d'Italia Spettante alla Scienza Naturale e Principalmente all'Agricoltura, alle Arti ed al Commercio* 4 (1792–93): 388–97.

42. See Giuseppe Antonini, "Opuscolo sopra i comunali di monte," *Raccolta di memorie delle Pubbliche Accademie di agricoltura* 1 (1789): 143–69; Pietro

Caronelli, "Memoria [. . .] in risposta al quesito del magistrato sopra i beni inculti [. . .]," *Raccolta di memorie delle Pubbliche Accademie di agricoltura* 15 (1795): 174–75; Bartolomeo Del Covolo, "Osservazioni sopra vari utili oggetti di patria agricoltura," *Nuovo Giornale d'Italia Spettante alla Scienza Naturale* 2 (1795–96): 345–68.

43. For Lombardy, see Cesare Beccaria, "Sulle miniere di ferro e sui boschi," [1783] in Beccaria, *Opere*, vol. 2 (Florence: Sansoni, 1958).

44. For Piedmont, see Perotti, *Delle cagioni,* 13–15.

45. For Venetia, see Carlo Carrera, "Memoria [. . .] sul quesito della Società georgica di Belluno, sulle cause e rimedi della scarsezza di legna e legnami," *Giornale d'Italia Spettante alla Scienza Naturale* 10 (1774): 389–91. For central Italy, see Adamo Fabbroni, "Dei beni comunitativi," *L'agricoltore* [Perugia-Assisi] 1 (1784), 20: 6–9.

46. Giovanni Scola, "Memoria [. . .] in risposta al quesito del magistrato sopra i beni inculti," *Magazzino Georgico* [Firenze] 2 (1784): 800.

47. About Vasco (1788), see Vecchio, *Il bosco,* 23–24. Melchiorre Gioia, *Filosofia della statistica,* vol. 2 (Milan: Pirotta, 1826), 117, wrote "in reference purely to private interests, trees of every kind of species must be cut when the yearly increase of their price is less than the yearly earnings you can get, plus the profit derived from the yearly value of the soil on which trees grow."

48. Delfico, *Memoria,* 1908, 664–65, 674–75.

49. Raffaele Pepe, "Dello stato e conservazione de' boschi della Provincia di Molise," in *Atti del R. Istituto d'incoraggiamento delle scienze naturali di Napoli,* vol. 1 (Naples: Trani, 1811), 211–12.

50. Carretti, "Dei boschi, e delle selve, e del modo di trarne partito, e distribuirli nell'economia rurale," *Memorie della Società di Agricoltura di Torino* 8 (1805): 316–19.

51. Giovanni Serafini, "Memoria, ed osservazioni sul miglioramento dei boschi nel territorio trentino," *Giornale di Agricoltura* [Milan] 1 (Fall 1807): 233–34.

52. Vincenzo Cuoco, "Rimboschimenti e bonifiche: Proposte," [1813?] in Cuoco, *Scritti vari,* ed. Nino Cortese and Fausto Nicolini (Bari: Laterza, 1924), 208–12.

53. Concerning this subject in Italy in that period, refer to (besides Bellenghi's work, already mentioned) Pietro Comparetti, *Saggio sulla coltura e governo de' boschi* (Padua: Brandolese, 1798); Gaetano Savi, *Trattato degli alberi della Toscana* (Pisa: n.p., 1801); Luigi Fornaini, *Della coltivazione degli abeti* (Florence: Stamperia Reale, 1804).

54. Salvatore Scuderi, "Trattato dei boschi dell'Etna," pt. 3, *Atti dell'Accademia Gioenia di Scienze Naturali di Catania* 3 (1829): 1–16.

55. Gian Domenico Romagnosi, "Regime economico politico dei boschi dell'Etna in Sicilia," in *Opere,* vol. 15 (Florence: Piatti, 1845), 613.

56. See, for example, Bruno Vecchio, "Un documento in materia forestale nell'Italia del secondo Ottocento: I dibattiti parlamentari, 1869–1877," *Storia Urbana* 69, no. 4 (1994): 177–204; Mario Sulli, Bruno Vecchio, and Alessandra Zanzi Sulli, "Forestry Legislation and Management in Italy, 1861–1923: Environmental Needs and Social Dynamics," in *JEV—Jahrbuch für europäische Verwaltungsgeschichte* 11 (1999): 111–38.

CHAPTER 7

Environmental Heritage of a Past Cultural Landscape

Alder Woods in the Upper Aveto Valley of the Northwestern Apennines

Roberta Cevasco

RECENTLY, A GOOD deal of attention has been paid to "cultural land-scapes" in European geographic and environmental studies. Much of this attention is due to the adoption of an administrative act called the European Landscape Convention, signed at Florence on 20 October 2000. This act reflects a number of European Union (EU) research projects de-voted to cultural landscapes, as shown by such initiatives as the European Thematic Network on Cultural Landscapes and Their Ecosystems (PAN) and the European Cultural Landscapes, Our Common European Cultural Landscape Heritage (ECL). It is in the context of heritage management and valorization policy rather than scientific circles that this late nineteenth-century concept of human geography has been readopted.

In its original meaning, a "cultural" landscape implicitly assumed the existence of a "natural" landscape. Generally, this distinction reflected a mis-understanding of the dynamic nature of most European rural landscapes since the late 1960s. For instance, the establishment of regional natural parks across Italy in the 1970s was premised on the concept of *naturalization*, that is, the spontaneous regrowth that follows abandonment of agro-sylvo-pastoral landscapes. Geographic spaces once devoted to production have been converted to leisure and renamed nature, becoming, in fact, postcultural landscapes. In southern Europe, especially in mountainous areas, various traditional ways of working the land disappeared during the twentieth century. In Italy's northwestern Apennines, the disappearance of pastoral systems began as early as the 1850s, when older land uses were abruptly replaced by forestry practices in Italy's preunified states.[1]

Many postcultural, pastoral landscapes became a type of wilderness and were unsustainable, as shown by the failures of recent naturalization policy.[2] Studying these cultural landscapes with regressive methods and topographic sensitivities (the two main tools available for analyzing historical fluxes in very small areas) allows us to develop a remarkably clear portrayal of the social and environmental processes involved.[3] This study presents a new understanding of former cultural systems by focusing on their environmental, technical, and social heritage. I argue that an understanding of cultural landscapes will enable us to better evaluate an area's environmental and cultural benefits.

The Alnocoltura Cycle

"Le *One* sono nei *Runkètti*"
(as heard in Roncolongo, springtime 2006)

The origins of cultural landscapes arise from former cultural environments through heritage and the processes of transmission, continuity, and discontinuity. Every single cultural landscape has been born from another cultural landscape. In other words, the geographic-historical qualities of a place, although invisible, have stamped an identity into its current landscape. Through what can be called a microanalytic approach, one can reveal and decode evidence of living organic material and energy flows in carefully circumscribed social and environmental systems.[4] Such evidence can be found, for example, as anomalies in the vegetation or in the soil stratigraphies.

The environmental heritage I discuss in the following case study is the current cover of white alder (*Alnus incana* Moench) in the upper Aveto Valley, within the larger Trebbia watershed of the northwestern Apennines. From these alder stands, which attract little attention from naturalists, one can re-create a vanished cultural landscape that depended on this single alder species as the system's central productive and reproductive element.[5]

The white alder in these mountains is outside its typical geographic and topographic range. *Alnus incana* occupies a northern-continental-Alpine distribution in Europe, and it forms only locally abundant populations in the northern Apennines. In the Aveto Valley (and within fragmented locations of the upper Trebbia watershed), this tree forms small, discontinuous plots in woodlands dominated by beech (*Fagus sylvatica*) and turkey oak (*Quercus cerris*), lying between eight hundred and twelve hundred meters above sea level. From the perspective of the network "Rete Natura 2000,"[6] which identifies ecological sites of European importance (SICs), current alder stands are viewed as relics of former alluvial forests because most biogeographers explain their distribution in purely physiographic terms.[7] Even though this tree reaches its southern limit in the Casentinesi Forests of Tuscany, the possibility of diffusion or enlargement of its range during historical times is not taken into account, meaning that social and political dimensions of its distribution are not considered. Nonetheless, the western limits of *Alnus incana,* as in Germany's Westphalia, has been explained as a legacy of earlier cultivation practices.[8]

Thanks to a microanalytic approach, we are able to document how the southern limits of the current white alder distribution can be considered the result of a historical environmental system characterized by the rotation of grain crops with pastures and woodlands. This rotation system, which in the Aveto Valley offers evidence for continual use over a span of two hundred years and perhaps much longer, is the source of the anomalous distribution of alder woods.

This land use system, which disappeared by the early twentieth century, is usually referred to as *alnocoltura*. The environmental heritage of this former cultural landscape is reflected in the ecological continuity of alder stands, even if these stands have become quite fragmented over the last hundred years.[9] Within the greater eastern Ligurian Apennine region of northern Italy, the alnocoltura system was centered on the upper Aveto Valley during the postmedieval era and was linked to a second agroforestry system, in which *black* alder (*Alnus glutinosa*) was coplanted with chestnuts across terraces. Indeed, remnants of this mixed woodland are still found in the region's more eastern, coastal valleys of Vara, Petronio, and Fontanabuona.[10] In this last valley, for instance, mixed chestnut and black alder woods can be traced to the efforts of an energetic local priest in the early nineteenth century, although certain farm records suggest that the nearby Graveglia Valley witnessed these forestry practices in the mid-eighteenth century.[11] Evidence for using black alder as a fertility enhancer is found as well in northeastern Italy, where black alder was planted in hay meadows until the 1950s in order to enrich soils while producing fodder. Although this soil-enhancing practice in that region has been linked to communities

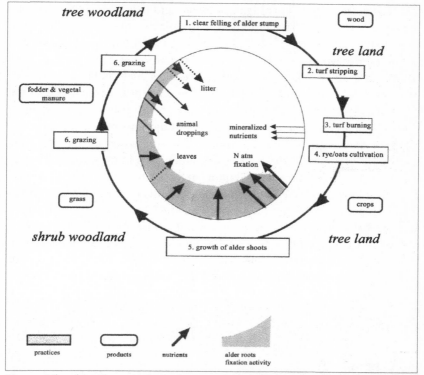

Fig. 7.1. The alnocoltura cycle in the 1820s in Val d'Aveto. Modified from Sabrina Bertolotto and Roberta Cevasco, "The 'Alnocoltura' System in the Ligurian Eastern Apennines: Archive Evidence," in *Methods and Approaches in Forest History*, ed. Mauro Agnoletti and Steve Anderson (New York: CABI Publishing, 2000)

with Slovenian origins, memories of alnocoltura in the Aveto Valley have been diluted and lost.[12]

At the beginning of this research, the historical reconstruction of the cultural cycle was carried out through archival documentation of the eighteenth and nineteenth centuries, within a study area devoted to tracking the composition, structure, and ecological functioning of the valley's woodlands (within the municipalities of S. Stefano and Rezzoaglio). Research initially focused on an eighteenth-century cartographic atlas, joining other information gleaned from archival records of the forestry administration of the Sardinia kingdom during the 1820s. This information allowed us to identify a network of sources relevant to sites already surveyed in the field.[13]

The management cycle carried out in the 1820s consisted of short rotation coppicing of the alder wood parcel (every three to twelve years), followed by controlled burning of branches and turf in order to sow temporary crops such as oats and rye. Pasture practice was allowed after the crop years. The owners of each plot identified their land as *bosco alberato di costi* (shrub woodland), *bosco alberato* (tree woodland), or *terra alberata* (tree land), which might also include products such as *fogliazzo* (leaves used for stalls), firewood, and fencing. The cycle was comparable to the practices of temporary cultivation known across Europe (as, for example, *debbio* [Italian] and *écobuage* [French]),[14] but the alnocoltura system in the Ligurian Apennines was more complex: it was based on local naturalistic knowledge of the fertilizing capacity of alder. This knowledge has mostly disappeared among current inhabitants of the Aveto Valley, with the system itself forgotten and the exact biological mechanism by which alder groves replenish soils remaining unknown.[15] The local dialect suggests that there is a gap between present and past cultural landscapes—the site *runkètti* quoted in the epigraph to this section denotes a specific alder (*one*) plot that conserves linguistic memory of the temporary cultivation system of *ronco*. Such words are still in use today and localize specific plots, but the

Fig. 7.2. Root nodules of white alder (*Alnus incana*), Moglie di Ertola site, Aveto Valley, Rezzoaglio, Genova, 1115 msl. From Andrea Cevasco et al., *Studio di fattibilità di un progetto per la conoscenza, conservazione e gestione delle zone umide liguri: Zone umide della Liguria come beni culturali*, vol. 1 (Genoa: Università degli Studi di Genova, LASA, Direzione Regionale per i Beni Culturali e Paesaggistici della Liguria, 2007)

local understanding of the ecological functioning of these woodlands is now interrupted.

Evidence of the alder's ability to enhance soil fertility is found in the agronomic-botanical literature after the fifteenth century. The adoption of alnocoltura in this region could be part of the changes taking place in summer pasture management during the early Middle Ages, when intensive and multiple fodder resource use systems were introduced, as the wooded meadows in the Apennines between Liguria, Emilia, and Tuscany (in the fifth and sixth centuries AD).[16] There is growing evidence that the alnocoltura system was practiced across Europe, as in Sweden where alders were used to enhance a pasture's productivity or in parts of Romania where farmers still rely on it.[17] In Finland, a similar cultural cycle of using rye through ecobuages in stands of *Alnus incana* has been discussed by George Kuhnholtz-Lordat consulting late nineteenth-century records, with the alder phase being considered a fallow period.[18] The cycle at work in the Aveto Valley, by contrast, was part of an intensive and multiple system of resource use involving pastoral, silvicultural, and agricultural activities. Today, a system comparable to alnocoltura is used in northwestern Yunnan, at the border of Tibet and Burma; at the village of Kending in the Dulong Valley, *Alnus nepalensis* is planted every five to seven years and rotated with buckwheat, millet, or maize.[19]

The study site shows the importance of jurisdictional rights and conflicts over the access to cultivation resources during the feudal regime.[20] Until the enactment of the 1927 law that abolished many common properties, temporary cultivation rights were determined by a local system of inheriting family commons (or *comunaglie*).[21] In the upper Aveto Valley during the first decades of the eighteenth century, making ronchi depended on the balance between family claims and larger seigneurial claims within the centuries-old problem of the seigneurial emphyteusis.

Traces in the Soil

In the early twentieth century, the alnocoltura system rapidly disappeared, generally fading from local memory and from forest classification systems. But the same plot of land described by early eighteenth-century sources can be explored with a historical microanalytic and archaeological approach.[22] The soils of the sites where alnocoltura existed often conserve ecological evidence of fire practices not linked with charcoal pits; charcoal particles, having a dimension of a few millimeters and found just under the surface, can be readily attributed to the burned remnants of a fire of alder branches that have been subsequently disturbed by hoeing.[23]

Archaeological evidence of special interest to the history of alnocoltura is shown by an alder stump, pointed out by a local farmer and careful observer of his mountains between the Trebbia and Aveto valleys; this farmer also made note of the semifossilized nature of this find, which did not undergo typical decomposition processes from year to year. This particular stump is rooted in an abandoned streambed of the Molineggi River, at a site called Pozzo, now a pasture belonging to inhabitants of the nearby hamlet of Ertola (Rezzoaglio municipality, Genoa). This site is within the same *perimetro d'acqua* (spatial distribution of watering rights) as the Moglie di Ertola, a previously studied, partially wet pasture located at 1,120 meters that includes peat layers and semifossilized fir trunks (*Abies alba*) dating from the Bronze Age (2920–2620 BC).[24] Radiocarbon analysis dated the alder stump to around 1550. Two sections were opened and analyzed in order to connect the stump to the surrounding stratigraphy. Results show that the strong deposits of fine materials accumulated in this small basin

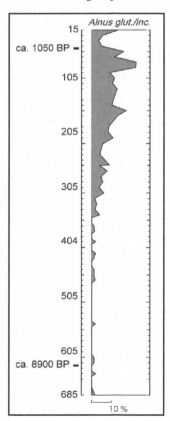

are surely anomalous and can be considered "archaeological" evidence for the practice of filling in wetlands with sediment, similar to a process called *colmata di monte* (artificial filling of a mountain slope with pipelines).[25] Further proof that such practices were common in this area comes from a document dated 1627 that describes how nearby inhabitants filled in Torrio Lake.[26] In order to correlate stratigraphy with vegetation types, the Moglie di Ertola site is currently undergoing pollen analysis.[27]

A pollen diagram already available from a peat bog on the opposite slope, located at Casanova (Trebbia Valley, Rovegno municipality), shows a progressive decline in alder pollen from the early Middle Ages, with this trend changing direction only in recent years. This phase of diminishing alder pollen beginning from one meter up is mirrored by increasing pollen from asters (*Compositae*)

Fig. 7.3. The *Alnus* curve in the pollen diagram from the Moglie di Ertola site. From Menozzi et al., *Studio di fattibilità*

and hazelnut (*Corylus*). The alder pollen decrease can be interpreted as either widespread removal of alder plots for promoting meadows, pastures, and cultivation of cereals (rye, wheat) or as short rotation coppicing within the alnocoltura cycle, which strengthened alders. To provide support for this second possibility, it will be necessary to show that the alnocoltura cycle induced a lower production of alder pollen. This second scenario may well be the case because alders do not flourish at least for the first two years and do not produce seeds for six to fifteen years after cutting.[28] Similar pollen results are shown at Lago Riane (Aveto Valley, near the village of S. Stefano d'Aveto), which in the last meter of sediment shows a decrease in alder and an increase in Graminaceae and beech (*Fagus*).[29] Here again, the best explanation may not be decreasing alder woodlands but an increasing cyclic use of alders, possibly connected with the settlement of a beech wooded meadow system, as proposed for the site of Prato Spilla.[30]

In the case of Moglie di Ertola, the situation is more complex due to the filling of the wetland site after the year AD 1000, when the current pasture was created. Pollen analyses in this case will have to account for the disturbance happening in the sediment around this period, corresponding to a depth of about fifty centimeters. This site seems to be key for sedimentary proof of the alnocoltura system in these slopes: it shows an evident decline of alder pollen together with the rise of grasses (Poaceae) and the appearance of cereals.[31] The increase of microcharcoal particles corroborates the existence of alnocoltura.[32]

Returning to the question about biological heritage of the cultural landscapes of the Aveto and Trebbia valleys, it is interesting to combine data from sedimentary and textual sources with the living ecological evidence of the alnocoltura system. The Moglie di Ertola area, with its series of pastures, lends itself to this multidisciplinary approach. In one of these large clearings now surrounded by a coppiced beech, there is a very large white alder stump (17.20 meters in circumference), which was probably still alive during alnocoltura days. Other evidence is found on nearby slopes, including geometric alder stands aligning to cairns, hawthorns, and local toponomy relative to ronchi. These evidences are the living memory of a cultural landscape that perpetuates itself even though the cultural system that created it is extinct.

Management Issues

Starting with these results, a specific application of our microanalytic approach has been proposed in local game management plans within the province of Genova.[33] It is obvious that the dramatic reduction of alder woods

Fig. 7.4. A white alder stump with a seventeen-meter circumference in the study area of Ertola, Aveto Valley. From Menozzi et al., *Studio di fattibilità*

occurring in the twentieth century had important effects also on animal populations, especially on avifauna. Residual alder plots can therefore serve as laboratories when combined with information about ecological relationships collected by game biologists. Game managers emphasize the importance of alder woods for woodcock (*Scolopax rusticula*) and snipe (*Gallinago gallinago*) because the nitrogen-rich soils sustain good populations of earthworms (*Lumbricus terrestris*).[34] These habitats attract woodcock because they are humid soils rather than permanent bogs and are thus able to withstand freezing and thereby promote earthworm growth, especially with the addition of bovine dung. These moist woodlands can be cyclically renewed through coppicing, and maintaining large clearings of mowed and grazed meadows promotes habitat diversity favorable to woodcock.[35] Grazing also keeps the ground open and limits the spreading of false brome (*Brachypodium*) thanks to animal droppings. These droppings and manures promote the growth of earthworms and associated microfauna.

This kind of habitat favorable to woodcock seems to have been similar to the cultural landscapes of alder woods subject to the alnocoltura system (and its associated grazing by sheep and goats) as was so widespread in the upper Aveto Valley and nearby Trebbia Valley until the end of the nineteenth century. Today, there is new interest in rearing a local, traditional cattle breed known as *Cabannina*, which is historically well adapted to the woodland and shrubland mountain pastures of the Aveto Valley.[36] This breed offers significant potential for managing alder woods. In these valleys, the historical cultural landscape of alnocoltura could be reevaluated and even reestablished in order to favor game, grow limited grains, and produce fodder with the goal of rearing Cabannina.

To conclude, cultural landscapes must be seen as part of a common European heritage,[37] and information on them should be disseminated in our educational programs. To avoid hiding the rich cultural legacy of landscapes behind their current static state,[38] it is important to distinguish the hidden landscape dimension—intended as the underpinning historical ecology—from habits, desires, myths, and dreams that were once or are today integral to these ecosystems. For conservation purposes, it is fundamental to acknowledge this living rural heritage by reconstructing the complexity of the past cultural landscapes and exposing the synergy of ecological and social processes that built them. Historical land uses still affecting the ecology of each site permeate the biodiversity and stability of these ecosystems. A careful assessment of such uses will contribute to their sustainable management.[39]

Notes

1. Diego Moreno, *Dal documento al terreno: Storia e archeologia dei sistemi agro-silvo-pastorali* (Bologna: Il Mulino, 1990).

2. On the problem of drift in the concept of cultural landscape within geographic and environmental studies, see Roberta Cevasco and Diego Moreno, "Microanalisi geo-storica o geografia culturale della copertura vegetale? Sull'eredità ambientale dei 'paesaggi culturali,'" *Trame dello spazio, Quaderni di Geografia Storica e Quantitativa* 3 (February 2007): 83–101. The topic is developed in a PhD project in progress at the University of Genoa's Doctoral School in Historical Sciences. Thanks are due to Cristina Bellini (at the University of Genoa) for her help with the translation.

3. Ross Balzaretti, Mark Pearce, and Charles Watkins, eds., *Ligurian Landscapes: Studies in Archaeology, Geography and History* (London: Accordia Research Institute, University of London, 2004).

4. Roberta Cevasco, "Nuove risorse per la geografia del turismo rurale: Ecologia storica e risorse ambientali nell'Appennino ligure-emiliano," *Bollettino della Società Geografica Italiana* 2 (2005): 345–74.

5. Diego Moreno, Roberta Cevasco, Sabrina Bertolotto, and Giuseppina Poggi, "Historical Ecology and Post-medieval Management Practices in Alder Woods (*Alnus incana (L.)* Moench) in the Northern Apennines, Italy," in *The Ecological History of European Forests,* ed. Keith J. Kirby and Charles Watkins (New York: CAB International, 1998), 185–201.

6. On its website the European Union defines Nature 2000 as "the largest coherent network of protected areas in the world." It is based on two European Union directives: the Birds Directive (1979) and the Habitats Directive (1991). Information from http://ec.europa.eu/environment/nature/index_en.htm (accessed 8 August 2009).

7. Mauro Mariotti, Attilio Arillo, Vincenzo Parisi, Elena Nicosia, and Giovanni Diviacco, eds., *Biodiversità in Liguria: La Rete Natura 2000* (Recco: Microart's, 2002). Locally, alder woods are recognized as an unstable phase in the dynamic series of beech and strictly dependent on coppicing and pasture; see Salvatore Gentile, *Note illustrative della carta della vegetazione dell'Alta Val d'Aveto (Appennino ligure)* (Rome: CNR, Collana del Programma Finalizzato "Promozione della Qualità dell'Ambiente," 1982).

8. Angelika Schwabe, "Monographie Alnus incana-reicher Waldgesellschaften in Europa: Variabilitat und Ahnlichkeiten einer azonal verbreiteten Gesellschaftsgruppe," *Phytocoenologia* 13, no. 2 (1985): 197–302.

9. According to the data collected by a national study of the 1880s, only in the village of S. Stefano d'Aveto did alder woods cover more than one thousand

hectares; see *Atti della Giunta per la Inchiesta Agraria e sulle condizioni della classe agricola,* vol. 10, fascicolo 1 (Rome: Forzani, 1883).

10. In the same Aveto Valley in the 1820s, the practice of coplanting alders with turkey oaks is documented: the specific statement of parcels according to the formula *terra alberata di cerri onati* (land with turkey oaks combined with alders) could be referring to the role of alders in promoting turkey oaks for producing leaves for *frasca* (leaf fodder).

11. As regards the Graveglia Valley, east of the Fontanabuona Valley, owner's instructions exist from the late eighteenth century about managing its chestnut woodlands; see Massimo Angelini, "I libri di famiglia di un erudito di provincia nel tardo Settecento," *Schede Umanistiche* 2 (1994): 107–37.

12. Marta Guidi and Pietro Piussi, "The Influence of Old Rural Land-Management Practices on the Natural Regeneration of Woodland on Abandoned Farmland in the Prealps of Friuli, Italy," in *Ecological Effects of Afforestation,* ed. Charles Watkins (Wallingford, UK: CAB International, 1993), 57–67; Pietro Piussi, "Piantagioni di ontano nero in prati falciabili nel Friuli orientale," *SM Annali di San Michele* 11(1998): 215–29. In the upper Vara Valley of Eastern Liguria, this use of black alder was still pursued in the 1960s; in Moreno, *Dal documento,* chap. 6.

13. Sabrina Bertolotto and Roberta Cevasco, "Fonti osservazionali e fonti testuali: Le 'Consegne dei Boschi' e il sistema dell' 'Alnocoltura' nell'Appennino Ligure Orientale (1822)," *Quaderni Storici* 103, no. 1 (2000): 87–108.

14. François Sigaut, *L'agriculture et le feu: Role et place du feu dans les techniques de préparation du champ de l'ancienne agriculture européenne* (Paris: Mouton, 1975), 320.

15. This fertilization capacity is now traced to the superficial roots that fix atmospheric nitrogen through the action of microorganisms *Frankia;* see C. Daniere, André Capellano, and André Moiroud, "Dynamique de l'azote dans un peuplement naturel d'Alnus incana (L.) Moench," *Acta Oecologica (Oecologia Plantarum)* 7, no. 2 (1986): 165–75.

16. John J. Lowe, Chiara Davite, Diego Moreno, and Roberto Maggi, "Holocene Pollen Stratigraphy and Human Interference on the Woodlands of the Northern Apennines, Italy," *The Holocene* 4, no. 2 (1994): 153–64; Diego Moreno and Chiara Davite, "Des 'saltus' aux 'alpes' dans les Apennins du Nord (Italie): Une hypothèse sur la phase du Haut-Moyen-Age dans le diagramme pollinique du site de Prato Spilla," in *L'homme et la nature au Moyen Age: Actes du V Congrès International d'Archéologie Médiévale,* ed. Michel Colardelle (Paris: Edition Errance, 1996), 138–43.

17. Thanks are due to Urban Emanuelsson for the information on this issue.

18. George Kuhnholtz-Lordat, *L'écran vert,* (Paris: Editions du Muséum, 1958).

19. Special thanks go to Joelle Smadja and Stéphane Gros for the information on alder cultivation in Yunnan.

20. Osvaldo Raggio, "Immagini e verità: Pratiche sociali, fatti giuridici e tecniche cartografiche," *Quaderni Storici* 108, no. 3 (2001): 843–76.

21. On common property, see Gabriella Corona's essay in this volume.

22. In particular, I am referring to the six maps conserved in the private archives of the Doria Pamphilj Landi family in Rome, produced by Marc'Antonio Fossa, judge and Doria's feudal officer in the Trebbia and Aveto valleys at the beginning of the eighteenth century (ca. 1700–1726). See also Roberta Cevasco and Vittorio Tigrino, "Lo spazio geografico concreto: Una discussione tra storia politico-sociale ed ecologia storica," *Quaderni Storici* 127, no. 1 (2008): 207–42.

23. Diego Moreno et al., "Historical Ecology and Post-medieval Management Practices."

24. In 2003, a project was promoted by the University of Genoa (Laboratorio di Archeologia e Storia Ambientale) in collaboration with the Direzione Regionale per i Beni Culturali e Paesaggistici della Liguria (and funded by the Ministero per i Beni e le Attività Culturali) on the importance of Ligurian wetlands as cultural landscapes. First results for the Moglie di Ertola site are found in Maria Angela Guido, Bruna Menozzi, Sara Scipioni, and Carlo Montanari, "Il sito 'Mogge di Ertola' come potenziale fonte per la storia ambientale del crinale Trebbia/Aveto," *Archeologia Postmedievale* 6 (2002): 11–116; Andrea De Pascale, Roberto Maggi, Carlo Montanari, and Diego Moreno, "Pollen, Herds, Jasper and Copper Mines: Economic and Environmental Changes during the 4th and 3rd Millennia BC in Liguria (NW Italy)," *Environmental Archaeology* 11, no. 1 (2006): 115–24; Cristina Bellini, Roberta Cevasco, Diego Moreno, Maria Angela Guido, and Carlo Montanari, "The Mogge di Ertola Site, High Aveto Valley, Ligurian Apennines (N. Italy): Bronze Age, Medieval and Present Cultural Landscapes," in *Cultural Landscapes of Europe: Fields of Demeter, Haunts of Pan*, ed. Knut Krzywinski, Michael O'Connell, and Hanjörg Küster (Bremen: Aschenbeck Media, 2009), 108–9.

25. Diego Moreno, "Improving Land with Water: Evidence of Historical 'Colmate di Monte' in the Trebbia-Aveto Watershed," poster discussed at the Second Workshop on Environmental History and Archaeology, Montebruno (Genoa), 22 May 2002.

26. Andrea Cevasco, Roberta Cevasco, Carlo Alberto Gemignoni, Maria Angelo Guido, Eleana Marullo, Bruna Menozzi, Chiara Molinari, Carlo Montanari, Diego Moreno, Sandra Placeteani, Anna Maria Stagno, and Elisabetta Roma, *Studio di fattibilità di un progetto per la conoscenza, conservazione e gestione delle zone umide liguri: Zone umide della Liguria come beni culturali,*

vol. 1 (Genoa: Università degli Studi di Genova, LASA, Direzione Regionale per i Beni Culturali e Paesaggistici della Liguria, 2007), 206.

27. Bruna Menozzi, Cristina Bellini, Andrea Cevasco, Roberta Cevasco, Andrea De Pascale, Maria Angela Guido, Roberto Maggi, Dagfinn Moe, Carlo Montanari, and Diego Moreno, "The Archaeology of a Peat Bog in Context: Contribution to the Study of Biodiversification Processes in Historical Time (Ligurian Apennine, NW Italy)," 4ème Congrès International d'Archéologie Médiévale et Moderne, Medieval Europe, Paris Sorbonne 2007, University of Paris 1 Panthéon–Sorbonne, available at http://medieval-europe-paris-2007. univ-paris1.fr (accessed 5 May 2009). Interesting evidences regarding alnocultura come from two peat bogs (Casanova and Lago Riane) already discussed in a historical ecological perspective. The discussion involved the pollen diagram from the Moglia di Casanova site, from Gillian Cruise, "Pollen Stratigraphy of Two Holocene Peat Sites in the Ligurian Apennines, Northern Italy," *Review of Palaeobotany and Palynology* 63, no. 3–4 (1990): 299–313; see also Gillian Cruise, "Environmental Change and Human Impact in the Upper Mountain Zone of the Ligurian Apennines: The Last 5000 Years," *Rivista di Studi Liguri* 57, no. 1–4 (1991): 175–94; Nick Branch's unpublished diagram, and one from the Lago Riane site, from Gentile et al., "Ricerche," in Cevasco et al., *Studio*. Special thanks go to Nick Branch for the opportunity to discuss his unpublished diagram.

28. This observation on the phenology of the alder is suggested by Dagfinn Moe (Bergen University) and concerns *Alnus incana* behavior in Norway. On the time of seed ripening, see Philip A. Tallantire, "The Palaeohistory of Grey Alder (*Alnus incana* (L.) Moench) and Black Alder (*A. glutinosa* (L.) Gaertn.) in Fennoscandia," *New Phytologist* 73, no. 3 (1974): 529–46.

29. Salvatore Gentile, Maria Angela Guido, Carlo Montanari, Gaudenzio Paola, Giulia Braggio Morucchio, and Mario Petrillo, "Ricerche geobotaniche e saggi di cartografia della vegetazione del piccolo bacino di Lago Riane (Liguria)," *Braun Blanquetia* 2 (1988): 77–104.

30. Lowe et al., "Holocene Pollen Stratigraphy," 153–64.

31. Cevasco and Moreno, "Microanalisi geo-storica o geografia culturale," 83–101.

32. Menozzi et al., "The Archaeology of a Peat Bog in Context."

33. Sabrina Bertolotto and Roberta Cevasco, "The 'Alnocoltura' System in the Ligurian Eastern Apennines: Archive Evidence," in *Methods and Approaches in Forest History*, eds. Mauro Agnoletti and Steve Anderson (New York: CABI Publishing, 2000), 189–202.

34. Woodcock hunters (*beccaccinai*) know the importance of alder woods, which form soft and humus-rich soil through decomposition of alder "fat" litter.

35. Paolo Casanova and Francesco Sorbetti Guerri, eds., *La caccia in Toscana negli ultimi settant'anni: Evoluzione sociale, dell'ambiente e della caccia* (Florence: Edizioni Polistampa, 2003).

36. Andrea Cevasco, Roberta Cevasco, Carlo Alberto Gemignani, Daniela Marrazzo, Alessandra Spinetti, and Anna Maria Stagno, "Archaeological and Ecological Evidence of Rearing Practices, Fodder and Water Resources Management in Post-medieval Ligurian Apennines (NW Italy)," paper presented at the 4ème Congrès International d'Archéologie Médiévale et Moderne, Paris 3–8 September 2007.

37. Krzywinski, O'Connell, Küster, eds, *Cultural Landscapes of Europe.*

38. Massimo Quaini, "Geografia culturale o geografia critica? Per una discussione sulle più recenti mode culturali in geografia," *Bollettino della Società Geografica Italiana* 10 (2005): 881–88.

39. Roberto Maggi, Carlo Montanari, and Diego Moreno, eds., "L'approccio storico-ambientale al patrimonio rurale delle aree protette: Materiali di studio dal secondo workshop on Environmental History and Archaeology," special issue of *Archeologia Postmedievale* 6 (2002).

CHAPTER 8

Act Locally, Think Nationally

A Brief History of Access Rights and Environmental Conflicts in Fascist Italy

Wilko Graf von Hardenberg

THIS ESSAY provides an overview of the evolution of nature conservation and resource management legislation and ideology in Italy during the Fascist Ventennio period (1923–43). Further, it explains the local environmental impact of Fascist policies through the analysis of two exemplary case studies: the Gran Paradiso National Park and the province of Novara. Crucial in the time line of the regime's interaction with the natural world was the period from 1929 to 1934, which marked a fracture in Italy's environmental history.

In 1976, Zeev Sternhell suggested that fascism represented the very first "environmentalist ideology of [the twentieth] century."[1] This interpretation of the relationship between fascism and environmentalism most probably arose from the fact that fascism, paradoxically, combined the attempt to modernize the industrial and agrarian systems with an ideological revolt against urbanism and industrialism. Anna Bramwell gave a short account of the possible existence of a generic fascist environmentalism. Italian Fascism seemed to her to have had a conflictual relationship with the natural world: citing Giovanni Gentile, she asserted that for Fascism, "nature was the enemy of human culture, and hence a danger to be fought" and a threat for "the autonomy of the state, and man's fully human culture."[2] Bramwell thus denied that Italian Fascists had any interest in environmental issues and concluded that National Socialism was the only fascist movement that had serious environmental concerns.

The question of whether Nazism may be interpreted as a movement that was intrinsically environment-friendly has been debated repeatedly since the mid-1980s.[3] In many cases, for example, Adolf Hitler's alleged love of animals and the drafting of a series of laws between 1933 and 1935 regarding the preservation of nature and the protection of animals have been used as proof of the existence of a "green wing" within the Nazi regime or even of a comprehensive Nazi allegiance to ecological policies. However, no actual, tight link may be traced between environmentalism and the government practices of any of the fascist and pseudo-fascist regimes that ruled over various European countries at different times in the twentieth century, Nazism included.

One of the main means used by the Italian Fascist regime to represent itself was the physical creation of a "New Italy," through environmental management and nature conservation. The transformation of wilderness into "productive nature" became one of the symbols of the regime, and the conservation of natural beauties (*bellezze naturali*) was seen as a propagandist means to consolidate national identity.[4] Ruralism and anti-industrialism, inspired also by sectors of Italian elites imbued with classical culture and neoidealistic aesthetics, represented important elements of Fascist ideology. Indeed, criticism of the modern way of life arose in Italy more from strictly aesthetic considerations than from concerns about the state of the environment or human health.[5] For instance, laws regulating the institution of national parks were rooted within the jurisprudence on the preservation of beauty, a concept encompassing artistic, historical, and environmental goods in a wider sense.[6] And ruralization was a matter of great importance in Fascist propaganda because of what were deemed to be its beneficial effects on the morale of the country and of its role as a symbol of the New Italy.

Environmental Legislation between Continuity and Rupture

Just two months after it assumed power in October 1922, Benito Mussolini's government established a national park on the Gran Paradiso massif, between the current provinces of Turin and Aosta in northwestern Italy,[7] and acknowledged the park instituted by the preservationist association Pro Montibus in the Abruzzi region.[8] In the following months, some Fascist

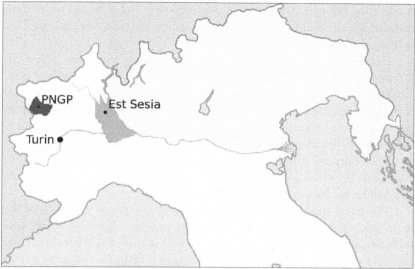

Map 8.1. Locations of the case studies

leaders attempted unsuccessfully to create a park in the mountainous area of the Sila in Calabria.[9] These early acts of nature conservation, the propaganda effort, and the Fascist resoluteness in decision making had a positive impact within the preservationist milieu. The similarity between the Fascists' enthusiasm for the project and the sudden interest for nature preservation shown by the Nazis just after their rise to power is noteworthy.[10] In both the German and Italian cases, the new authoritarian regimes adopted assertive decision-making strategies to impress public opinion. However, most of the laws and the decrees they drafted in their early years were not original outcomes of their ideologies but rather the products of earlier cultural and social developments.

It was easy for the Fascist regime to depict itself as the savior of Italy's nature, marking its distance from the allegedly "wavering liberal ruling class,"[11] and to rank the creation of the parks among its most outstanding accomplishments. The institution of the national parks was, however, not so much a Fascist success as the outgrowth of the debate on nature conservation that flourished during the last years of the Liberal era, of the king's decision to donate his hunting reserves, and of the private initiative of a group of conservation enthusiasts. Moreover, the creation of these protected areas was set within an international trend toward the constitution of national parks started in the late nineteenth century in the United States.[12] As James Sievert writes with respect to the creation of Italy's parks, "That 1922 also marked the fall of Liberal Italy is a coincidence. But it is also more than that. Fascism brought changes to Italian society that did not bode well for nature conservation."[13]

Despite the regime's initial activism, innovative legislative actions in the environmental field were rare under Fascist rule, just as they had been during the Liberal era.[14] Moreover, the Gran Paradiso and Abruzzi national parks were abandoned to their destiny soon after their creation, only to be put under direct state control in 1934 when their autonomous administrations were disbanded and substituted by the Milizia Forestale Nazionale (National Forestry Militia), instituted in 1926 by the regime as a section of the Fascist paramilitary Milizia Volontaria di Sicurezza Nazionale (Voluntary Militia for National Security).

The trend toward the modernization of agricultural practices of the 1920s and 1930s derived from the Fascist regime's desire to reach self-sufficiency in the supply of resources, as well as from the Liberal era's last push toward a technocratic way of thinking, especially in civil service. Two of the most publicized modernizing agrarian policies were the *bonifica integrale* (integral land reclamation) and the *battaglia del grano* (battle for wheat). In the former project, humid areas were drained, ancient forests were cut down, new forests were planted, and the soil was heavily treated with chemical fertilizers, all to improve the agricultural output and to increase the surface of arable land.

In 1925, the regime launched the battaglia del grano with the goal of fostering the production of grains, especially in unsuitable mountainous areas, to improve Italy's independence from imports. This policy may be seen as the first step of the Fascist autarkic policy, even if the latter was not officially declared until 1936. The battaglia del grano greatly favored the owners of large estates in southern Italy while damaging small landowners and tenants, in patent contradiction to the propagandized aim of setting up a smallholders economy, specialized in traditional, more profitable niche productions. Moreover, the battaglia del grano also damaged mountain ecology: grain farming in the mountains increased erosion, worsening the conditions of the watersheds.[15]

Land reclamation in its various forms had been widespread across Italian history, slowly but steadily transforming the landscape. Traditionally, such reclamation had been financed mainly by landowners and private enterprises, but during the Fascist era, it became a form of permanent public works under the catchword *bonifica integrale,* in an alleged effort to impose a thorough rearrangement of the national territory.[16] This concept not only included drainage of marshy areas but also the consolidation of mountain streams, construction of common irrigation works, general improvement of agricultural areas, and the redefinition of lease contracts. The *bonifica integrale* promoted any activity deemed necessary for creating new cultivable lands and also for defending and improving existing ones.[17] In addition, its various forms of reclamation and drainage represented a make-work policy or "a huge job-creation scheme,"[18] aimed at ceding lands to impoverished agrarian workers while favoring a small-landholder economy that did not jeopardize the interests of large estates. Indeed, large estates were a more fundamental part of Fascism's social base than economically viable land management or sensible agrarian reform.[19]

The actual results of Fascist agrarian policies have been widely criticized and dismissed as nonsystematic, if not counterproductive.[20] The reclamation works intended to modernize the Pontine Marshes near Rome, for example, were in fact carried out in a totally incompetent way, destroying much of the natural humus of the area and neglecting the needs of the original local inhabitants.[21] As can be inferred from the following data, massive industrialization led to the decline of the very agrarian world that Fascist ideology claimed to promote. Agriculture represented 34 percent of the gross national product (GNP) in 1921 and 27 percent in 1938, whereas industry represented 24 percent in 1921 and 31 percent in 1938. The *bonifica integrale* was, somehow, the fig leaf covering up the shortfalls of the allegedly ruralist Fascist policies.[22]

Reforestation programs were intended mainly for creating ecological conditions that promoted the smooth functioning and development of hydropower plants. This policy was strongly supported by the electric industry lobby. Between 1925 and 1940, more than half a million hectares were reforested, mainly in the Alps, where most of Italy's hydropower plants were located.[23] Mountain dwellers, subject to the powers of external lobbies, lost their motivation to seek an autonomous equilibrium with their environment. In fact, reforestation became virtually the only issue that the Fascist regime entertained when considering the problems of mountainous areas, thereby neglecting the real interests and needs of local populations.[24]

Between 1924 and 1927, the regime drafted specific legislation on common properties and user rights that augmented the central government's power, taking the control of resources out of the hands of commoners. For example, customary property and use rights had to be declared within two years; otherwise, they would be lost.[25] A further attempt to go beyond traditional rights to access resources was made in 1933, when a decree required that water be considered a public good when it was meant for collective uses.[26] Any traditional form of commons management was thus dismantled or put under the direct control of the state. By contrast, the Fascist regime's bonifica integrale fostered the establishment of irrigation consortia, which were a more modern form of the commons. Moreover, in 1924, following an existing Liberal tradition, the regime promulgated Decree 456/1924, which transformed perennial water rights into fee-subjected state concessions, creating major conflicts with privileged landowners and tenants.

In January 1934,[27] in the midst of the bonifica integrale of the Pontine Marshes, the regime decided to preserve a small section of ancient forests and marshes, both as a nostalgic remnant of how the area looked during Roman times and as propaganda for marking the successes of the bonifica.[28] Thus was born the third Italian national park: the Parco Nazionale del Circeo. A little more than a year later, in April 1935,[29] the regime founded the Parco Nazionale dello Stelvio in the Alps of Trentino, lying nearly continuous with the Swiss National Park of Engadina. Stelvio was a sort of belated realization of the park that had been planned in the nearby Livigno Valley since the beginning of the century.[30] The two new national parks did not play a strict preservationist role, as they were mostly intended to foster outdoor tourism.[31] Moreover, the new parks could guarantee the Milizia Forestale Nazionale a stage for enacting its power politics.[32] As Sievert explains it, these parks were "the cynical expression of a Fascist regime that set up parks for show rather than conservation."[33] In fact, even if there was a large symbolic motive for establishing them, this was not the only reason for creating parks and protected areas, as was also true in the case of the Circeo and Stelvio parks.

In 1933, a first attempt to issue a law on the protection of natural and panoramic attractions and reform the Liberal law of 1922 (Law 778/1922) was stopped by the intervention of the Ministero della Giustizia (Ministry of Justice); ministry officials were worried by the economic difficulties arising from the need to grant monetary compensation to farmers because of regulations imposed on their properties for nature protection.[34] The first comprehensive Fascist law on nature conservation was thus issued only in 1939 (Law 1497/1939), in an effort to correct the ineffectiveness of the 1922 law established for preventing the destruction of panoramic views.[35] The new law represented an exception with respect to the general tendencies of nature conservation during Fascist rule. In a rare move toward bureaucratic decentralization, it relegated nature protection to the preparation of territorial landscape plans, or *piani territoriali paesistici,* with the aim of integrating protection of both the panoramic and the ecological features of landscapes.[36]

It is difficult, if not impossible, to determine the efficacy of the new law, since the Fascist regime fell just four years after its promulgation. During World War II, the law became a dead issue and had no real corrective effect on the negative consequences that an industrial war machine was inflicting on the natural world—nor any real effect on the raw environmental consequences that would stem from an urgent, postwar reconstruction effort. Even if it had been possible to promote the Fascist era's evolving concepts about protecting natural attractions and landscapes into an autonomous preservation ideology, the inherent contradictions between the interests of the industrial and agrarian bourgeoisie and the principles stated by Law 1497/1939 would seem to have been insurmountable, especially when confronted by a rising sentiment for defending private property. Moreover, this law was rendered ineffective because the commissions responsible for its enforcement also represented the groups and lobbies that needed to be controlled.[37]

Two Exemplary Case Studies

In analyzing the impact of Fascist policies on entitlements to resources at the local level, I present two very different case studies. The goal in exploring these cases is to highlight the interwoven issues of access rights and nature administration as accurately and amply as possible, without focusing on any single aspect or context. The Gran Paradiso National Park, on the one hand, and the rice paddies of Novara Province, on the other, present a spectrum of land use challenges running from protected area management to agroecosystem cultivation.

Gran Paradiso National Park was created as a symbol of Italian nature and identity, in accordance with Law 778/1922, but also to preserve rare animal species while supporting research activities and promoting tourism. Theoretically, the park's enabling act also defended the economic interests of the local people by allowing them to use land within the park for agricultural and pastoral purposes. Any stricter form of park preservation would have been unrealistic in an area with as long and significant a human presence as that of the Gran Paradiso massif. However, the park was established largely by an elite group of scientists, hunters, and tourists who wanted to preserve a set of symbolic, aesthetic, and ecosystemic values they believed were being wasted and destroyed by the local population. Yet as Karl Jacoby pointed out in an American context, what elite park enthusiasts saw as simply theft and/or destruction of public property was considered by local villagers as customary practices being improperly limited by state authority. The vision of a new state-managed landscape, promoted in the early twentieth century by technocrats and conservationists, required the creation of a new body of legislation that unveiled a completely new category of crimes.[38]

The aims of the park were interpreted differently over time, with a marked change coming about 1934. By reading the archival documents, one has the impression that the park was becoming a sort of hunting reserve or game farm by 1929 and that the administration of hunters had become the park administration's main activity. The park's policies changed again in 1934 when the Milizia Forestale was put in charge of these Alpine valleys. Despite optimistic plans made by the Milizia for improving surveillance of park users, the period from 1934 to 1945 was marked by frequent changes of top-level administrators, along with poor execution of daily preservation tasks and diminished scientific research.

In its initial years, the Gran Paradiso National Park went through a complex period of controversy and struggle. The main problem stemmed from the fact that the park was created by joining various public and private properties, even though the latter had been included without consulting the owners. These private-public origins greatly affected the traditional hunting, fishing, and grazing uses of local communities, sparking major conflicts between locals, park authorities, and the regime. As Jacoby remarked, mapping out a boundary and declaring vast state and private properties a park was much easier than properly managing it: "Landscapes do not magically reshape themselves in accordance with the desires expressed in legislation."[39] Popular protests at Gran Paradiso normally involved merely poaching or boycotting park rules, but from time to time, the situation escalated into violent conflicts. Another strategy pursued by rebellious villagers was to take advantage of the Fascist regime's hierarchical structure and of local connections for advancing their own interests. Moreover, the existence of multiple power nodes within the Fascist regime allowed villagers to play different levels of command against one another.[40] Between 1922 and 1926, local communities repeatedly attempted to assert their rights through formal means, such as making claims, submitting requests to institutional boards of arbitration, refusing to appoint representatives, and engaging administrators more sympathetic to local needs. In September 1926, several incidents of poisoning ibex—the wild Alpine sheep and the park's icon—were considered acts of sabotage, and they sent a clear message to park officials about how harsh local opposition had become. This convinced authorities in the park and higher up to grant locals more user rights, along with other concessions, a decision that reduced popular discontent for some years. After 1934, the Milizia ceased payments of subsidies, sparking a new round of protests, even if open expression of dissent had become more difficult:

the Fascist totalitarian project was almost realized by this point, with most local protests being aimed at the central government and promising foreseeable consequences. Occasionally, the risk of widespread popular unrest convinced central authorities to revert to more subtle diplomatic means, such as a liberal donation granted by Mussolini in 1935.

With regard to the park's animal numbers, which for some was the best indication of a successful park, the number of ibex initially grew from 2,370 in 1922 to 3,865 in 1933. After 1934, when the Milizia took direct control of the park, the number abruptly fell: in 1941, just 1,708 ibex roamed the park, and in 1945, only 419 lived there. Despite various projects carried out by the Milizia to improve conservation within the park, the consequences of higher poaching rates, a worse surveillance service, lower ibex birthrates, continuous military drills, shameful relationships with villagers, and total detachment from local conditions brought the ibex population in the Italian Alps almost to extinction.[41] Under Fascist rule, one can detect two very different periods with regard to the management of the ecosystem. The first, partially autonomous period was inspired by scientific management that resulted in a sort of rebirth of the ibex population; the second period was marked by a regime that chose to disband autonomous park administration, initiating a major decline.

The style of managing the park and its conflicts between 1922 and 1934 was not manifestly influenced by Fascist ideology. Despite the park's

Fig. 8.1. An ibex selection hunt in the 1930s. Archivio Fotografico del Parco Nazionale Gran Paradiso, album 185, photo 240; courtesy of the Parco Nazionale Gran Paradiso

Fig. 8.2. Adult ibex in the repopulation paddock in Cogne, Valnontey, ca. 1930. Archivio Fotografico del Parco Nazionale Gran Paradiso, album 185, photo 245. Courtesy of the Parco Nazionale Gran Paradiso

financial problems and the regime's attempts to deprive them of authority, the park administrators succeeded in preserving their autonomy until 1934. Thus, the administration was, to a certain point, able to pursue management goals that followed scientific, not ideological, principles. It may well have been this absence of a clear ideological imprint in park management that led to the power takeover of 1934. Mussolini's regime held that central management of the park would lead to an eminently Fascist way of nature conservation, which would draw praise at the international level. In a certain sense, this project succeeded. But the problem was that the Fascist management style, combined with increasing economic problems and indifferent attitudes toward preservation, produced disastrous effects on the ibex population. As in the case of American conservation, it may be said that Italy's early park administrators "often pursued environmental quality at the expense of social justice."[42] But in the longer term, the Italian administrators were not even successful in enhancing environmental quality. In fact, if the decline of the ibex was not necessarily an ecological disaster, it was surely an indicator of the failure of the park's efforts at preserving its totemic animal.

Fascist attempts to modernize Italy's agriculture, by modifying traditional rights to resource access, kindled deep social conflicts between landowners and tenants. The modes of resource use and the structure of access rights (as controlled by such regulating bodies as irrigation consortia, government, and farmer unions) underwent major changes during the period of Fascist rule. Nevertheless, these changes were not properly Fascist goals but the result of activities of allegedly apolitical technocrats who entered civil service just before the Fascist takeover. These representatives of a technical bourgeoisie were more than happy to use Fascist authoritarianism to implement their knowledge and modernize the country. It should be pointed out that from a social point of view, even if the reforms set up by the technocrats can be considered rather incoherent, their implementation was bound to trigger a process of radical change and modernization in the water distribution system. Such modernization could have changed the existing feudal privileges, creating a more equitable and thus more sustainable system of access to resources. However, it is doubtful that Mussolini's government was really in a position to implement reforms that favored more equity and more inclusion of local communities in decision-making processes. It seems improbable that the regime would have had a real interest in enforcing technocrat reforms that contrasted with the economic interests of Fascism's social base, such as the large-estate farmers of northern Italy's rice plains.

The Est Sesia irrigation consortium in Novara Province was set up to coordinate the tasks involved in distributing resources as fairly as possible among the users.[43] This consortium may therefore be seen as a means derived by the users themselves for responding to the economic and social changes brought on by World War I. Earlier, the resistance shown by many land users hindered the creation of a general coordination agency for the whole hydrologic basin, especially because of personal conflicts and fear of financial losses by farmers and minor consortia alike. In the postwar period of economic decline, times were ripe to challenge the status quo due to the rise of a strong worker's movement, the creation of a centralized and authoritarian regime, and the need to defend local interests against the greed of the consortia in Vercelli and Lombardy. Until the end of the Belle Époque, the system was based on a mix of feudal concessions, private ownership, state-driven resource distribution, and small nonnetworked consortia, such as the Cavo Montebello consortium. Even if this system was suboptimal for developing rice agriculture, it made it possible to satisfy a large number of demands relating to distribution of power, the maintenance of relationships and networks, and the control of land and laborers.

Even though the Est Sesia consortium was established as an autonomous irrigators' cooperative, it became strictly bound to the will of the

Fig. 8.3. Fixing works of the Canale Cavour, organized by Est Sesia after the Sesia flood of 7 June 1923. Archivio Storico delle Acque e delle Terre Irrigue, Fondo "Est Sesia," 1033/2/5, photo 5. Courtesy of the Associazione Irrigazione Est Sesia

regime's bureaucracy in 1929. And even if the new management imperative limited the consortium's ability to maintain a good relationship with its members, it also guaranteed its survival in a period of harsh competition with other user interests. The establishment of Est Sesia was also the beginning of a more rational use of irrigation water in the region.

There were two ways to improve the water distribution system: by nationalizing private canals and by abolishing monopolistic user rights. In fact, a more equitable and efficient distribution system could only come from establishing a coordination agency that managed a hydrographically sound commons—linked to watershed boundaries[44]—in combination with a reformed system that transferred disproportionate feudal rights into fee-based state concessions.[45] This latter development may be ascribed to the legislators of the Fascist period, even if they were not able to substantially modify the system in the short period of time they were in power. And even if the Fascist regime almost succeeded in creating a new basis for water distribution, ongoing social conflicts were largely responsible for blocking both prerequisites, and the regime fell before the task was accomplished.

In both Novara and Gran Paradiso, the landowners and tenants attempted to defend their traditional rights from changes that they felt would damage their economic interests. However, there were also important differences in

Fig. 8.4. Irrigation ditch near Ponzana after being lined with concrete by Est Sesia. Archivio Fotografico Est Sesia, album Lavori 4, photo 23. Courtesy of the Associazione Irrigazione Est Sesia

the two case studies. In Novara, it was primarily the large-estate owners and tenants who defended their traditional privileges, whereas in Gran Paradiso National Park, a wider sector of the community was engaged in the conflict. A major factor in arousing the conflict in the park was a reaction against external forces: the landowners held that the state could not take over access rights they had previously granted to the king. Gran Paradiso villagers also felt that because wildlife consumed their pastures, they were the only ones who were paying for the park. But in the case of Novara, the central government and the consortia made cooperative efforts to improve the effectiveness and overall equity of the distribution system. However, these efforts clashed with the economic interests of the large landowners, who were able to benefit from their networks of power as well as spend large sums in court cases, thereby delaying the implementation of the proposed reforms.

In the two case studies, user groups employed different networks of relationships to influence sectors of the Fascist regime. It must be noted how land users of Gran Paradiso enjoyed less powerful and extensive networks of relationships than the farmers of Novara—that is, villagers at Gran Paradiso had less social capital.[46] Park authorities could easily circumvent these networks by resorting to their own contacts within higher levels of the Fascist state and by using its top-down structure to deter locals from claiming rights. The park authorities' greater access to social capital and their greater ability to affect a wider range of human resources gave them an advantage in confronting social conflict. This situation induced Gran Paradiso communities to express discontent through more radical means, such as sabotage. Manifested at the level of physical resources, this sabotage may be interpreted as an effort to overcome the limits posed by competing interests that maintained greater control of human resources. As morally questionable as the sabotage may have been, this response was equally as (or more) successful than the refined lobbying strategies used by the rice farmers in maintaining traditional access to resources—or in obtaining fair compensation for the loss of access. In these ways, actors as diverse as large-estate farmers and mountain communities succeeded in convincing Italy's Fascist regime to search for compromises in resolving the economic conflicts arising from access to natural resources.

INDEPENDENT FROM ideological issues and political commitments, the Fascist regime's impact on the environment may be seen as a modernizing one, both because its policies tended to modify traditional and customary rules of access and because it aimed at radical, permanent transformation of the environment. Yet the Fascist policies may also be seen as antimodern for the regressive effect they had on the standard of living and on social opportunities for wide sectors of the population, as well as for the authoritarian way in which they were implemented: by reducing the role of society in the decision-making processes. The general approach of the Fascist regime toward nature conservation and natural resource management tended toward centralizing the decision-making process.

In Italy between the two world wars, national interest became the only thing to safeguard; the interests of local populations could be sacrificed on the altar of either landscape conservation or industrial progress.[47] In fact, what may be learned from the history of the Fascist regime's relationship with the environment, in particular from the preceding case studies, is that policies of centralization that ignore the primary needs of local communities and their ability to manage local landscapes are doomed to face bitter social conflict. Such policies are most likely to lead, in the long term, to ecologically and socially unsustainable practices.

This process of centralization reached its zenith in 1933 and 1934 when, as we have seen, existing parks were subjected to strict government control, new and inefficient national parks were established, and common properties were either privatized or put under state control. Liberal conservation had, by this point, lost its momentum and disappeared from the public scene.

Furthermore, the Fascist project of gathering funds for invading Ethiopia together with resistance from large-estate owners effectively blocked advances in the bonifica integrale and agrarian reform, which became limited to areas dependent on high publicity. As a result of these developments, even the propaganda-supported concept of "productive nature" suffered a major setback. As noted previously, economic motivations were a large reason why the law on natural attractions was not implemented until 1939.

The attempts made by the Fascist regime to impose a different system of access rights to natural resources (water, pastureland, game) were inherently attempts to change environmental policy. The allocation of access rights to natural resources affects not only the efficiency of resource use but also the level of social conflict within society. There are different reasons why local communities may oppose state attempts to modify their traditional modes of resource use: such communities may want to defend traditional systems of resource management, they may be frustrated at being continually subjected to external forces, or they may be reacting to what they consider unfair practices or different interpretations of the natural world. A central authority's ability to overcome traditional user rights for improving efficiency or equality therefore depends on its willingness to deal with transition costs. Such costs may be borne financially or socially, and they depend on the degree to which local users comply with their demands.

Conflict will vary according to the level of confrontation. Those who feel wronged can resort to formal compensation claims, to informal political lobbying, and to direct acts of sabotage. Regardless of the kind of social conflict, disputes can be resolved through decision-making mechanisms internal to a community or through external entities such as courts, local state officers, central bureaucracies, and government. In Italy in the 1920s and 1930s, local communities that disputed resource access often took advantage of the Fascist state's multiplicity of power centers for promoting their own interests. In an allegedly totalitarian Fascist regime, then, it was still possible for local villagers to utilize their social network for exerting pressure toward a favorable result. In conclusion, even in an authoritarian regime, the rational use of human and physical resources allowed local communities to resist accepting a new system of access rights, or at least it allowed them to accept monetary compensation.

Notes

1. Zeev Sternhell, "Fascist Ideology," in *Fascism: A Reader's Guide,* ed. Walter Laqueur (London: Wildwood House, 1976), 341.

2. Anna Bramwell, *Ecology in the 20th Century: A History* (New Haven, CT: Yale University Press, 1989), 34.

3. See Anna Bramwell, *Blood and Soil* (Bourne End, UK: Kensal, 1985); Jost Hermand, *Grüne Utopien in Deutschland: Zur Geschichte des ökologischen Bewusstseins* (Frankfurt am Main: Fischer Taschenbuch Verlag, 1991); Simon Schama, *Landscape and Memory* (London: HarperCollins, 1995); Karl Ditt, "Nature Conservation in England and Germany: Forerunner of Environmental Protection," *Contemporary European History* 5, no. 1 (1996): 1–28; Karl Ditt, "The Perception and Conservation of Nature in the Third Reich," *Planning Perspectives* 15, no. 2 (2000): 161–87; Paul Josephson and Thomas Zeller, "The Transformation of Nature under Hitler and Stalin," in *Science and Ideology: A Comparative History*, ed. Mark Walker (London: Routledge, 2003), 124–55; Joachim Radkau and Frank Uekötter, eds., *Naturschutz und Nationalsozialismus* (Frankfurt: Campus, 2003); Franz-Josef Brüggemeier, Marc Cioc, and Thomas Zeller, eds., *How Green Were the Nazis?* (Athens: Ohio University Press, 2005).

4. Gabriele Zanetto, Francesco Vallerani, and Stefano Soriani, *Nature, Environment, Landscape: European Attitudes and Discourses in the Modern Period—The Italian Case, 1920–1970* (Padua: University of Padua, 1996), 9.

5. Andrea Saba, "Cultura, natura, riciclaggio: Il fascismo e l'ambiente dal movimento ruralista alle necessità autarchiche," in *Storia ambientale: Una nuova frontiera storiografica*, ed. Andrea Saba and Edgar H. Meyer (Milan: Teti Editore, 2001), 75.

6. See also Luigi Piccioni's essay in this volume.

7. Regio Decreto-Legge (RDL) 1584/1922.

8. Regio Decreto (RD) 257/1923.

9. Even if some reports state that the park was officially established in 1923 and Michele Bianchi, patron of Calabrian politics, was referred to as its director, a national park was not established on the Sila until 1968. See *Verbale dell'adunanza* (Notes from a meeting of the royal commission managing the park), 25 January 1924 (Archivio del Parco Nazionale del Gran Paradiso [APNGP], Aosta, Italy, Verbali d'adunanza); Luigi Piccioni, e-mail message to the author, 29 March 2004.

10. Edeltraud Klueting, "Die gesetzlichen Regelungen der nationalsozialistischen Reichsregierung für den Tierschutz, den Naturschutz und den Umweltschutz," in *Naturschutz und Nationalsozialismus*, 77; Douglas Weiner, "Demythologizing Environmentalism," *Journal of the History of Biology* 25, no. 3 (1992): 385–411.

11. Luigi Piccioni, *Il volto amato della Patria: Il primo movimento per la protezione della natura in Italia, 1880–1934* (Camerino: Universitàdi Camerino, 1999), 246.

12. Patrizia Dogliani, "Territorio e identità nazionale: Parchi naturali e parchi storici nelle regioni d'Europa e del Nord America," *Memoria e Ricerca* 1 (1998): 7–38.

13. James Sievert, *The Origins of Nature Conservation in Italy* (Bern: Peter Lang, 2000), 11.

14. Piccioni, *Il volto amato,* 246; Sandra Sicoli, "La formazione dello Stato unitario e il problema della conservazione," in *Verso una gestione dei beni culturali come servizio pubblico,* eds. Roberto Togni and Augusto Rossari (Milan: Garzanti, 1978), 11.

15. Oscar Gaspari, "Il bosco come 'male necessario': Alberi e uomini nella montagna italiana," *Memoria e Ricerca* 1 (1998): 68–69.

16. For an introduction to the concept of bonifica integrale, see Manlio Rossi-Doria, *Cinquant'anni di bonifica,* ed. Gian Giacomo Dell'Angelo (Rome: Laterza, 1989), and Giuseppe Barone, *Mezzogiorno e modernizzazione: Elettricità, irrigazione e bonifica nell'Italia contemporanea* (Turin: Einaudi, 1986).

17. Francesco Socrate, "Carlo Petrocchi," in *I protagonisti dell'intervento pubblico in Italia,* ed. Alberto Mortara (Milan: CIRIEC–Franco Angeli, 1984); "Bonifica integrale," in *Dizionario del Fascismo: A–K,* ed. Victoria De Grazia and Sergio Luzzato (Turin: Einaudi, 2002).

18. Martin Clark, *Modern Italy, 1871–1995* (London: Longman, 1984), 270.

19. Paola Magnarelli, "Arrigo Serpieri," in *I protagonisti dell'intervento pubblico,* 309–327.

20. Carl Levy, "From Fascism to 'Post-Fascists': Italian Roads to Modernity," in *Fascist Italy and Nazi Germany,* ed. Richard Bessel (New York: Cambridge University Press, 1996), 171–72. For a conclusive critique of Fascist land reclamation policy, see Paul Corner, "Fascist Agrarian Policy and the Italian Economy in the Inter-war Years," in *Gramsci and Italy's Passive Revolution,* ed. John Davis (London: Croom Helm, 1979), 239–74; Gustavo Corni, "La politica agraria del Fascismo: Un confronto tra Italia e Germania," *Studi Storici* 28, no. 2 (1987): 384–421; Vera Zamagni, *Dalla periferia al centro* (Bologna: Il Mulino, 1990), chap. 8.

21. Saba, "Cultura," 85. On the Pontine Marshes, see also Piero Bevilacqua's essay in this volume.

22. Luigi Preti, *Le lotte agrarie nella valle Padana* (Turin: Einaudi, 1973), 477.

23. Gaspari, "Il bosco," 72; Alberto Mura, *Ordinamento forestale e problemi montani* (Milan: Giuffrè, 1973), 45–53.

24. RD 23/1926. Gaspari, "Il bosco," 69–71.

25. RD 751/1924 and Law 1766/1927. Carlo Vanzetti, *Storia dell'agricoltura italiana* (Bologna: Edagricole, 1986), 692. On commons, see Corona's essay in this volume.

26. RD 1775/1933, §1. Teresa Isenburg, *Acque e Stato: Energia, bonifiche, irrigazione in Italia fra 1930 e 1950* (Milan: Franco Angeli, 1981), 107–8.

27. Law 285/1934.

28. Of the 20,700 hectares in the Pontine Marshes that were formerly covered in forests, only 3,270 were preserved, and 700 hectares were reforested with alien species. See Saba, "Cultura," 85.

29. Law 740/1935.

30. Sievert, *Origins*, 200.

31. Dogliani, "Territorio," 34.

32. Piccioni, *Il volto amato*, 265–68.

33. Sievert, *Origins*, 200.

34. Guido Melis, *Storia dell'amministrazione italiana 1861–1993* (Bologna: Il Mulino, 1996), 332.

35. Francesco Ventura, "Alle origini della tutela delle 'bellezze naturali' in Italia," *Storia Urbana* 40, no. 3 (1987): 31.

36. Melis, *Storia dell'amministrazione*, 351–53.

37. Saba, "Cultura," 77–78.

38. Karl Jacoby, *Crimes against Nature: Squatters, Poachers, Thieves, and the Hidden History of American Conservation* (Berkeley: University of California Press, 2001), 2.

39. Ibid., 29.

40. Once more, the similarity with the German case may be noticed: the polycratic reality of the Nazi state structure, as opposed to the totalitarian myth, had a major role in defining the actual implementation of the regime's environmental policies. See Frank Uekötter, "Einleitung," in *Naturschutz und Nationalsozialismus*; Uekötter, "Polycentrism in Full Swing: Air Pollution in Nazi Germany," in Brüggemeier, *How Green Were the Nazis?* 101–28.

41. "Diagrammi delle variazioni degli stambecchi, delle guardaparco e degli amministratori del Parco Nazionale del Gran Paradiso dal 1922 al . . ." n.d., APNGP XI/2.

42. Jacoby, *Crimes*, 198.

43. The history of environmental conflicts in the province of Novara has been reconstructed on the basis of documents conserved at the Archivio Storico delle Acque e delle Terre Irrigue (ASATI).

44. Conflicts frequently arose between the Est Sesia and the Cavo Montebello, the other principal irrigation consortium in the watershed. The Consorzio Cavo Montebello lost its independent management status in 1933 when a government commissioner was appointed, and it lost its autonomy in 1939 when it was absorbed by the Est Sesia.

45. RDL 456/1924.

46. James Coleman, "Social Capital in the Creation of Human Capital," *American Journal of Sociology* 94, no. S1 (January 1988): S95–S120.

47. Gaspari, "Il bosco," 78.

Pollution, Industry, and Urban Environment

CHAPTER 9

Dealing with Industrial Pollution in Italy, 1880–1940

Simone Neri Serneri

INDUSTRIAL PRODUCTION has been a crucial theme of contemporary environmental history for some time. There has been a profound transformation in the way resources are used, both in the enormous quantity of raw materials mobilized and waste produced and in their manipulation by developing technologies.[1] The role of industries in changing the territorial and environmental foundations of increasingly vast areas has been no less relevant.[2] In general, industrial development has paralleled urban development because industrial products radically modified ways of constructing contemporary cities, along with living and working conditions of urban society. The placement of factories, in particular, steered the adaptation of infrastructural networks and the functional division of surrounding areas, together with the requirements of waste disposal.[3]

The Italian Case

This essay considers the environmental impact of industrial plants in Italy during the first decades of industrialization. The Italian case is fully

representative of a larger European experience that shares a twofold pe-
culiarity: the contemporary urban network is an extension of that which
came before it rather than being a recent and original formation (as in
the American or Australian experience), and environmental pollution
problems have existed since the early modern age.[4] Relationships between
industrialization and urban development were therefore particularly important in Europe and in Italy specifically, especially given the large role of
the industrial sector in European economic development. But this simultaneous industrial and urban development also created strong controversy.
The scientific culture of the epoch, dominated as it was by the hygienist
paradigm and oriented toward urban reform, was largely responsible for
this controversy.[5] Central and local authorities were also involved, concerned as they were not only with guarding public health but also with
encouraging nascent industrial activities that were supposed to improve
social welfare. Finally, numerous other influential actors were involved,
including industrial entrepreneurs, technicians, and citizens whose health,
personal property, or economic activities were threatened by emissions.

The Italian case, however, shows some peculiarities, since industrialization and urbanization proceeded later and less intensively than in central and
western Europe. Moreover, Italian legislation, despite its centralist approach,
was not as cogent as elsewhere, and public opinion rarely mobilized on the
issues of industrial pollution.

The environmental impact of industry became a concern in the 1880s
when the rate of industrial production enlarged, ushering in a period of still
greater expansion between 1896 and 1909.[6] Thereafter, industry gradually
became more widespread up until the 1950s, at which time a second wave
of rapid, intense industrialization considerably changed the parameters of
environmental issues and the reactions to them.

Legislation governing industrial emissions was introduced in the late
1880s (following similar legislation in central and western Europe), at a time
when their effects on public health were becoming increasingly relevant. It
was precisely this health perspective that pushed environmental issues to
the forefront. Although industrial effects on health were already attracting
some attention, by the early twentieth century, they assumed much greater
proportions. In those years, mechanical advances and the appearance of
water turbines and advanced chemical industries coupled with urban transformation became an opportunity for testing the cultural and legislative
approaches formulated a couple of decades earlier.

In the 1930s, industry progressed further, particularly when it arrived
in certain technologically advanced sectors.[7] These latest developments were

also reflected in the state and in perceptions of environmental issues, as well as in the cultural and regulatory instruments that were quickly becoming obsolete.

Legislation Governing "Unhealthy Industries"

The public health measures issued by the Francesco Crispi government in 1888 also introduced regulations regarding so-called unhealthy industries. Until then, the consequences of industrial activity had been regulated by a complicated network of legislation. The heterogeneity of these various statutes and directives, and their limited application, underlined the need for a more general legislative mandate, comparable to that of other European countries.[8]

The provisions of 1888 reflected a health-based perspective that sought to prevent direct harm to public health. Such provisions considered natural resources (such as water or air) as goods to be protected in a healthful state and destined for direct and immediate use by the public. The provisions did not aim to mitigate large-scale ecological imbalances. They were simply meant to ensure the sufficient supply of natural resources for sanitary and dietary uses. This explains the founding criteria of the legislation (within and beyond Italy) that required isolating harmful industries from population centers, both to avoid risks to public health and to dilute and disperse harmful effluents in the environment.

The 1888 measure, in referring to French legislation and its centralist approach on the same matter, mandated that "workshops or factories which produce unhealthy fumes or in some other way endanger the health of inhabitants" be listed within a register under two categories.[9] The first category included industries "to be isolated in the countryside or distant from dwellings; the second included those that required special safeguards for the safety of the neighborhood." The Ministry of the Interior, being responsible for public health, was to compile this list and update it every three years.

The first category included more than fifty industrial activities, usually singled out because of the dangerous nature of their products or raw materials but in some cases because of their manufacturing processes (for example, distillation or fermentation). Some industries produced particularly irritating and burning fumes, toxic minerals, dust-producing or potentially infectious materials, and rotting or fermenting substances. The second category included approximately sixty activities that either used or produced such by-products as mildly toxic acids, easily handled organic materials, manageable poisons, controllable combustibles, and so forth.

The list was published in 1895, and it reflected the general intent of the health authorities, despite making special exceptions for certain entrepreneurs who were at least partly supported by advisory bodies to the Ministry of Agriculture and Industry. Health authorities had in fact already ceased compiling a more detailed list, maintaining that certain categories were sufficiently comprehensive and that certain activities were not practiced in Italy. For his part, the spokesman for the Higher Industrial Council succeeded in imposing a more permissive classification of industries and a more limited application of the law, arguing that the new measure should not apply to dangerous substances or to those that contaminated water because both concerns were being addressed by other laws.[10]

Also noteworthy are the trends among chambers of commerce and local representatives of entrepreneurs. The Turin Chamber of Commerce, for instance, like many others, sought to shorten the lists as much as possible. It called attention to the possibility of suffocating industrial development, to the capability of industrialists to regulate their own activities, and to the faith in economic and technological progress to mitigate damaging effects of industrial production. In contrast, the Milan Chamber of Commerce pointed out the importance of public health and even requested that more industries be included in the first category, specifically stating that this two-part classification would stimulate technological progress. In fact, the legislation's underlying principle—the importance of moving health-damaging industries away from inhabited areas—was almost universally approved. Nonetheless, this law created short-term punitive effects, since it raised costs considerably and isolated some industries from other economic activities.[11] The law also stipulated that a first-category industry could continue operating in an inhabited area if "the industrialist was able to demonstrate that, thanks to newly developed methods and special precautions, his business did not cause harm to the surrounding area."[12] A provision such as this did meet the aim of limiting health hazards caused by industries to their surrounding areas.

In sum, the set of productions identified in the list and the principle of isolating unhealthy industries demonstrate how relationships between industry and environment were established at the time that Italy began producing modern wastes. However, most manufacturing practices remained traditional. As a result, the environmental and sanitary problems of industrial activity stemmed from the rudimentary level of technology and the concentrated presence of many small plants. These factors explain why the regulation of unhealthy industries was so widely requested and why there was so much effort dedicated to establishing criteria useful in lawsuits requesting damages.[13] Such factors also explain why the legislation proved substantially inadequate in the face of heightening industrialization in the following decade.

Another legislative initiative addressing impacts of industrial waste proved to be equally ineffective. The original 1888 sanitation law and subsequent regulations pertaining to application permitted industrial plants to release wastewater into lakes, canals, and watercourses "destined for domestic use or consumption" only if this water was first subjected to "total, effective purification" and only if "special precautions were prescribed for each case by the local sanitation code."[14] As a result of these new regulations, it was possible to discharge in the city and its environs "properly purified" industrial water into any watercourse, whereas sewage and wastewater could only be discharged into watercourses "covered and lined with impermeable walls." Local authorities were to establish the minimum distance from dwellings that impure water could be discharged into watercourses, according to their flow and speed as well as "their capacity for self-purification and the level of impurity of the water emitted." If careful analysis demonstrated that the capacity for self-purification was insufficient for downstream inhabitants, authorities could demand that the water be purified. Coastal cities were likewise prohibited from discharging wastewater into the sea. Lastly, all purification was to be carried out "according to the methods suitable for each industry." Such methods were to be chosen by the industrialists, but it was the task of the public authorities to verify their effectiveness. Italian legislation aimed to guarantee public authorities control of the matter so as to avoid major injuries to public health. Yet in contrast to German, British, and American policies, Italian policies did not mandate that public authorities promote industrial development along with social and environmental compatibility.[15]

How Effective Were Public Authorities?

It is noteworthy that regulations governing "unhealthy industries" remained practically unchanged until the 1960s, which is another difference between Italy and other industrialized countries. The Sanitary Law Consolidation Act, which took effect in 1934, simply reaffirmed existing legislation. Its main effect was to emphasize the power of the *podestà* (the local official appointed by the Fascist government) to prescribe "executive regulations in order to prevent or avoid damage or risk" to public health and to enforce such regulations "when vapors, gases or other fumes, impure water, solid or liquid waste originating from workshops or factories endanger or harm public health."[16] Since the damage was often difficult to assess, local authorities had a good deal of discretion on whether to intervene.

The absence of revisions implies the tacit choice to deal with the effects of industrial activity on a case-by-case basis. The aim was to reconcile public health and industrial interests by means of administrative provisions, which were often influenced by the disproportionate economic and political sway of the people involved.

The overall legal mechanism of the legislation was, however, marginally effective. First, the norms did not prescribe any preventive permission (a crucial difference from French and German legislation)[17] but rather gave entrepreneurs total freedom of initiative while investing public authorities with the task of classifying, checking, and eventually reprimanding "health-damaging" industrial activities once they were established. This legislation also involved a number of private and public protagonists and frequently set off various administrative provisions and petitions that could reach the highest levels of the central administration. Disputes were capable of dragging on for years due to the time required to adopt provisions, to review opinions of advisory bodies (and sometimes those of investigative commissions because of unreliable data), and to verify the effectiveness of the technologies imposed upon the plants. Since the petitions against authorities' provisions suspended the provisions themselves, it was always challenging to limit possible harmful emissions.

Public authorities were involved in this procedure at three levels. At the top level were the central authorities, who intervened only in the last stages of a hierarchical petition or to solicit prefects to enforce the law and ensure fairness in the legal proceedings. The prefects were the second level, and as representatives of the central government, they were supposed to deal directly with the local authorities—except that prefects typically enforced legal provisions within a wide range, either because of pressure by local interests or because they felt that measures for protecting public health should not compromise local economic or social interests. At the third level were the local authorities, who were responsible for applying the legislation within their territorial confines. It was their job to classify current and proposed plants and to verify that regulations were being following (for example, emitting at minimum distances from inhabited areas or following precautions to avoid damaging health).

Municipalities encountered obvious practical and financial difficulties in carrying out these tasks, which also required a corps of qualified personnel, since, unlike in most of the other industrialized countries, there were not any governmental inspectors.[18] Only large municipalities maintained a bureau of public health; others relied on a health officer or provincial medical doctor. In most cases, tacit understandings prevailed for satisfying the powers that be, except when public health was in evident danger. Since industrialists were only obliged to give notice of their activities but not to await permission to act, municipal authorities only intervened in exceptional cases. The law nonetheless required an assessment of each plant. This stipulation complicated the work of the municipal authorities, who were repeatedly forced to report negative industrial practices even though such industries represented precious employment opportunities, especially in small towns.

Moreover, municipal authorities were supposed to identify "special precautions" that allowed industries to maintain a central location, as well as to highlight regulations that would exempt industries of the second category from lawsuits. In fact, the record shows that only one such exempting regulation was adopted, that of the city of Turin in 1907, which may well have been the first and last such regulation until 1940. As Italy's largest industrial city, Turin was granted an exception, but it was also home to the best school for hygienists in Italy.[19] The fact that the city's sanitation bureau carried out inspections and/or filed case reports for 157 industrial plants in 1902, made 108 requests for classifying health-damaging industries, and examined 34 workshops in 1906 demonstrates the effort required to enforce legislation at Turin,[20] as well as the challenges of enforcing it elsewhere.[21]

The situation may have been even more challenging beyond Turin. The sanitary regulations in Milan, Como, Brescia, Genoa, Florence, Naples, and other similar cities simply repeated the provisions of the central government's legislation. In other municipalities, no mention was even made of health-damaging industries, which probably reflected both limited industrial activity in these places and negligence on the part of local administrators.[22] However, mention should be made of cities that permitted exceptions to restrictive regulations, which can be interpreted as a testimony of the political power of certain industries, even in the 1910s. Such was the case of Campello sul Clitunno, a rural village in Umbria that depended on a chemical plant, or the towns of Lucera and Lucca, which depended on brick and paper works, respectively.[23]

The increasing complexity of industrial activity soon revealed other weak points in the legislation. For example, it was unclear which industries should be included on the list of unhealthy industries and whether this list was absolute or indicative. It was usually considered absolute, but there were cases to the contrary, even when involving the central authorities. Between 1906 and 1908, a plant in Savona that galvanized iron was not included on the list, since such processes were relatively new and still rare in Italy, and in 1913, a rather hazardous calcium carbide factory was also missing from the list.[24] But authorities considered the list indicative, stating correctly that if it were treated otherwise, the list would be continually outdated; thus, they included the Savona factory on the list and registered it in the first category, for it produced waste rich in hydrochloric acid. The ministry's technicians, for their part, confirmed the need to include galvanization on the list, but they failed to specify the category because, they explained, the first category included factories that produced noxious acids, whereas the second category included industries that produced wastewater mixed with acid.[25] Such considerations underscored the shortcomings and contradictions of the classification.

Another weak point of the legislation was the time required to implement the provisions, particularly when it came to moving certain plants away from inhabited areas. Beginning in 1903, a period of five years was stipulated as the legal time limit, but by 1910 and with many plants still unmoved, the issue was not resolved. The Ministry of Agriculture, Industry, and Trade requested a grace period of ten years for industries that were required to move away. This was largely because the issue involved match factories, mostly of modest or insignificant size.[26] These small plants were destined to disappear, due in part to imminent prohibitions against white phosphorous, at the same time that larger and more successful plants were favored with maximum compliance periods, in the expectation that safeguards could be adopted in the meantime. In the end, a 1912 decree skirted the phosphorous issue, entrusting municipal authorities with the task of settling it case by case.[27]

The greatest defect in the procedure was probably the fact that although unhealthy industries were supposed to respect certain criteria, this could only be verified after the plants were built. And at that point, it became enormously difficult to bring about substantial modifications, particularly if these involved relocating or shutting down a recently opened plant. Industrial entrepreneurs sought general approval from health authorities beforehand, but they could not fully guarantee what effects their production would have. Moreover, health authorities, for their part, had no ability to prevent construction of a potentially dangerous plant or to solicit modifications in advance in order to reduce emissions.[28] This situation often resulted in a stalemate. One illustrative case occurred in Maglie, where a factory for extracting oil from olive residues using carbon sulfide was to be built in a rural area. Protests began when the project was announced in 1915, and lawsuits were still pending two years later when the ministry declared itself unable to pass judgment on the case; it added that the factory needed to await completion before verifying the alleged safety of the chemical process so as to determine stipulations on where should be located.[29] An analogous case arose in 1904 in the center of Portici, where a factory for the production of superphosphates, acids, and soda sulfates was constructed according to provisions suggested by the local administration; however, those provisions soon proved to be too lax for preventing excessive harmful emissions.[30] It would be fair to conclude that the public authority's power to direct locations of industrial production was far from effective or coherent.

The Location of Industrial Activities

How was the territorial distribution of so-called unhealthy industries affected by the policy of relocating them away from inhabited areas? First, as we have seen, this policy was not exactly binding. Second, the original disadvantages of placing factories in the countryside became less and less detrimental due to improvements in transportation and the self-sufficiency of certain activities, such as the chemical sector, which actually benefited from the lack of regulation resulting from its presumed isolation. In fact, the concept of isolation reflected the territorial conditions that existed at the beginning of the industrial age, when manufacturing was concentrated in city centers or in villages but in both cases took place in inhabited areas whose limits had remained unchanged for centuries. Beyond these areas stretched the countryside, with its woodlands and pastures. Industrial and urban development would serve to erase these borders and the very concept of isolation.

The ambiguity of isolation was demonstrated by the disputes concerning the distance required between a factory and inhabited areas. The meagerness of this minimum required distance is striking: one hundred meters in Genoa, two hundred in Vicenza, five hundred in Bari, or usually from two to three hundred meters in most cases, when it was not simply a designated location beyond the railroad tracks or main roadway. Furthermore, what was the precise meaning of *inhabited area*? Were single rural houses included or just a specified number of houses? Some local regulations established a minimum required distance from any dwelling, but the ubiquity of scattered buildings across the Italian countryside led to countless controversies.[31]

Indeed, potentially health-damaging factories were never completely isolated. Even when factory emissions did not directly affect inhabitants, they might poison crops or contaminate water destined for livestock or fishing. Precisely because such factories were considered isolated, they were free to release emissions unchecked over entire valleys, eventually reaching

rural dwellings and small villages despite the considerable distances involved. In some places, rivers or streams transported harmful substances
for kilometers. An important case involved a chemical plant in Cengio that
since the 1910s had severely contaminated the Bormida River, affecting
the entire valley's economy for many decades.[32] Other examples include
a paper factory in Chiaravalle near Ancona and another one in Serra San
Bruno in Calabria, which dumped waste in the Ancinale River,[33] and the
plant of Collestatte near Terni that produced calcium carbide, cyanamide,
and ammonium sulfate, which became the subject of drawn-out legal
battles between 1910 and 1919 on the part of local public agencies defending
small-scale farmers.[34]

Health-damaging industries were also concentrated in areas surrounding cities because of the legislation. And factories that had originally been
located away from population centers witnessed the arrival of more and
more plants, roads, railways, and cheap housing projects. In the outskirts
of large and small industrial cities alike, as at Padua, Leghorn, Savona,
and Porto Empedocle, the effects of such trends were clear and provoked
repeated protest.[35]

The quantities and varieties of industrial contaminants multiplied, affecting ever-larger areas. In the mid-1920s, complex controversies erupted
over Lake Orta at the foot of the Alps, involving industrial plants making
use of its water or treating it as a dumping ground, and local towns relying
on it for domestic and agricultural water supplies as well as for receiving
sewage. This water body rapidly reached a state of irreversible damage.[36]
Much of this story was repeated during the 1930s in Lombardy's Olona
River valley, which counted at least 65 industrial plants and a hydroelectric
power plant over a distance of about twenty-five kilometers, with a city
of 150,000 inhabitants and 150 other industrial plants lying a short distance away. Even as the river become inadequate for providing energy to
these industries, it continued being a convenient conduit for "waste, to the
point that in several areas its water was of a turquoise or violet color, with
iridescent reflections that would have seemed beautiful had they not been
dirtied by oil slicks."[37]

During the 1920s, the spread of urban and industrial development was
already making it impossible to isolate health-damaging industries and to
implement measures that would contain the hazards of industrialization.
The criterion of isolation had not only proven itself hazardous, it also
encouraged a process of environmental degradation across the countryside that had invited further unfettered industrial growth.[38]

Did Technology Help?

The reserve mechanism stipulated by the legislation of 1888 was of little help. As mentioned earlier, the hardship of being banished from the town center could be avoided by adopting any "modern" method of disposal to eliminate harmful effluents. It was hoped that the progress of technology would create a more effective technique for containing potential damage.

In reality, technological progress is often nonlinear. Thus, when entrusting it to reduce emissions, the most immediate result was tolerance, dictated by the need to verify innovations. Such was the case when industries either were forced to or chose to adopt opportune measures. In fact, the uncertainty of technological progress seemed in some way justified by the equal uncertainty regarding the harmful effects of pollution. As a result of these uncertainties, administrative and judiciary measures were taken to avoid closing or relocating a plant so that potential negative effects could be shifted from the entrepreneurs, workers, and local economy to the less perceptible and latent effects of harmful emissions.

The main difficulty when attempting to evaluate the adequacy of measures taken for limiting health hazards lay in evaluating the precise extent of the hazard. The level of knowledge and the social perception of existing damage encouraged authorities, technicians, and the public to concentrate on the most severe cases, while overlooking others of minor relevance or of long-range or recurring nature (such as those associated with seasonal or irregular production cycles). Similarly, although actual damage was measured, potential damage was not taken into consideration. Or an inspector might state that bothersome acidic fumes had, for the moment, caused no damage.[39] Certain emissions were not always unambiguously harmful, and the source of damaging pollution could not always be identified.[40]

Contradictory opinions and reports often reflected conflicts of interest, but they also reflected inadequate knowledge about tolerable concentrations of toxic substances as well as inadequate instruments for measuring these concentrations. Knowledge was also lacking about all the details of manufacturing processes, so that polluting substances or alternative processes could not always be identified. In this respect, technical and theoretical methodologies gave way to empiricism, with less than satisfactory results.[41]

This series of complications often brought about the following sequence of events. Protests against harmful emissions led to intervention by the authorities. Inspectors were sent, orders were given to carry out changes, and such changes were granted a "reasonable time span." Then the industrial modifications were inspected, and harmful emissions diminished or disappeared.

But eventually, the emissions reappeared—for reasons ranging from negligent management of facilities to simple inadequacy of modifications—and that led to a new round of health-damaging procedures. Between the 1910s and the 1930s, this was the round of events at the infamous cases of Portici, Montebelluna, Collestatte, the Bormida Valley, Lake Orta, and Mori.[42]

In reviewing complaints about unhealthy industries, one can identify three distinct and often concomitant approaches to containing harmful emissions: the denial, external, and technological approaches. The denial approach combined faith in technology and in nature with a systematic undervaluation of the damage caused by emissions, primarily in the name of societal tolerance. From this perspective, it even became possible to praise the antiseptic properties of acidic fumes and the healing qualities of water containing resinous waste. Health-damaging emissions could be justified by comparing them with others produced in nearby plants. Nearly unlimited trust was placed in the "self-purifying capacity" of air or water. Or the supposed harmless nature of certain emissions seemed confirmed by the fact that workers could tolerate contact with them.

The external approach was widespread even among competent technicians and authorities. It tended to overlook the most immediate effects of industrial activity and aimed to smooth over the conflicting requests for natural resources by industry and other economic or public uses so as to satisfy all parties involved. But by failing to update manufacturing processes, this approach downplayed the question of damage to natural resources while emphasizing the discovery of new supplies. For example, it was common to prescribe that industrial wastes be dumped into alternative watercourses not destined for public or agricultural use.[43] In another common practice, compensation was given to immediate sufferers, such as fishermen along a certain watercourse, and water requirements for drinking, agriculture, and stock farming were then sought in other springs and wells.[44] In the long run, such short-term solutions proved disastrous because they failed to reduce pollution and expanded contaminated areas. Priority given to industrialization was not joined by a simultaneous policy of long-range resource and waste management.

Only the technological approach could improve manufacturing methods while decreasing emissions. The conception, application, and effectiveness of such an approach were determined by a variety of factors, including scientific knowledge, technical feasibility, and economic outcome. Devices were usually proposed by technicians put in charge by local or central authorities, who were sometimes earnestly assisted by the factories' own technical planners or directors.

Various types of devices were utilized, sometimes simultaneously. Some devices simply collected powdery emissions so as to prevent their dispersion and facilitate their collection. Others reduced the harmfulness of pollutants by diluting them, as by adding water to waste liquids. Still others moved the emissions farther away, thereby delaying their damaging effects or facilitating their dispersion. Such was the case with ever-higher chimneys and smokestacks and ever-longer drainage pipes extending into the sea or lake, serving to transport rather than reduce pollution. The rather widespread and legal practice of dumping wastes into wells—especially the most harmful and long-lived wastes—was motivated by a similar goal but one that risked permanently damaging groundwater.[45] In general, these devices counted on the ability of air and water to purify themselves through the biological breakdown of polluting agents and then sought to delay their diffusion, which nonetheless took place quite rapidly. As in the United States and the United Kingdom, the only substantial measures for mitigating water pollution in Italy were the construction of modern waterworks and sewage systems.[46]

The most complex techniques attempted to reduce the quantity of waste and collect their harmful components. Such techniques consisted mostly of clarification processes that utilized filters, fans, condensers, and absorbents so as to concentrate the primary waste and initiate its oxidation. The best (though rarely chosen) solution was to utilize alternative raw materials that produced less waste, which could in turn be consumed in other manufacturing processes. The ability to apply complex techniques greatly depended on the precise operations of the plant and on the magnitude of its production. Often, such techniques were discontinued due to technical or economic reasons. A sampling of the historical record suggests that when such technologies were installed, pollutants were reduced to give at least temporary respite from their most destructive effects. Yet such technologies were rarely adequate for reducing an industry's environmental impact; instead, they proved much more effective as support to reassure the public concerned about industrial pollution.[47]

The 1930s: Toward New Scenarios

In the 1930s, industrial pollution's visibility was reduced through a combination of the bureaucratic authoritarianism of the Fascist regime; social habituation to harmful emissions; and the increasing division of urban areas into affluent neighborhoods, low-cost housing areas, and industrial zones.[48] Yet a quick estimate of overall industrial production shows that waste production had grown considerably,[49] with health-damaging industries (though not necessarily classified as such) growing from twenty thousand in 1911 to twenty-seven thousand in 1937.[50]

These structural transformations were accompanied by changes in public intervention: administrative governance and territorial planning were both strengthened, which also fostered industrialization and resource management. The location of industrial facilities would become considerably dependent on the economic and political priorities of the regime. In addition to Italy's first area of industrialization, located largely in the "industrial triangle" of Piedmont, Lombardy, and Liguria, new "areas of intense industrialization" grew as tangible evidence of the Fascist industrial policy.[51] Arising from executive discretionary power and private enterprise, these new industrial areas generated direct consequences for territorial and environmental planning. Such was the case with the law requiring authorization for new industrial plants (in 1933), the law for industrial development in central and south Italy (in 1941), and legislation that introduced town planning and industrial zoning (in 1941). During the 1930s, at least seven industrial areas (Venice, Livorno, Bolzano, Apuania, Ferrara, Palermo, and Rome) were established outside the industrial triangle in order to stimulate and extend industrialization across Italy. By facilitating loans, designating industrial plants as public works, providing public services and infrastructure, and selecting permissible industries, the Fascist regime aimed at streamlining industrial activity while encouraging productive and functional integration and reducing costs and infrastructures.

The environmental implications of these new industrial settlements are easy to imagine but are yet to be researched in depth. The day's experts in health and resource issues turned their attention to these and other industrial areas, whether of regional importance like those described previously or of local importance in the outskirts of numerous cities. Taking advantage of such areas had seemed the best way both to move health-damaging industries away from cities and to cluster certain types of manufacturers so that supply and waste disposal requirements could be shared. These trends presented a considerable advantage, since it was becoming increasingly difficult in Italy to find "a superficial watercourse in which it was possible to dump liquid waste without first performing purification procedures."[52]

In reality, despite ongoing legislative developments and despite the tacit acceptance of public opinion, the problem of industrial pollution was not going away. Significantly, scientific research had begun to define more reliable criteria for measuring and tolerating industrial emissions. But in their official meetings, even health officials preferred to simply ignore the new scientific findings.[53]

Italy's first phase of industrialization closed in silence.[54] The legislation of 1888 had led to a policy that stipulated the dispersion of supposedly containable or tolerable industrial wastes and was justified by the limited level of industrialization and the relative isolation of health-damaging industries. Once these conditions were no longer present, the problem was systematically concealed. Italy's approach to the environmental problems posed by industrial development during the first half of the twentieth century was marked less by its status as a relative latecomer and more by the weakness of its normative instruments. Because of the gradual pace and countrywide distribution of industrial development, these weak legal and institutional instruments did not become apparent until the second great wave of industrialization in the 1950s.

Notes

1. See Theodore Steinberg, *Nature Incorporated: Industrialization and the Waters of New England* (New York: Cambridge University Press, 1991). See also Gerald Markowitz and David Rosner, *Deceit and Denial: The Deadly Politics of Industrial Pollution* (Berkeley: University of California Press, 2002); David Stradling, *Smokestacks and Progressives: Environmentalists, Engineers, and Air Quality in America, 1881–1951* (Baltimore, MD: Johns Hopkins University Press, 1999); Joachim Radkau, *Technik in Deutschland*, vol. 18, *Jahrhundert bis zur Gegenwart* (Frankfurt: Suhrkamp, 1989).

2. For general surveys, see Joel A. Tarr, ed., *Devastation and Renewal: An Environmental History of Pittsburgh and Its Region* (Pittsburgh: University of Pittsburgh Press, 2003); Franz-Josef Brüggemeier, *Das unendliche Meer der Lufte: Luftverschmutzung, Industrialisierung und Risikodebatten im 19. Jahrhundert* (Essen, Germany: Klartext, 1996); Ulrike Gilhaus, *"Schmerzenskinder der Industrie": Umweltverschmutzung, Umweltpolitik und sozialer Protest im Industriezeitalter in Westfalen, 1845–1914* (Paderborn, Germany: Schöning, 1995); John Opie, *Nature's Nation: An Environmental History of the United States* (Fort Worth, TX: Harcourt, Brace, 1998).

3. This argument is taken up by Joel A. Tarr, *The Search for the Ultimate Sink: Urban Pollution in Historical Perspective* (Akron, OH: University of Akron Press, 1996); Martin Melosi, *The Sanitary City: Urban Infrastructure in America from Colonial Times to the Present* (Baltimore, MD: Johns Hopkins University Press, 2000); Bill Luckin, "Pollution in the City," in *The Cambridge Urban History of Britain*, vol. 3, *1840–1950*, ed. Martin Daunton (New York: Cambridge University Press, 2000), 207–28; Harold L. Platt, *Shock Cities: The Environmental Transformation and Reform of Manchester and Chicago* (Chicago: University of Chicago Press, 2005). An overview of the Italian case is found in Simone Neri

Serneri, *Incorporare la natura: Storie ambientali del Novecento* (Rome: Carocci, 2005), and Gabriella Corona and Simone Neri Serneri, eds., *Storia e ambiente: Città, risorse e territori nell'Italia contemporanea* (Rome: Carocci, 2007).

4. See also Christoph Bernhardt, "Umweltprobleme in der neuren europäischen Stadtgeschichte," in *Environmental Problems in European Cities in the 19th and 20th Centuries,* ed. Christoph Bernhardt (New York: Waxmann, 2001), 8; Christoph Bernhardt and Geneviève Massard-Guilbaud, eds., *The Modern Demon: Pollution in Urban and Industrial European Societies* (Clermont-Ferrand, France: Presses Universitaires Blaise-Pascal, 2002); Dieter Schott, Bill Luckin, and Geneviève Massard-Guilbaud, eds., *Resources of the City: Contributions to an Environmental History of Modern Europe* (Aldershot, UK: Ashgate, 2005); and Geneviève Massard-Guilbaud and Peter Thorsheim, eds., "European Urban Environmental History," special issue of *Journal of Urban History* 33, no. 5 (2007).

5. This has been demonstrated by, among others, Christopher Hamlin, *A Science of Impurity: Water Analysis in Nineteenth Century Britain* (Berkeley: University of California Press, 1990).

6. Vera Zamagni, *The Economic History of Italy, 1860–1990* (New York: Oxford University Press, 1993), 76–78.

7. Ibid., 274–75.

8. Iljia Mieck, "Luftverunreinigung und Immissionsschutz in Frankreich und Preussen zur Zeit der frühen Industrialisierung," *Technikgeschichte* 48 (1981): 239–51, and Iljia Mieck, "Die Anfänge der Umweltschutzgesetzgebung in Frankreich," *Francia* 9 (1981): 331–67; Geneviève Massard-Guilbaud, "French Local Authorities and the Challenge of Industrial Pollution (1810–1917)," in *Urban Governance: Britain and Beyond,* ed. Richard Trainor and Robert J. Morris (Aldershot, UK: Ashgate, 2000), 151–64.

9. Public Sanitation Law (22 December 1888), art. 38. The list was issued in 1895.

10. See documentation in the Italian Central State Archives, Ministero dell'Interno, Direzione Generale Sanità Pubblica (hereafter Dgsp), 1867–1900, 239.

11. Camera di Commercio di Milano, *Sulla determinazione delle industrie da dichiararsi insalubri* (Milan, 1894); Giovan B. Cereseto, *La legislazione sanitaria in Italia* (Turin: Unione Tipografico Editrice, 1910), 644–74.

12. Public Sanitation Law (22 December 1888), art. 38.

13. Dgsp, 1867–1900, 239: "Norme per gli stabilimenti insalubri e contravenzioni, 1890–1897."

14. In particular, see Public Sanitation Law (22 December 1888), art. 40 and 44, and Ministero dell'Interno, Direzione Generale Sanità Pubblica, *Istruzioni ministeriali sull'igiene del suolo e dell'abitato* (Brescia: n.p., 1901).

15. Tarr, *Search*, 358–74; Martin V. Melosi, *Effluent America: Cities, Industry, Energy, and the Environment* (Pittsburgh, PA: University of Pittsburgh Press, 2001), 62–67, 106–18; Brüggemeier, *Das unendliche Meer der Lufte*, esp. 224–35, 299.

16. As established by art. 217.

17. Massard-Guilbaud, "French Local Authorities"; Brüggemeier, *Das unendliche Meer der Lufte*.

18. Even at that time, this was considered one of the main defects of the legislation; see Francesco Bertarelli, "Per una nuova legge delle industrie insalubri," *Critica Sociale*, 16 July 1907.

19. In fact, Luigi Pagliani, its founder, had acted as the first head of the General Health Directorate in the Ministry of the Interior, established in 1887, and Francesco Abba, the author of the regulation for health-damaging industries, had worked at the same directory for many years.

20. *Relazione sulle condizioni igienico-sanitarie del Comune di Torino, Biennio 1902–1903* (Turin, 1905); *Annuario del Municipio di Torino, 1906–1907* (Turin, 1907).

21. Dgsp, 1882–1915, 867: Torino; Paolo Frascani, "La disciplina delle industrie insalubri nella legislazione sanitaria italiana (1865–1910)," in *Salute e classi lavoratrici in Italia dall'Unità al fascismo*, ed. Maria Luisa Berti and Ada Gigli Marchetti (Milan: Franco Angeli, 1982), 725–26; Enrico Jevina, "Dei vapori o gas nocivi provenienti dai camini delle fabbriche," *Rivista di Ingegneria Sanitaria* 3–4 (1909).

22. Dgsp, 1910–20, 559: Campobasso.

23. Dgsp, 1910–20, 611 bis: 2; 1882–1915, 867: Foggia, 867: Lucca.

24. Dgsp, 1910–20, 611 bis: 18 "Varzo (Novara)." A similar occurrence took place in the case of a salting plant for dairy products that was not included on the list in spite of the hydrogen sulphate, hydrogen phosphate, and ammonia emissions it produced; see Dgsp, 1882–1915, 867: Noicattaro.

25. Dgsp, 1882–1915, 869: Savona.

26. In reality, such understatements inspire considerable doubts. See Dgsp: 1867–1900, 239: 1915.

27. Dgsp, 1867–1900, 239: 1915.

28. In Germany, the need for a preliminary authorization seems to have encouraged case-by-case agreement among industrialists and authorities in order to introduce some disposals against pollution; see Brüggemeier, *Das unendliche Meer der Lufte*, 299–309.

29. Dgsp, 1910–20, 611: 1.

30. The controversy, which was pending at least until 1909, is in Dgsp, 1910–20, 611: 9.

31. Dgsp, 1867–1900, 239: 1915; Dgsp, 1882–1915, 867: Civitavecchia, and 868: 2; Municipio di Genova, Regolamento locale d'igiene, *Igiene del suolo e dell'abitato* (Genoa, 1912), art. 48.

32. Pier P. Poggio, ed., *Una storia ad alto rischio: L'ACNA e la Valle Bormida* (Turin: Edizioni Gruppo Abele, 1996).

33. Dgsp, 1882–1915, 867: Chiaravalle, and 868: 19.

34. Dgsp, 1910–20, 611 bis: Collestatte; Monica Giansanti, "Industria e ambiente: Il caso della 'Carburo' a Collestatte e Papigno (1896–1930)," *Proposte e Ricerche* 37, no. 2 (1996): 189–215.

35. See, respectively, Dgsp, 1882–1915, 869: Padova; 1910–20, 611: Livorno; 610 bis: Savona; 611: Porto Empedocle.

36. Central State Archive (Rome), Ministero dell'Interno, Istituto Superiore di Sanità (hereafter ISS), Analisi delle acque, 33.

37. Mauro Francesco, *Industrie ed ubicazioni* (Milan: Hoepli, 1944) 1:118–19.

38. Frascani, "La disciplina," 721.

39. Dgsp, 1882–1915, 866: Ravenna.

40. See, among many others, the case of the complaint lodged in 1901 by the Società Regionale Veneta per la Pesca ed Acquicoltura against a plant allegedly polluting the waters of the Retrone River, in Dgsp, 1882–1915, 867: Vicenza.

41. As examples, see the case cited at note 37 and also the previously mentioned case of the chemical works at Portici, in Dgsp, 611: 9.

42. Dgsp, 1910–20, 611 bis: Montebelluna, and 611: Collestatte; ISS, Analisi delle acque, 33: Inconvenienti igienici, Lago d'Orta'; Giuseppe De Luigi, Edgar Meyer, and Andrea Saba, "Nasce una coscienza ambientale? La Società italiana dell'alluminio e l'inquinamento della Val Lagarina (1928–1938)," *Società e Storia* 67 (1995): 75–110.

43. Dgsp, 1882–1915, 867: Regolamento per la concia delle pelli (1904).

44. Dgsp, 1882–1915, 867: Chiaravalle, and 869: Padova; Dgsp, 1910–20, 610 bis: Ferrara (1907–10).

45. Poggio, *Una storia ad alto rischio;* Dgsp, 1882–1915, 867: Vicenza, and 768: Padova, Este.

46. Tarr, *Search,* 53–56; Melosi, *Sanitary City;* Luckin, "Pollution," 213–20; Platt, *Shock Cities,* 408–41.

47. Dgsp, 1910–20, 610 bis: Savona, Società Carboni Fossili; ISS, Analisi delle acque, 33: Inconvenienti igienici, 1924–38: Lago d'Orta; Dgsp, 1910–20, 611: 9, Napoli, and 611 bis8 (Portogruaro, 1914) and 611 bis: 18 (Montebelluna 1909). Analog evaluations concerning Germany are in Gilhaus, "*Schmerzenskinder der Industrie,*" 530–33.

48. Notoriously, zoning was a common trend in the industrialized countries, and it resulted in a way of admitting or tolerating pollution in specific urban

areas; cf. Franz-Josef Brüggemeier, "Umweltprobleme und Zonenplanung in Deutschland: Der Aufstieg und die Herrschaft eines Konzepts, 1800–1914," in *Environmental Problems in European Cities*, 143–64; Stephen Mosley, *The Chimney of the World: A History of Smoke Pollution in Victorian and Edwardian Manchester* (Cambridge, UK: White Horse Press, 2001), 144–45.

49. Between 1918 and 1938, the industrial contribution to the Italian gross domestic product rose from 24.9 percent to 30.3 percent. See Zamagni, *Economic History*, 32–38.

50. These numbers are based on the industrial censuses of 1911 and 1937.

51. For more on this subject, see Simone Neri Serneri, "Industrial Pollution and Urbanization: Ancient and New Industrial Areas in Early 20th Century Italy," in *Environmental Problems in European Cities*, 174–82.

52. Ernesto Bertarelli, *Trattato d'igiene* (Milan: Treves, 1938), 376–78.

53. Ibid., 626–28. See also Ernesto Bertarelli, "Rilievi e considerazioni intorno ai criteri da seguirsi per il riversamento delle acque luride nel mare, nei laghi, nei fiumi," *Annali d'Igiene* 44 (April 1934).

54. A collection of essays specially devoted to the environmental impact of Italian industry in the second half of twentieth century is Salvatore Adorno and Simone Neri Serneri, eds., *Industria, ambiente e territorio: Per una storia ambientale delle aree industriali in Italia* (Bologna: Il Mulino, 2009).

CHAPTER 10

Petrochemical Modernity in Sicily

Salvatore Adorno

BEGINNING IN 1949, Sicily's southeastern coast between Augusta and Siracusa was the protagonist in a story of sudden and tumultuous industrial development, creating one of the biggest European petrochemical centers in a twenty-year period. Between 1956 and 1959 alone, some 130 billion lire (about $200 million at 1959 exchange rates) were invested in industrial plants in this area, representing 15 percent of all industrial investments in southern Italy during the period and financed largely by special credit mechanisms of the Sicilian Regional Parliament (Assemblea Regionale Siciliana). Between 1951 and 1961, the number of people employed by these industries amounted to about 13,000 workers, pushing up the employment rate by more than 7 percent. By the 1970s, petrochemical plants with names such as Raisom, Sincat, and Celene, owned variously by Esso, Montedison, and other companies, spread across some 2,700 hectares of coastal Sicily.[1]

In November 1990, the area was declared an environmental emergency. The declaration of risk and the successive cleanup plan showed extremely high levels of air, water, and land pollution, resulting in a profoundly disrupted ecological equilibrium. A water emergency stemming from indiscriminate

Map 10.1. Location of petrochemical industries, Augusta, Sicily

use of aquifers resulted in a subsiding water table and increasing levels of salinity. Industrial emissions of micro- and macropollutants caused frequent temperature inversions along with photosynthetic ozone and nonmethane hydrocarbons. Organic and inorganic dust accumulated. Illegal waste disposal along with petroleum and mercury by-products degraded marine waters, resulting in eutrophic processes and genetic transformation of sea life. The lack of a safety zone between storage areas and population centers exacerbated human exposures to industrial and urban wastes. The whole area presented high seismic risks, and beyond that, industrial plants were sited near precious natural and archaeological resources, such as the Greek ruins of Megara Iblea.[2]

Comparing this image with those offered in the 1960s by the rather cheerful analyses of industrialization provided by Gabriele Morello, Eugenio Peggio, Mario Mazzarino, Valentino Parlato, and Franco Leonardi, one can understand the gap that had grown between the expectations and the problems in the intervening thirty years.[3]

The perspectives of these sociologists and economists described the sudden and traumatic transition from a primarily agricultural society to an industrial one. But this transition was told in terms of rising incomes, increasing consumer capacities, and improving employment rates. And even when these analysts acknowledged the imbalances of the new development models, such as the connections to interests of private monopolies, the risks of developing a local economy based only on the chemical industry, and the challenges of heavily subsidized industries, they painted a basically optimistic picture of Sicily's petrochemical development. It should be noted that those studies were silent with regard to environmental costs and hazards, reflecting just how absent such concerns were during those years. There was almost no mention of theoretical considerations or popular opinions regarding environmental threats. Only since the 1970s has the environmental question begun gaining political and social ground, becoming a key consideration in the process of industrialization. The environmental question would eventually supersede other considerations centered on employment and development.

Indeed, during the second half of the seventies, development and environment came to be seen as interrelated: on the one hand was the economic crisis of chemicals worsened by an international oil embargo,[4] and on the other were the first signs of a national environmental crisis, manifested in the chemical spills at Seveso and Manfredonia, along with local Sicilian fish die-offs, neonatal malformations, industrial plant fires, large-scale poisonings, and recognition of dropping water tables.[5] At this stage, the data gathered on environmental and health indicators were intertwined with legal sanctions for environmental violations. The knowledge and measurement of environmental phenomena, together with respect for and application of regulations, took a central role in the building of a new awareness of environmental questions as a strategic object for development. The rest of this paper focuses on the ramifications of this new environmental awareness.[6]

Air Pollution: Laws and Environmental Networks

It is well known that the Italian legislative process has been prone to delay in matters dealing with environmental protection, as well as in the fragmentation and limited effectiveness of implementing regulations to control pollution, at least up to the 1970s. One might consider the consequences that such delays had on the highly industrialized area of Siracusa. Air pollution was regulated in Italy by the so-called 615 antismog law of July 13, 1966, and the successive DPR n.322, 15 April 1971.[7] This latter law established a limit to the saturation of some pollutants and required the provincial government to monitor the level of pollution in industrial areas. This high limit reflected the alarming level of environmental pollution saturation. For individual plants, emission limits were calculated by noting the lowest possible emissions obtainable with the best available technologies for purification and reduction and then obliging companies to conform to these standards in order to avoid penal sanctions and fines. The assessment and verification of these standards for each plant were relegated to a regional organization, the Regional Committees against Atmospheric Pollution (CRIA), to which industries were obliged to communicate information on both their abatement technology and the obtainable levels of reduction. The provincial government had the task of monitoring and communicating to CRIA the overall levels of pollutant saturation in the areas over which it had jurisdiction.[8]

Without going into definitions of legal jurisdiction, it should be emphasized that the 615 law identified a typological classification of towns that were listed in documents called Chart A and Chart B and were subject to the regulations; all others were temporarily excluded. In Sicily, Catania and Palermo were registered on a chart, whereas several other cities with industrial plants were excluded, such as Siracusa, Augusta, Melilli, Milazzo, and Gela. Consequently, up to 1975 or 1976, the industrial coastal towns such as Augusta, Siracusa, and Melilli were never subjected to any specific environmental regulations concerning air emissions. Miscellaneous other laws and regulations about hygiene dating back to the Liberal and Fascist periods were also completely inadequate and mostly ineffective in dealing with new problems.[9]

One can trace the way in which Siracusa's coastal townships became registered on the chart through two sources: the national parliamentary inquiries of 1976 and a contemporary investigation made by the Sicilian Regional Parliament's sixth legislative Commission. The national parliamentary inquiries of October 1976, which arose from local and national emergencies, focused on the environmental condition of the coast of Siracusa.[10] From such information, it became apparent that this area had remained exempt from the regulations in force. The fact that these areas had been excluded from the 615 law meant that the industries in question did not need to present requests for building licenses or make readings of gaseous emissions. It was only after 1975 (following their insertion into Chart A) that the plants of Esso, Montedison, and Liquichimica started to submit emission reports according to law. The inquiries clarified, moreover, that up until that time, the only form of environmental monitoring being done was carried out by the industries themselves, without any governmental detection networks.

It appears that Montedison, after 1968, and the ISAB (Sicilian Industry of Asphalt and Bitumen) petrochemical plant and the Enel electric plant of Priolo, after the mid-1970s, had privately detected sulphuric dioxide through fixed and mobile networks.[11] In 1976, a syndicated private detection network called CIPA (Industrial Consortium for Environmental Protection) was established and brought together the Esso, Liquichimica, and Montedison plants with twenty-five automatic fixed stations for detecting sulphur anhydrite and a mobile station for detecting sulphur anhydrite, dust, and nitric oxide.[12] The Enel plant was also working to integrate itself into the CIPA network. Meanwhile, a public monitoring network was still missing.[13]

The parliamentary inquiry emphasized the ambiguous role of the industries, which were both controllers and controlled. It revealed that the private monitoring networks had focused exclusively on sulphur anhydrite to the exclusion of all other toxic substances, even if the Ministry of Health had expressed the need to monitor sulphur dioxide, dust, nitrogen, hydrogen sulphide, mercaptan, nonmethane hydrocarbons, sulphur oxides, and heavy metals. Each of these substances was considered a potential effluent of the industrial processes being carried out in the area. Because of this industry-centered control system, the ministry's declarations that pollution levels had remained safe were considered absolutely unreliable.

The results of the 1976 investigation about the environmental conditions of its industrial areas were greatly appreciated by the parliamentary group of the Sicilian Communist Party. With these first results, an understanding of Sicily's environmental condition began to emerge. The investigation underlined not only the serious state of the Siracusa-Augusta coast but also the condition of the cities of Gela and Milazzo, which were suffering from indiscriminate air and water pollutants. After declaring the "inadequacy and insufficiency" of the regulations,[14] the commission of investigation ordered a thorough collection of data, including the mapping of discharges into the air, sea, and rivers, and proposed a public monitoring network. Subsequent inspections in the industrial area acknowledged the state of emergency, forcing the inclusion of several more areas in Chart A. Siracusa and Augusta were added on 15 July 1975 and Melilli on 25 May 1976. By the time the 615 law came into full force in these areas, public concerns about air pollution had noticeably increased. Professor Marcello Carapezza of the University of Palermo, an adviser to the provincial government, complained again in 1979 that four survey networks in the industrial area did not cooperate and that air pollution levels were high.[15]

After 1976, Public Defender Antonino Condorelli started legal proceedings against both the provincial government, for failure to supervise air pollution inspection, and members of the Sicilian CRIA, for not identifying relationships between pollutant emissions and existing technology—both requirements of the 615 law. In the prosecution, Condorelli denounced "the scandalous inaction" and "inertia" of the public administration, emphasizing its "cultural lag" in dealing with the environmental question. He also highlighted the imbalance between employment benefits and environmental and public health concerns.[16] Thanks to Condorelli's political and cultural investigations, the time was right for beginning the first investigation of the social ramifications of air pollution.

This research, initiated by the Italian National Health Institute (ISS) in 1981, began with the monitoring of the industrial plants of the Siracusa-Augusta coastal strip and the immediate hinterland.[17] The research had the objective of interpreting information gathered in past years and streamlining statistical surveys with the CIPA network. Analysis of data gathered during monitoring and comparison with contemporary national and international standards certified widespread presence of pollutants, including relatively high concentrations of mercury vapor and above-average concentrations of nickel.[18] The researchers' conclusion recommended reducing polluting emissions while extending research to other pollutants not yet measured.

The investigation reinforced the potential dangers of several pollutants, including benzene, but it did not consider other dangerous compounds such as polycyclic aromatic hydrocarbons.

Today's rising standards of air pollution monitoring suggest that many pollutants were not registered in the 1980s, so even more serious pollutants may have been present. Nevertheless, these research results created a turning point in environmental awareness.

Legal Proceedings

The trials opened by the Court of Augusta in 1979 and 1980, together with the broader application of the 615 law along the Siracusan coast, marked a pause in the growing contamination of this area. The Merli Law on water pollution had been issued in 1976, and other social and economic measures had also been added around that time.[19] In the same period, an unemployment crisis was superimposed on the environmental crisis based on petrochemicals. These forces propelled the public toward a bona fide environmental movement. In turn, local governments were becoming much more involved in environmental questions. In this phase, the public opinion aroused strong reactions from the local councils, which were responsible for addressing environmental concerns. Amplified by TV and radio programming, social tensions were upsetting the harmony of this industrial zone.[20] Even certain levels of the industrial bureaucracy began to take notice, understanding the need to adapt themselves to the new regulations and realizing that the environmental question had implications for long-term development.

In this context, the inquiries made by Condorelli became important. He confronted the complex range of industrial problems and traced various investigative veins. The first investigation focused on the responsibility of the public administration to monitor local air pollution emissions. A second investigation looked at the responsibility of private management in causing water pollution. A third concerned the consequences of these emissions on human health (such as tumors and birth defects). A fourth looked into the indiscriminate lowering of the water table.

Following the Merli Law and the extension of the 615 law to the province of Siracusa, the cases conducted by Condorelli became crucial for defining the legality of the proceedings and for controlling how the new laws were enforced. It is possible to trace the consequences that his judicial mark had for other incident levels, which reflected more general concerns about the environmental effort. In addition, Condorelli's legal inquiries spawned a detailed monitoring of local environmental conditions, thereby supplying the first objective measures of pollution levels and possible effects on inhabitants, as well as expanding the general awareness of environmental problems. These court cases also stimulated political action, motivating decision makers and industrial leaders to tighten regulations while planning for environmental remediation and restoration. Such was the case in designing and constructing a nearby water purification plant. Although thirty years of inertia were difficult to surmount, the late 1970s became a decisive moment in terms of perceiving environmental problems and identifying possible solutions.

Water Pollution: Environmental and Epidemiological Investigations

Another example of how judicial inquiries in that period helped identify responsibility and locate compromises can be found in regard to water pollution. The problems of water pollution were made clear both by frequent fish blights at the Port of Augusta and by neonatal poisonings and birth defects ascribable to consuming fish that had ingested mercury and other pollutants dumped into the sea.

A 1978 report offers us the first good picture of seawater pollution near Augusta, after the Montedison, Esso, and Liquichimica facilities had dumped waste without precautions or protection for thirty years.[21] The northern part of the port near Augusta did not have elevated levels of pollution except for lead and mercury, but the southern part of the coast showed elevated concentrations of both, together with noxious hydrocarbons. Elevated concentrations of hydrocarbons were also found in the strip between the coast and the open sea. The report's alarming conclusion confirmed that pollution in the bay "constituted a problem to which a solution could no longer be procrastinated."[22]

After 1980, Public Defender Condorelli commissioned research on fish blight as part of an investigation. This research aimed to verify not only the presence of pollutants in the bay's sediments but also the accumulation of heavy metals in the port's marine organisms.[23] Special attention was given to mercury. Toxic materials were found in all of these substances, with sediments being loaded with hydrocarbons, heavy metals, and mercury—up to the high level of 153 ppm.[24] Heavy metals were also found in fish, though in much lower levels. The existence of highly contaminated sediments and relatively low bioaccumulation was explained by the fact that fish samples had been collected by trawling directly after a blight, which had served to eliminate much of the former fish population. Indeed, very few fish could be caught at all. Bioaccumulation requires extensive residence in an environment, and the long-resident fish had already died.

According to investigators, the Port of Augusta was in a precarious state not only because of the shoreline dumping of chemicals and heavy metals but also because of the heavy traffic of large oil tankers, frequent harbor excavations, and widespread construction of docks and offshore dams, which all served to weaken the local flora and fauna. In the words of the investigators: "Systematic blight, scarcity of benthos, high levels of heavy metals in sediments in some organisms, along with other information already collected

... permit a correct evaluation of the situation as a whole, which is that of a highly degraded environment." Concentrations of toxic materials, the investigators added, "represent a serious reason for worrying about the foreseeable consequences to human health, when bio-accumulation manifests itself through the trophic chain."[25] Gianni Moriani, an expert from the University of Venice, noted in a local newspaper that the blights were "a biological indicator of a process of pollution that had been going on for thirty years." He observed three kinds of pollution dumped into the bay: eighty-two tons of mineral oils contributed by the Montedison plant (impeding the passage of oxygen); phosphate, nitrogenous wastes, silicon, and heavy metals (triggering eutrophication processes); and phenols and organic solvents, arsenic, and finally mercury, which entered the food chain through fish.[26]

Subsequent legal proceedings, along with more recent investigations tied to the reclamation of Priolo, confirmed that mercury is a dominant element in the environmental emergency of the Port of Augusta.[27] Legambiente—the largest Italian environmental organization—reported that about five hundred tons of mercury had been dumped into the sea by Montedison's sodium chloride plant, mostly between 1958 and 1980.[28] Inquiries conducted in 2004 by the Institute for Scientific Research on Maritime Ecosystems (ICRAM) detected "strong contamination mainly due to mercury and heavy hydrocarbons, and secondarily due to chlorobenzene, light hydrocarbons, polychlorobifenyls, and arsenic."[29] Also present in smaller quantities were dioxin, BTEX (benzene, tolvene, ethylbenzene, and xylenes), furan, and chlorinated aliphatic compounds. The investigations noted that mercury was concentrated in the first fifty centimeters of sediment and in the southern part of the port, whereas concentrations in the northern part were also "worrisome."[30] The data showed that in marine life, mercury could be found in all the species analyzed.[31]

It should be pointed out that the Department of Health in the early 1970s (before the Merli Law) had already indicated the importance of monitoring and controlling mercury dumping, for it was well aware of the capacity of bioaccumulation and cognizant of the disasters at Minamata, Japan.[32] Not surprisingly, the defense strategy in the trials of the 1980s was aimed at delegitimizing the accusations regarding the presence of mercury, while focusing on a handful of contradictory results in sediment and fish samples. And being unable to deny the port's advanced environmental degradation, the defendants emphasized less important crimes and health effects, such as eutrophication. Even the local press stressed this last effect as the main outcome of water pollution, dedicating much less attention to the presence of mercury.

The fact that mercury had already become a crucial issue in Sicily is shown by a petition filed by Giacinto Franco, a physician from Augusta's Muscatello Hospital. He noticed an increase in the number of congenital birth defects compared to previous years. The court then urged the Ministry of Health to establish a commission to track infant malformations, adding the province of Siracusa to the monitoring program of the Italian Center of Congenital Malformations (IPIMC). Until 1989, this center tabulated data on birth defects; in 1990, the Sicilian register of birth defects took over this task, thereby providing a long and detailed historical database. Such data indicate that the Siracusa area has witnessed a significant upward shift in birth defects in the circulatory and digestive systems, compared to the regional and national averages.[33] Recent medical research has indicated a possible connection between hypospadias (a urethra birth defect) and the bioaccumulation of mercury.[34]

Studies are also accumulating on deaths caused by or related to tumors. According to research commissioned by Condorelli, the mortality rate due to cancer in Augusta went from 8.9 percent between 1950 and 1955 to 23.7 percent between 1976 and 1980, peaking at 29.9 percent in 1980. Males were predominately more affected by tumors, especially of the lung, but this research was not able to verify a direct relationship between increasing cancer rates and rising environmental pollution. Investigations were subsequently extended both to the 1980–88 period and in the town of Priolo. Many other studies have since been conducted by the World Health Organization, the Ministry of Health, and ENEA (National Council for New Technology, Energy and the Environment), designed to find correlations between risks of lung cancer and residency in industrial areas. Results suggest that, at least in the Megara area, links exist between tumors of the pleura and exposure to asbestos manufactured in a nearby plant.[35] In the case of tumors and birth defects, we are reminded of the importance of place for human inhabitation and of the need for greater political and social responsibility when developing that place.

Notes

1. For a brief history of the construction projects and the economic and financial forces that promoted them, see Salvatore Adorno, "Imprenditori e impresa a Siracusa in età contemporanea: Note e riflessioni," in *Gli archivi di impresa in Sicilia: Una risorsa per la conoscenza e lo sviluppo*, ed. Gaetano Calabrese (Milan: Franco Angeli, 2007), 201–17.

2. "Piano di risanamento ambientale delle aree ad elevato rischio di crisi ambientale nel territorio di Augusta-Priolo-Melilli-Siracusa," *Supplemento*

Ordinario alla Gazzetta Ufficiale della Repubblica Italiana, gen. ser. 100, 2 May 1995; "Accordo di programma per l'attuazione del piano di risanamento di aree a rischio di crisi ambientale nel territorio dei comuni di Priolo, Augusta, Melilli, Floridia, Solarino, e Siracusa," *Gazzetta Ufficiale della Regione Siciliana,* 13 April 1996.

3. Gabriele Morello, *L'industrializzazione nella provincia di Siracusa* (Bologna: Il Mulino, 1962); Eugenio Peggio, Mario Mazzarino, and Valentino Parlato, *Industrializzazione e sottosviluppo: Il progresso tecnologico in una provincia meridionale* (Turin: Einaudi, 1960); Franco Leonardi, "Operai nuovi: Studio sociologico sulla nuova forza lavoro industriale nell'area siracusana," in *Problemi dell'economia siciliana,* ed. Paolo Sylos Labini (Milan: Feltrinelli, 1966): 1029–1239. On Augusta in particular, see Severino Santiapichi and Giovanni Vaccaro, *Augusta: Industrializzazione in Sicilia* (Palermo: Flaccovio, 1962).

4. On the Italian petrochemical cycle and the crisis of the 1970s, see Geoffrey J. Pizzorni, ed., *L'industria chimica italiana nel novecento* (Milan: Franco Angeli, 2006), and in particular the essay by Angelo Moioli, "La frontiera della petrolchimica italiana nel secondo dopoguerra," 73–101. See also Renato Giannetti, "Imprese e politica industriale: La petrolchimica italiana negli anni settanta," in *Radici storiche ed esperienza dell'intervento straordinario nel Mezzogiorno,* ed. Leandra D'Antone (Naples: Bibliopolis, 1996), 499–525.

5. In 1976, two environmental disasters occurred, at Seveso, Lombardy, and at Manfredonia, Puglia, attracting international attention and swaying Italian public opinion on topics related to security and pollution. A toxic dioxin cloud from the ICMESA plant formed over Seveso, and in Manfredonia, ten tons of arsenic spilled from the Dauna plant. On Seveso, besides Laura Centemeri's essay in this volume, see Daniele Biacchessi, *La fabbrica dei profumi: La verità su Seveso, l'Icmesa, la diossina* (Milan: Baldini Castoldi, 1995), as well as the film *Seveso 10 luglio 1976: Una storia da raccontare,* dir. Fabio Tosetto, 54 min., Legambiente Lombardia, 2004, DVD. On Manfredonia, see Maria Gabriella Rienzo, *Manfredonia: Industria o ambiente? Per la composizione di un conflitto* (Naples: Edizioni Scientifiche Italiane, 2005). On the birth of the Italian environmental question in petrochemical areas, see the case of Marghera, in Felice Casson, *La fabbrica dei veleni: Storie e segreti di Porto Marghera* (Milan: Sperling and Kupfer, 2007).

6. On these topics, see Salvatore Adorno, "Il polo industriale di Augusta-Siracusa: Risorse e crisi ambientale," in *Storia e ambiente: Città, risorse e territori nell'Italia contemporanea,* ed. Gabriella Corona and Simone Neri Serneri (Rome: Carocci, 2007): 195–217.

7. See Rodolfo Lewanski, "Il difficile avvio di una politica ambientale in Italia," in *L'industria e l'ambiente,* ed. Bruno Dente and Pippo Ranci (Bologna: Il Mulino, 1992), 27–78.

8. The CRIA were institutions established in every region, according to articles 5 and 6 of the 615 law of 1966, with the task of checking and monitoring pollution. Each was headed by the president of the region. Internally, they represented the local public health institutions, the chambers of commerce, and the outlying agencies responsible for traffic control, fire control, and weather forecasting. They could make use of consultants and experts in the environmental field.

9. On those rules, see Simone Neri Serneri's essay in this volume.

10. Atti parlamentari, Camera dei Deputati, settima legislatura, discussioni, seduta del 5 ottobre 1976, *Svolgimento di interpellanze e interrogazioni sull'inquinamento nell' area industriale di Siracusa*, 851–78, available at http://legislature.camera.it/_dati/leg07/lavori/stenografici/sed0016/sed0016.pdf (accessed 30 August 2009); Capria, Bandiera, Calabrò, Castelliana, Coarallo, Lo Bello, Santagati, Sgarlata spoke during the parliamentary enquiry.

11. Enel was created in 1962 to nationalize the Italian electric industry. Then, in 1992, Enel became a joint-stock company. On the data gathered on Montedison, see D. Sordelli, A. Giuffrida, and L. Fossi, *Ricerche sull'inquinamento atmosferico nella zona di Priolo* (n.p.: Montedison, 1976).

12. On the CIPA network (an industrial consortium for environmental protection), see the pamphlet *Cipa: La cultura dell'aria* (Siracusa: G and G Stampa, 1990). The network was established on 27 September 1974 under the auspices and by the will of the association of industrialists of the province of Siracusa, with the objective of monitoring an area of about 150 square kilometers.

13. Atti parlamentari, Camera dei Deputati, settima legislatura, discussioni, seduta del 5 ottobre 1976, *Svolgimento di interpellanze e interrogazioni sull'inquinamento dell' area industriale di Siracusa*, 862, with the intervention of the undersecretary of health, Ferdinando Russo, available at http://legislature.camera.it/_dati/leg07/lavori/stenografici/sed0016/sed0016.pdf (accessed 30 August 2009).

14. See Gruppo Parlamentare Comunista all'Assemblea Regionale Siciliana, ed., *I comunisti per la tutela dell'ambiente nelle aree industriali* (Palermo: Arti Grafiche A. Renna, 1980). A picture of the environmental conditions of the territory in those years can be found in Marcello Marsili and Antonio Andolfi, *Immagine ambientale: Siracusa—Polo industriale e qualità della vita* (Ferrara: Edizioni CDS, 1985); Marcello Marsili, "Condizioni d'inquinamento da aerosol in un'area industrializzata," *Acqua Aria*, no. 10 (1981) and no. 1 (1982); Marsili, "Indicatori di inquinamento nell'area industriale di Siracusa," *Acqua Aria*, nos. 1–2 (1984).

15. See the report on the intervention of Carapezza at the convention of Catania on the "Sviluppo industriale e tutela ambientale," quoted in *Diario*

di Siracusa, 10 November 1979. Marcello Carapezza, geochemist and rector of the University of Palermo, was an expert on volcanic and seismic risk. In the 1970s, when the devastating effects on humans and the environment were just beginning to be perceived, he focused his studies on researching the balance between humans and nature.

16. Some material on the investigation is published in Marsili and Andolfi, *Immagine ambientale*. In particular, see also *Sentenza del pretore di Augusta Antonino Condorelli n. 77/bis/80 del 18 febbraio 1980*. I am grateful to Dr. Corrado Giuliano and his law firm in Siracusa for the opportunity to access this document, conserved in their professional archive. The document can also be accessed at the Court of Augusta.

17. Istituto Superiore di Sanità, *Indagine sullo stato di inquinamento atmosferico nella fascia costiera da Augusta a Siracusa ed il suo immediato entroterra*, typewritten, (1982), in possession of the author. This document can be consulted at the Environmental Protection Office of the Siracusan Regional Province, XII area. The industrial plants to be subjected to monitoring were the Liquichimica of Augusta, the Italian Esso, the thermoelectrical Enel plant of Priolo, the Montedison (the Montedipe, Montepolimeri, and the Fertimont plants), the Isab, and the CoGeMa.

18. Ibid., 84.

19. Regarding the Merli Law, see Gianfranco Amendola, *Inquinati e inquinatori: Storia e cronaca della legge Merli* (Rome: Nis, 1980).

20. Regarding this subject, see *Siamo 10.000 operai della Montedison di Priolo*, ed. Gruppo di Intervento contro la Nocività in Fabbrica e nell'Ambiente di Radio Libera Siracusa (Siracusa: Tipografia Sagandurra, 1976).

21. Salvatore Sciacca and Roberto Fallico, "Presenza e concentrazione di sostanze inquinanti di origine industriale nei fanghi della rada di Augusta (Siracusa)," *Inquinamento* 20, no. 6 (1978): 33–38. Salvatore Sciacca, hygienist and professor on the Faculty of Medicine and Surgery at the University of Catania, had conducted, up to the 1970s, numerous epidemiological investigations of the industrial area between Siracusa and Augusta.

22. Ibid., 37.

23. Aristeo Renzoni, Roberto Minervini, and Vito Consoli, *Relazione tecnica preliminare sulle indagini effettuate nella Rada di Augusta*, 8 November 1980, typewritten, in possession of the author. The assignment was given to Professor Aristeo Renzoni, Dr. Roberto Minervini from the Anatomy Department of the University of Siena, and Dr. Vito Consoli of the Co.I.P.A. of Rome, following measure 1802/79r.g. of the magistrate's court of Augusta concerning the fish blight in September and October 1979. In the 1960s, Renzoni, a biologist, studied the biological fundamentals of mussel farming in the gulf of Naples;

he was a scholar of ecology and the processes for the preservation of nature and its resources and a member of the Faculty for the Science of Natural and Physical Mathematics at the University of Siena; there, he was the director of the botanic garden between 1984 and 1989. In particular, see Renzoni, *Contaminants in the Environment: A Multidisciplinary Assessment of Risk to Man and Other Organisms* (Boca Raton, FL: Lewis Publishers, 1994).

24. Ibid., 27.

25. Ibid.

26. "A Siracusa si berrà solo acqua minerale," *Diario di Siracusa,* 20 November 1979.

27. ICRAM, *Elaborazione e valutazione dei risultati della caratterizzazione ambientale della rada di Augusta—Aree prioritarie ai fini della progettazione degli interventi di messa in sicurezza di emergenza: Sito di interesse nazionale di Priolo,* August 2005, Bol-Pr-Si-PR-Rada di Augusta–01.04, in the author's possession.

28. Legambiente, "Stop al mercurio: La campagna italiana per la riconversione del clorosoda," ed. Stefano Ciafani, Katia Le Donne, and Emanuela Cherubini, available at http://www.legambiente.eu/documenti/2006/0612_Stop_Mercurio/stop_al_mercurio_dossier_legambiente.pdf (accessed 5 May 2009). For more general material on pollution by mercury, see Nicola Pirrone and Kathryn R. Mahaffey, eds., *Dynamics of Mercury Pollution on Regional and Global Scales: Atmospheric Processes and Human Exposures around the World* (New York: Spinger-Verlag, 2006).

29. ICRAM, *Elaborazioni,* 30.

30. Ibid.

31. Ibid., 82.

32. See the circular letter no. 12, 1971, of the Ministero della Sanità, DGSIP div. 5. On the Minamata disaster, see Pirrone and Mahaffey, eds., *Dynamics of Mercury Pollution on Regional and Global Scales;* also, John R. McNeill, *Something New under the Sun: An Environmental History of the Twentieth Century World* (New York: W. W. Norton, 2000), 138–40.

33. The data are published in Comitato Cittadino contro il Termovalorizzatore, *Dossier informativo per le autorità preposte, gli organismi di informazione e i cittadini residenti nella zona industriale di Augusta-Priolo-Melilli-Siracusa: Breve storia e situazione del polo industriale Augusta–Priolo–Melilli,* typescript (2004), also available at Ideasolidale, http://www.ideasolidale.it/pop/Associazione/Termovalorizzatore/Breve%20storia%20del%20polo%20industriale.doc (accessed 5 May 2009).

34. Fabrizio Bianchi, Sebastiano Bianca, Nunzia Linzalone, and Anselmo Madeddu, "Sorveglianza delle malformazioni congenite in Italia: Un

approfondimento nella provincia di Siracusa," *EP* 28, no 1 (2004): 27–33. See also Fabrizio Bianchi, Sebastiano Bianca, Gabriella Dondaroni, Nunzia Linzalone, and Anna Pierini, "Malformazioni congenite nei nati residenti del comune di Gela," *EP* 30, no. 1 (2006): 19–26.

35. About the epidemiological investigations regarding the industrial area, see Anselmo Madeddu, Lisa Contarino, Francesco Tisano, and Salvatore Sciacca, *La salute di Aretusa e . . . i padroni del tempo: Atlante della mortalità per tumori e per patologie cronico degenerative in provincia di Siracusa nel quinquennio 1995–1999* (Siracusa: Provincia Regionale di Siracusa, 2002); Madeddu, Contarino, Tisano, and Sciacca, *La peste, gli untori e l'immaginario: Atlante della mortalità per tumori e per patologie cronico degenerative in provincia di Siracusa dal 1995*, vol. 2, *Aggiornamento 2000–2002* (Siracusa: Provincia Regionale di Siracusa, 2003). On asbestos and health in Italy, see also Piero Bevilacqua's essay in this volume.

CHAPTER 11

The Seveso Disaster Legacy

Laura Centemeri

IN THE history of the environment as a public problem, industrial disasters have been insufficiently explored.[1] Such disasters are nonetheless crucial because their collective interpretation weaves together technical and scientific issues, problems of social justice, and controversies concerning conflicting "common goods" by destabilizing the equilibria that have formed between these elements.[2] These disequilibria lead to episodes of normative and cognitive uncertainty and thereby provide an opportunity for social critique and social change, especially by sparking public debates on rules, institutions, and representations about technical progress. In short, industrial disasters become opportunities for rethinking the types of compromises between "orders of worth"—in particular, industrial and civic—upon which a society rests.[3]

Yet there is still little acknowledgment of the social change that industrial disasters can trigger. What kind of social change such disasters produce in the mid-to-long term and how these disasters produce such changes are questions that often go unaddressed.[4] Moreover, an industrial disaster occurs in a specific locality even though its potential social and political effects can reach far beyond that place. The environment affected by a disaster is usually limited and circumscribed, but as a threat to the environment—to nature—this disaster causes widespread concerns.[5] The collective explanation of the industrial accident and of its specific character and narrative takes place at different scales. The specific scale should not be considered simply a reflection of the researcher's lens. Every scale implies a need to address a different stage of the disaster as an event that requires a different collective solution.

As pointed out in the anthropological literature on this topic, "disasters offer the investigator amazing situations in which to analyze hypotheses pertaining to the constitution of society and culture."[6] These studies address disasters not just as events but also as processes in which symbolic and social resources are enacted by the affected population in an effort to re-create an order after the disruptions caused by catastrophe. Political cultures play a role in these dynamics because they provide collective frames of interpretation of the event—and of the responses needed—and articulate the local and specific experiences of victims to more general issues. At the same time, political cultures are tested by the event in their capacity to address societal issues made visible through the experience of the disaster.

Starting from these premises, this essay examines the role of political cultures in the local social dynamics triggered by the Seveso disaster.[7] The recovery of the town of Seveso after the industrial accident of 10 July 1976 is a topic usually overlooked in the literature devoted to the disaster, which to date has centered mostly on how this event led to stricter European Union (EU) policies about environmental responsibility.[8] Indeed, Seveso is considered a kind of symbol of the European environmentalist struggle. Yet for Italy's own environmental movement, this event has overtones of defeat because of the failure to match the "general stakes" of the disaster with its "local sensibility."[9] In fact, at the local level, the disaster has triggered a harsh conflict between, on the one hand, the large majority of the affected population and, on the other, social movements mobilized to support victims as well as public authorities in charge of the response. As I aim to show here, this conflict has prompted local environmental activism to change toward a "localist pathway" of political engagement[10] that sought in the 1990s to promote a dialogue between the way disaster has been experienced by the affected population and more general social issues raised by the accident.

After a concise reconstruction of the disaster dynamics, I shall focus on the local forms of mobilization in response to the crisis, pointing out the processes that support the prevailing interpretation of dioxin damage as a threat to the local culture and identity. I will then consider how this connection between environmental damage and local identity has been at the heart of the renewal of political action for a group of Seveso environmental activists, engaged in promoting local green policies and practices. By way of conclusion, I will then address the key role played by the construction of a shared memory of the disaster in an effort to promote more sustainable paths of local development.

The Dioxin Crisis in Seveso and Its Management

Seveso is a town of twenty thousand inhabitants located north of Milan, the regional capital of Lombardy, in the area known as Brianza Milanese. The Brianza is a subregion with a strong Catholic cultural tradition, specializing in the manufacture and design of furniture, together with a tradition of small, family-owned firms.[11] After World War II, chemical industries began to install their plants in this area, given the rich water resources and good infrastructure.

The accident at the core of the Seveso disaster occurred in the chemical plant of the ICMESA (Industrie Chimiche Meda Società Azionaria) company (located in the adjoining town of Meda), owned by Givaudan, a subsidiary of the Swiss multinational Roche. On Saturday, 10 July 1976, at around 12:30 a.m., the ICMESA trichlorophenol reactor released a toxic cloud of dioxin and other pollutants due to a sudden exothermic reaction that caused a failure of the safety valve. Various poisons were dispersed by wind to settle on buildings and backyards in the towns of Meda, Cesano Maderno, Desio, and the most heavily afflicted location of all, Seveso.

As the Italian Parliamentary Commission on the Seveso Disaster has documented, the accident can be traced to Roche making inadequate safety investments in the ICMESA plant.[12] This negligence is made all the more serious when one realizes that the health risks of trichlorophenol were well known from previous industrial accidents. These risks revolve around the chemical produced in the process of synthesizing trichlorophenol: dioxin.

In 1976, the extremely harmful effects of dioxin on human health were predicted largely on the basis of toxicological evidence. Epidemiological studies with dioxin were still scarce and limited to tracking cohorts of industrial workers (all adult males) accidentally exposed to high concentrations of dioxin.[13] Seveso's large-scale dioxin contamination, affecting an entire population, was without precedent: scientists were unable to anticipate the damages (on the environment, animals, men, women, children, and human fetuses), and they were unable to identify procedures for decontamination. There were no instruments yet available for measuring dioxin levels in human blood.[14] As a result, there was a "radical uncertainty" about the consequences of dioxin contamination on human health and the environment,[15] as well as their duration in space and in time. Only dioxin's extreme toxicity had been proven in the laboratory.

The frightening scenario did not take shape immediately after the accident. The toxic cloud passed by largely unnoticed, considered by inhabitants of Seveso and Meda as a typical nuisance (one in a long series), though perhaps a bit more annoying because of its nasty smell. Givaudan engineers reassured local authorities that everything was under control:[16] the rest of the production work continued normally in the ICMESA plant. A "week of silence" passed.[17] In the meantime, strange events were taking place in the nearby area. Leaves suddenly began falling; small animals, such as birds and cats, were dying; and a mysterious skin disease (chloracne) was affecting children. Anxiety grew in the population, and Roche's efforts failed to avoid a "desectorialisation of the crisis" on technical to political fronts.[18] On 19 July—nine days after the spill—Roche experts informed Italian authorities that the accident at the ICMESA plant had caused widespread dioxin contamination. Evacuation of part of Seveso and Meda's population was highly recommended.

The evacuation began on 24 July. Seven hundred inhabitants of Seveso and Meda were forced to leave their houses and all their personal belongings. Two hundred people never returned to their houses, which were eventually demolished during cleanup operations. "Risk zones" were created, based on

Fig. 11.1. Decontamination (in Seveso), anonymous photographer. Courtesy of the Ente Regionale per i Servizi all'Agricoltura e Alle Foreste (ERSAF), Lombardy

Fig. 11.2. Risk Zone A, Dino Fracchia, photographer. Courtesy of ERSAF, Lombardy

the estimated trajectory of the toxic cloud and random tests of dioxin concentration in the ground but also based on practical feasibility, so that toxic boundaries turned out to be oddly rectilinear.[19] Given the suspected teratogenic effects of dioxin, pregnant women in the contaminated area (within the first trimester) were given "free choice" to ask for a medical abortion, even though abortion was still considered a crime in Italy. In fact, the Italian movement for decriminalizing abortion was at its peak at that time.[20] In an emotionally packed atmosphere, about thirty women from the contaminated area decided to voluntarily interrupt their pregnancy.[21]

The Lombardy regional authorities' management of the dioxin crisis was marked by bureaucracy and technical dependency.[22] Committees of experts were created and asked to supply solutions with respect to health risk, decontamination, and socioeconomic problems. Each committee was required to give its advice unanimously so that the only thing the Regional Council had to do was to approve their recommendations, and no discussion on alternative technical choices was allowed. Decisions of a true political nature were therefore taken inside the committees, meaning that these were not just advisory bodies. Likewise, a special technical body was created (the Seveso Special Bureau) in order to implement the adopted measures. Lastly, government stability at regional and national levels was a priority, thereby narrowing the windows of opportunity for institutional change opened by the crisis.[23] In the end, there was little visibility in the decision-making process, which offered few chances for ordinary citizens to add their input, despite the fact that such decisions strongly affected their everyday lives.

Given the enormous scientific uncertainty surrounding dioxin, it was clear to everyone that most decisions taken at Seveso could not rely on much objectivity. Nevertheless, scientific controversies about dioxin hazards were widely discussed in the media. The insistence by public authorities that decision criteria were purely scientific and technical, followed by a period of erratic and contradictory decision making, convinced the public that dioxin was mainly a false scare and a political trick. Allowing abortions despite uncertainties about the risk to fetuses was considered to be evidence of the manipulation of the crisis.

Abortion became the central issue in the public debate, so that more general health issues surrounding dioxin, including the risks from pollution damages, slipped into the background. The dioxin catastrophe became a question of "allowing women to abort or not"; it was not about the hidden costs of industrialization.[24]

Considered from the perspective of the government-citizen dialogue, management of the dioxin crisis in Seveso was a good example of a bad way to handle a chemical emergency. Nonetheless, the environmental recovery was ultimately successful, with a complete cleanup of the contaminated area and little transformation of the local socioeconomic fabric.[25]

From Disaster to Cultural Conflict: Rival Interpretations of the Dioxin Crisis

In Europe, the dioxin crisis at Seveso marked the appearance of a new kind of environmental damage—one that might produce delayed rather than immediate effects. Damaging chemical effects might extend to future generations.[26] The specifics of the damage and the supranational features of the disaster accelerated the process of assigning environmental responsibility to the European Union, an issue that was not envisioned in the 1957 Treaty of Rome. The Seveso disaster was especially influential in establishing the category of "major accident hazards of certain industrial activities" regulated through Directive 82/501/CEE (or the Seveso Directive). In its design, this 1982 directive echoed some of the issues brought out by the Seveso disaster and, in particular, the crucial role played by information in risk management.[27] The Seveso disaster is widely interpreted as an "information disaster." Given the secrecy about what was happening inside ICMESA, public authorities had insufficient information for intervening in a timely manner. At the local level, too, the lack of information was crucial, especially because there was little information generated by citizens for use in making public decisions.

Social movements already active in the Italian political scene along with several left-wing political parties mobilized in Seveso. One result was the establishment of the Scientific Technical Popular Committee (STPC) to look after the interests of the victims. One of the most important actors in this mobilization was Medicina Democratica (MD), a movement that arose out of a large coalition between scientists and workers to lobby issues related to health damages stemming from industrial production, within and beyond plants.[28] Underlying this agenda was a social critique of capitalistic exploitation and its hidden costs. But this frame found little to no reception among Seveso victims, thus reducing the weight of MD's public arguments and, more generally, its influence at the national level.[29] How does one explain this failure?

The leftist activists held up the Seveso disaster as a typical "capitalistic crime," as a clear example of the capitalist system of injustice.[30] Seveso people were asked to join an existing cause, that of the class struggle. In the way leftists were framing the crisis, people from Seveso could exist in the public space only as victims of irreparable damage. In this respect, leftist radicals were as incapable as public authorities of comprehending what Seveso people considered to be the priority in responding to the dioxin crisis—preserving their town as a specific community. Neither public authorities nor radical leftists, given their interpretative frames, were able to account for this dimension of "attachment" to place and community.[31]

In response to the scientific uncertainties of the dioxin risk, there emerged a grassroots mobilization of people from a strong Catholic background. They asked public authorities to consider the seriousness not only of health risks but also of their community's uprooting. Yet no arenas to

Fig. 11.3. "Seveso says . . . ," anonymous photographer. Courtesy of ERSAF, Lombardy

publicly discuss and mediate these issues were opened, which caused intense grassroots protest.

In this protest, a central role was assumed by activists of the Catholic movement called Comunione e Liberazione (CL).[32] For CL adherents, the disaster was not a crime but a test for the community. They felt themselves under attack as a community and believed they needed to stick to their values, territory, and tradition as a response. CL asked public authorities to recognize the community's right to actively be part of the response to the dioxin crisis, appealing to the subsidiary principle (or belief that policy decisions should be made at the most local level). In actual fact, CL activists organized their own services for supporting families harmed by the disaster, and they tried to maintain communitarian cohesion. The harm done by dioxin was thus seen as damage to a community, not to individuals. From this perspective, the return to a good community life was considered the best indication of recovery from the dioxin horror, beyond the actual cleanup of contaminated areas. This idea of dioxin damage as a community threat parallels the idea of recovery based on privatizing the disaster's controversial implications, particularly its future health effects. Such health damages are left to individuals to bear alone. In the collective effort to "resist and move on," the problematic issues revealed by the event (especially as measured by ongoing chemical pollution of the territory) seemed to be erased.

A Return to Seveso: Activist Trajectories

After the accident, only a small number of inhabitants chose to leave Seveso, among them a small group of young Seveso activists who had participated in the mobilization promoted by the STPC. The accident had pushed them into political action, yet the response of most Seveso people made them believe that "in Seveso it was not possible to carry on the struggle necessary to change the institutional system so as to avoid repeating a similar accident" (interview with LB).

In fact, from the perspective of the political ecology of STPC, industrial damage of the environment was proof that the capitalist system needed to be radically changed. Concerns for nature or territory were of dubious validity because such issues were matters of "bourgeois conservationism."[33] Needing to face conflicts stirred up by the disaster in the people of Seveso, these young activists lacked a vocabulary capable of translating into political issues the attachment to place that their fellow citizens claimed to be a "common good" requiring protection. Indeed, their political culture condemned this very attachment as an obstacle to joining the general cause of the class struggle.

During the 1980s, these young activists embraced new political agendas, in particular international cooperation and feminism. Participants in these political experiences shared the belief that practice was a form of political engagement.

At the beginning of the 1990s, the group of activists returned to Seveso with a new political project, that of making the experience of the disaster a basis for social and economic change toward a model of urban sustainable development, produced within the local community. Since the time of the accident and thanks to their recent political experiences, their previous way of conceiving political action on environmental issues had changed dramatically, largely because of feminist influences.[34] The emphasis that Italian feminism puts on the "practice of relationships" as a form of "primary political action" led to a redefinition of the very terms of the issue of environment, far from the frameworks of both political and conservationist ecology.[35] The idea here is that of *taking care* of a concrete and local environment through practices that give birth to new relationships between human beings and between human beings and their environment. The emphasis is no longer on the concept of political duty, nor on the abstract concept of the right action to be taken as a guide for political engagement. Rather, political action must be rooted and must take shape in everyday life practices that are political per se because they build and change contexts through changing relationships.

One of the Seveso activists described this change in focus of political action, and the need for change, as follows:

> At the time of the accident, we were unable to understand the importance of the "practical" dimension. We launched into an ideological extrapolation of the environmental question in order to fight a global struggle. We didn't consider, or didn't consider enough, the vital interests linked to everyday life, that were affected by the dioxin event. This is the reason why we did not succeed in our attempt to interact with the people. This is the reason why I decided to leave Seveso, because my political action at that time was intended to change a lot of things: it was not enough for me to change a small aspect of living in my neighborhood. But after a few years, I began to see my political action as rootless. There was a sort of gap: my political action was becoming more and more universal, but every time I came back to Seveso I had less and less to share with the people living there. (interview with MM)

The new political attitude of the group became consolidated through a series of local experiences of new political engagement. First of all, there was the creation in Seveso of a local section of Legambiente, named after Laura Conti, one of the preeminent figures in the STPC and a communist, environmentalist, and feminist.[36] Then, in 1991 and 1992, the group became engaged in restoring a small wooded area in Seveso, Fosso del Ronchetto, that was being used as a waste dump. The Fosso del Ronchetto experience was a turning point. Legambiente activists made themselves visible in the eyes of the local community; the restoration project provided the opportunity for meeting citizens and getting them interested in Legambiente activities. At the same time, the activists established a new kind of relationship with local institutions. They assumed a direct and formal responsibility in doing things for the community, an attitude far from their former critical and conflictual logic of action. In fact, the town council gave the local Legambiente section formal responsibility for the recovery and management of the woods. From this point, the Legambiente activists in 1995 formed Natur&, a "social enterprise" meant to offer "innovative environmental and social services" (Statute of the Natur& Association, art. 4). This choice marked the shift of Legambiente activists toward a model of "localist and access organizations,"[37] very similar to that of some of the organizations linked to the CL movement.

Direct action in the local context, through supplying services, is considered by activists as one of the ways to promote a greener model of economic development. Direct involvement in the local political arena is the other. In 1996, the group of activists turned to the local political arena, as a local branch of the national Green Party. But in 1999, the group left the Greens and contributed to the creation of a "civic list" not directly linked to any national political party in order to support a candidate for town mayor; this candidate was a bridging figure, strongly linked to the Catholic movement CL but also to local environmentalism. The civic list won the elections, and one of the activists was put in charge of the municipality's social and environmental policies. Among his first decisions, he chose to promote an Agenda 21 process together with the other municipalities involved in the accident of 1976 (Cesano Maderno, Desio, and Meda). In Agenda 21, the work on the collective memory of the disaster is explicitly promoted as a milestone in the local move toward a more sustainable model of development. Thus, in 2002, the Agenda 21 process sponsored the project known as the Seveso Bridge of Memory, which was promoted and realized by the Seveso section of Legambiente.

The Construction of "Discreet" Memory

The issue of the memory of the ICMESA accident is especially linked to one place, the Oak Wood, a forty-two-hectare plot of forest in the urban center of Seveso that was artificially created over the most contaminated area—the site of two subterranean dumps filled with the toxic wastes produced during the decontamination procedures. In 1996, the wood was opened to the public without any kind of "memory inscription" testifying to its origin.[38] Legambiente activists highly criticized this kind of "indiscriminate opening": "We never agreed with the choice of an indiscriminate opening of the park, composed of folkloristic and purely recreational events. Instead, we proposed since 1996 to make it a space of environmental education for preserving and safeguarding the memory of the disaster. The idea that one could forget what was hidden under its soil, and perhaps even build houses on it, has always been greatly disturbing for us" (interview with GB).

The Seveso Bridge of Memory project was developed in 1999 and 2000 by these activists as a way to oppose what seemed to be a sort of collective pressure to erase the disaster's memory, starting with the normalization of the Oak Wood. They then asked local town councils to finance the creation of an archive of the disaster as well as a "memory footpath" in the Oak Wood, complete with displays telling the accident's story through texts and photos.

Given the aim of defining a commonly shared memory of the event, the texts and photos were written and chosen by Legambiente activists together with an oversight committee composed of ten people from Seveso. These people were considered representative of the local community but uninvolved in politics or public institutions at the time of the accident. Once the displays were created, they were presented to the larger community of Seveso for further opinions and suggestions.

The process that led to the opening of the memory footpath in 2004 showed how Legambiente activists aimed to place the IMCESA event at the center of a new collective identity for the Seveso community. The inscriptions on the displays fix the ICMESA accident as a test for the local community, successfully overcome. According to one of the project's organizers, the inhabitants of Seveso now acknowledge the importance of what happened in the context of more general issues—such as sustainability—in order to make better decisions in the future. The dioxin incident is therefore considered a tragedy as well as an "opportunity for change": the attachment to place shown by Seveso inhabitants at the time of the accident could now be the starting point for promoting a green model of local development (interview with MM). Thus, the people of Seveso can "positively" identify themselves with the ICMESA event, confirming that this was not merely a painful tragedy but also a moment in which the community recognized the value of its attachment to the land, making it an active instrument of change. The Oak Wood is celebrated as a victory, a symbol of a community rooted in the territory and of an environmentalism dependent on this same attachment to the land, thereby opening it to broader issues of sustainability.

Yet this process of memory building, with its celebration of a community's attachment to its territory, conceals controversial issues. First of all, this attachment has not been a choice but an adaptive response for the affected population, justified largely by the economic and social difficulties people confronted in relocating elsewhere. Second, this adaptive response reduces the issue of dioxin's long-term health effects to personal problems or troubles, thereby accounting for the lack of collective effort to ask for a full disclosure of the disaster's damages. The controversial nature of this process of memory building is well expressed in the words of one of the committee members: "The memory we are writing here must be a *discreet memory,* respectful of personal suffering. In this process, we must try to avoid reopening old wounds, avoid forcing people to confront painful or sorrowful things they want to forget. We must avoid the nihilism that assumes recovery from this damage is impossible, stressing instead the resilience of civic community" (interview with FT).

From this perspective, one of the main problems that the Seveso disaster made collectively obvious is that health and environmental damages stemming from chemical plants in Brianza have never been adequately addressed or compensated, politically or symbolically. In spite of that, the health and environmental aftermath of industrial pollution, its costs, and the need for justice and reparation are issues that, just as in the past, the local community does not wish to address today.

Notes

1. Marco Armiero and Stefania Barca, *Storia dell'ambiente: Una introduzione* (Rome: Carocci, 2004), 156–64.

2. See Sheila Jasanoff, ed., *Learning from Disaster: Risk Management after Bhopal* (Philadelphia: University of Pennsylvania Press, 1994), esp. the introduction, 1–21.

3. See also Luc Boltanski and Eve Chiapello, *Le nouvel esprit du capitalisme* (Paris: Gallimard, 1999), translated by Gregory Elliott as *The New Spirit of Capitalism* (London: Verso Books, 2005); Luc Boltanski and Laurent Thévenot, *De la justification* (Paris: Gallimard, 1991), translated by Catherine Porter as *On Justification* (Princeton, NJ: Princeton University Press, 2005).

4. The sociological literature on industrial disasters is abundant but mainly oriented toward disasters as organizational phenomena; see, for instance, Charles Perrow, *Normal Accidents: Living with High Risk Technologies* (New York: Basic Books, 1984), and Diane Vaughan, "The Dark Side of Organizations: Mistake,

Misconduct, and Disaster," *Annual Review of Sociology* 25 (August 1999): 271–305. On industrial disasters as moral and political objects of analysis, see Barbara Allen, *Uneasy Alchemy: Citizens and Experts in Louisiana's Chemical Corridor Dispute* (Cambridge, MA: MIT Press, 2003), and Paul Jobin, *Maladies industrielles et renouveau syndical au Japon* (Paris: Editions de l'EHESS, 2006).

5. As pointed out by Francis Chateauraynaud and Didier Torny, catastrophes can be "localized" or "distributed," as was the case at Chernobyl; see Chateauraynaud and Torny, *Les sombres precurseurs: Une sociologie pragmatique de l'alerte et du risque* (Paris: Editions de l'EHESS, 1999), 48. See also Laurent Thévenot, Michael Moody, and Claudette LaFaye, "Forms of Valuing Nature: Arguments and Modes of Justification in Environmental Disputes," in *Rethinking Comparative Cultural Sociology: Repertoires of Evaluation in France and the United States*, ed. Michèle Lamont and Laurent Thévenot (New York: Cambridge University Press, 2000), 213–28.

6. Anthony Oliver-Smith and Susanna M. Hoffman, "Anthropology and the Angry Earth: An Overview," in *The Angry Earth: Disaster in Anthropological Perspective*, ed. Anthony Oliver-Smith and Susanna M. Hoffman (New York: Routledge, 1999), 11.

7. The analysis I develop in this contribution is a synthesis of my PhD dissertation about the collective responses to the Seveso disaster; see Centemeri, *Ritorno a Seveso: Il danno ambientale, il suo riconoscimento, la sua riparazione* (Milan: Bruno Mondadori Editore, 2006).

8. Bruna De Marchi, "Seveso: From Pollution to Regulation," *International Journal of Environment and Pollution* 7, no. 4 (1997): 526–37, and De Marchi, Silvio Funtowicz, and Jerome Ravetz, "Seveso: A Paradoxical Classic Disaster," in *The Long Road to Recovery: Community Responses to Industrial Disaster*, ed. James K. Mitchell (New York: United Nations University Press, 1996), 86–120.

9. Andrea Poggio, *Ambientalismo* (Milan: Bibliografica, 1996), 54. See also Mario Diani, *Isole nell'arcipelago: Il movimento ecologista in Italia* (Bologna: Il Mulino, 1988), 73–74, and Giovanni Lodi, "L'azione ecologista in Italia: Dal protezionismo storico alle Liste Verdi," in *La sfida verde: Il movimento ecologista in Italia*, ed. Roberto Biorcio and Giovanni Lodi (Padua: Liviana Editrice, 1998), 17–26.

10. David Hess, *Alternative Pathways in Science and Industry: Activism, Innovation, and the Environment in an Era of Globalization* (Cambridge, MA: MIT Press, 2007), esp. 171–234.

11. Arnaldo Bagnasco, *Tre Italie: La problematica territoriale dello sviluppo italiano* (Bologna: Il Mulino, 1977).

12. Relazione conclusiva della Commissione Parlamentare di inchiesta sulla fuga di sostanze tossiche avvenuta il 10 luglio 1976 nello stabilimento ICMESA

e sui rischi potenziali per la salute e per l'ambiente derivanti da attività industriali, Atti Parlamentari, VII legislatura, doc. XXIII, n.6, 1978; Jörg Sambeth, *Zwischenfall in Seveso* (Zurich: Unionsverlag, 2004).

13. Sergio Zedda, "La lezione della cloracne," in *ICMESA: Una rapina di salute, di lavoro e di territorio* (Milan: Mazzotta, 1976), 17–43.

14. Paolo Mocarelli, "Seveso: A Teaching Story," *Chemosphere* 43, nos. 4–7 (2001): 391–402.

15. Michel Callon, Yannick Barthe, and Pierre Lascoumes, *Agir dans un monde incertain: Essai sur la démocratie technique* (Paris: Seuil, 2001), translated by Graham Burchell as *Acting in an Uncertain World: An Essay on Technical Democracy* (Cambridge, MA: MIT Press, 2009), esp. 21–22.

16. Francesco Rocca, *I giorni della diossina,* supplement to *Quaderni Bianchi* 2 (1980) (Milan: Centro Studi A. Grandi, 1980).

17. Massimiliano Fratter, *Memorie da sotto il bosco* (Milan: Auditorium, 2006), 8–20.

18. Michel Dobry, *Sociologie des crises politiques* (Paris: Presse de la FNSP, 1986), 39–40.

19. Zone A (108 hectares, 736 inhabitants) was evacuated; Zone B (269 hectares, 4,600 inhabitants) was not evacuated, but inhabitants were forced to follow strict rules of conduct (including "abstention from procreation"); Zone of Respect (1,430 hectares, 31,800 inhabitants) was not evacuated, but inhabitants were forced to follow some precautionary rules of conduct.

20. Only in 1978, with Law 194, were voluntary pregnancy terminations legally admitted.

21. Marcella Ferrara, *Le donne di Seveso* (Rome: Editori Riuniti, 1977), 1–10.

22. Laura Conti, *Visto da Seveso: L'evento straordinario e l'ordinaria amministrazione* (Milan: Feltrinelli, 1977).

23. Centemeri, *Ritorno a Seveso,* 87–96. In 1976, the Italian government was based on a coalition of "national solidarity." This was a government led by the Christian Democratic Party with external support by the Communist Party. The need for this large coalition was in part explained by the growing terrorist menace to Italian institutions. On this, see Paul Ginsborg, *Storia d'Italia dal dopoguerra a oggi: Società e politica, 1943–1988* (Turin: Einaudi, 1989), 507–20, translated as *A History of Contemporary Italy: Society and Politics, 1943–1988* (New York: Penguin Books, 1990).

24. Conti, *Visto da Seveso,* 73–75.

25. The issue of Seveso's dioxin consequences on health is still controversial; see Pier Alberto Bertazzi, Dario Consonni, Silvia Bachetti, Maurizia Rubagotti, Andrea Baccarelli, Carlo Zocchetti, and Angela C. Pesatori, "Health Effects of Dioxin Exposure: A 20-Year Mortality Study," *American Journal of*

Epidemiology 153, no. 11 (2001): 1031–44, and Kyle Steenland, Pier Alberto Bertazzi, Andrea Baccarelli, and Manolis Kogevinas, "Dioxin Revisited: Developments since the 1997 IARC Classification of Dioxin as a Human Carcinogen," *Environmental Health Perspectives* 112, no. 13 (2004): 1265–68. Environmental recovery was aided by the rapid and generous compensation voluntarily offered by Roche to a large fraction of the damaged parties, both private and public, even though the compensation issue is still unresolved at Seveso; Centemeri, *Ritorno a Seveso*, 135–58. It is important to point out that Roche never admitted its responsibility for the disaster in a court of law.

26. Patrick Lagadec, *La civilisation du risque* (Paris: Seuil, 1981), chap. 1.

27. Josée van Eijndhoven, "Disaster Prevention in Europe," in *Learning from Disaster*, 113–32.

28. MD is a movement born in the 1970s that brings together industrial workers, citizens, scientists, and intellectuals. MD saw the importance of developing participatory forms of knowledge production for industrial health issues. On linked health-work issues in Italian industrial history, see Stefania Barca, "Health, Labor, and Social Justice: Environmental Costs of Italian Economic Growth, 1958–2000," *Agrarian Studies Colloquium 2005–2006*, Program in Agrarian Studies, Yale University, available at http://www.yale.edu/agrarianstudies/papers/26italiangrowth.pdf (accessed 5 May 2009).

29. Giovanni Bignami, "Se il seme non è morto: Giulio Maccacaro e il Movimento per la Salute," in *Atti del Convegno "Attualità del pensiero e dell'opera di Giulio A. Maccacaro"* (Milan: Cooperativa Centro per la Salute Giulio A. Maccacaro Editore, 1988), 215–27. On the importance of the mobilization of victims as a form of pressure leading to "external incentives" for political action with regard to health and environmental issues, see Michael R. Reich, "Mobilizing for Environmental Policy in Italy and Japan," *Comparative Politics* 16, no. 4 (1984): 379–402.

30. Giulio Maccacaro, "Seveso un crimine di pace," *Sapere* 796 (November–December 1976): 6.

31. Laurent Thévenot, "The Plurality of Cognitive Formats and Engagements: Moving between the Familiar and the Public," *European Journal of Social Theory* 10, no. 3 (2007): 409–24.

32. Comunione e Liberazione is a Catholic movement born in Italy in the 1950s and particularly active in Lombardy. One of its distinguishing traits is the development of *opere*, or social services made available through voluntary organizations. Relations between CL and the state have always been rather conflictual. In the opinion of CL, the state cannot and should not take part in society's organization: "In order for the Christian spirit to develop, the State must limit its presence in people lives," in Salvatore Abruzzese, *Comunione e Liberazione* (Rome: Laterza, 1991), 171.

33. Diani, *Isole,* 73–74.

34. The 1980s were marked by a deep change in Italian environmentalism as well as in other political cultures, as reported in Franco Livorsi, *Il mito della nuova terra: Cultura, idee e problemi dell'ambientalismo* (Milan: Giuffrè, 2000), chaps. 16 and 17. The specific characteristic of the Seveso activists is the strong link between feminism and environmentalism. This alliance is not something that exists at the national scale.

35. Libreria delle Donne di Milano, *Non credere di avere dei diritti* (Turin: Rosenberg and Sellier, 1987), chap. 1.

36. Legambiente is the most important environmentalist organization in Italy today. On the recent development of Italian environmentalism, see Donatella Della Porta and Mario Diani, *Movimenti senza protesta? L'ambientalismo in Italia* (Bologna: Il Mulino, 2004). Laura Conti (1921–93) was an important figure in the story of the Seveso accident. She was at the time a representative in the regional council for the Communist Party in Lombardy. Conti was a feminist activist and one of the first Italian environmentalist activists. On her life, see also the introduction to this volume, note 12.

37. Hess, *Alternative Pathways,* 173.

38. Paul Connerton, *How Societies Remember* (New York: Cambridge University Press: 1989), esp. chap. 3.

Landscape, Culture,

and Environmentalism

CHAPTER 12

A "Natural" Capitalism

Water and the Making of the Italian Industrial Landscape

Stefania Barca

> We need different ideas because we need different relationships.
> —Raymond Williams, *Ideas of Nature*

Capitalism in the Apennines

Italy's many waterfalls cascade down more than six thousand kilometers of rivers and streams that drain the country's mostly mountainous and hilly terrain.[1] This hydrologic characteristic, along with a substantial lack of mineral resources, has played a crucial role in the development of energy systems used by Italian industry, namely, a historical reliance on water-power. The first industrial survey, completed in 1911, suggested the importance of hydraulic energy at that time: water occupied 59 percent of all the power potential installed in factories, and 11 percent of this waterpower came from hydromechanical engines (both vertical wheels and turbines); the rest came from hydroelectricity. Though lacking comparable data for the nineteenth century, we can readily argue that before hydroelectricity became available in the 1880s, virtually all the waterpower used in industry came from mechanical energy developed directly along rivers.[2]

Thus, the making of Italian industrial capitalism can be traced to the Alpine and Apennine valleys, where textiles, paper, iron, and other products were processed with the aid of hydraulic machines. Beginning in the early nineteenth century, industrial entrepreneurs appeared in a number of these valleys, where they accomplished the gradual concentration and mechanization of the production process, thereby creating the factory system. At the end of that century, Italian mills began to replace hydromechanical technology with hydroelectric technology, a transformation that required several decades to be completed. Starting in the first decade of the twentieth century, big hydroelectric projects were developed to exploit so-called white coal and to tame the torrents of the Apennines.[3] But it was only after World War II, with the availability of cheap imported oil, that the Italian industrial sector substantially shifted to fossil energy. This long energy transition, from water to fossil fuels, is the main ecological feature of Italian industrialization, yet its implications in socioenvironmental terms have not been fully explored.[4]

In the following pages, I argue that by viewing the industrialization of Italy from the perspective of river valleys, we can get a much deeper and more comprehensive idea of what the new mode of production meant in terms of society-nature relationships. Looking beyond the steam paradigm and giving far greater importance to ecological relations of production, we can see an Industrial Revolution taking shape in the country,[5] as the hydraulic machines in the mountain valleys became the core of a new mode of production: the factory system.[6]

Looking for data on the increase of energy consumption and national income and having found them only at the end of the nineteenth century—when coal imports steadily increased—economic historians have generally dismissed the idea that the waterpower era was a stage of the Industrial Revolution in Italy.[7] In this essay, I offer a counterargument to this interpretation. Starting from the striking quantitative importance of waterpower for Italian factories, I will look at the watermill—what I call the "machine in the river"[8]—as the locus of the Italian Industrial Revolution, considering the latter as a process involving the mutual transformation of the mode of production *and* of society-nature relationships. This dual process materialized at different moments in different places throughout the nineteenth century; thus, it is quite meaningless to use the term *revolution* in a national sense, also considering that the Italian nation-state dates only from 1860. Rather, if we look at the industrialization process from the perspective of the many different *places* in the Italian Alps and Apennines where it took shape, then we will see that the socioecological transformations linked to the emerging water-powered factory system had revolutionary characters. This revolution involved three interrelated processes: (1) the appropriation of water, that is, its incorporation within the capitalist property system in the form of mechanical energy; (2) the mechanization of labor, that is, its disciplining by means of harnessing it to the hydraulic machine; and (3) the invention of an industrial narrative, that is, a new discourse of society-nature relations.

I will focus here on the third point, for the aesthetic and the landscapes of waterpower were essential, though usually neglected, elements of the way in which the Industrial Revolution has been perceived. The image of the waterwheel, for example, immediately evokes the idea of a traditional, even idyllic rural world, in which it appears as a seminatural feature of the landscape.[9] Watermills are thus not associated with the "satanic mills" that formed the imagery of the English Industrial Revolution or with the landscape that "carboniferous" capitalism produced.[10] Conversely, a narrative of the Industrial Revolution unproblematically linked to steam technology is obviously ill equipped to account for the waterpower story. It is a particularly challenging and unusual mental exercise to associate the waterwheel with long hours of labor, with the bodies of women and children working under the incessant pounding of waterpower-driven machines, with the loss of a direct relationship to nature as a means of livelihood and the loss of control over one's own physical work—in sum, with the social ecology of the nineteenth-century factory. To do this, we first must deconstruct the cultural and the aesthetic categories that were built around waterpower and served to obscure the real nature of the transformation.

In this essay, I focus on a crucial aspect of early industrial capitalism: the making of its ecological consciousness,[11] seen from the vantage point of one of the earliest locations of the Italian factory system, the Liri Valley. This case reveals how the political-economic vision of the river—as a flow of mechanical energy and thus as natural capital[12]—mixed with visions of the landscape, giving rise to a particular narrative of industrialization. Beyond being places for the making of industrial capitalism and political economy, Italian river valleys were also the loci of poetry, painting, archaeology, natural history studies, literature, and travel. At a time when disciplinary boundaries were beginning to separate these different visions, the emerging narrative of Italian river valley landscapes acted as a unifying discourse, developing interdependently with the discourse of political economy and so contributing to a distinct ecological consciousness of industrial capitalism. To support this hypothesis, I consider the narrative of the industrial landscape as it emerged in the Liri Valley, where it reflected a pastoral ideal of industrialization, suggesting the total compatibility between nature and progress.

The Machine in the River: Naturalizing Capitalism in the Liri Valley

The Liri-Fibreno basin, located at the northern border of the Kingdom of the Two Sicilies, was one of the internal valleys of the Apennines where waterpower was used to convert domestic productions into a factory system. The industrial transformation of the Liri Valley began in the early nineteenth century, under the influence of Napoleonic rule and of antifeudal reformism, which had returned running waters to ancient Roman law, classifying them as no one's property.[13] Freed from the fetters of feudalism, water resources became an open access resource, and they were individually appropriated by landowners and mill owners along the riverbanks. As in other early industrial areas, the private appropriation of the river soon revealed its ecological contradictions, in three interrelated spheres: (1) rather than enhancing the overall efficiency of the economic system, water enclosures produced a high level of litigation and high transaction costs; (2) they also produced inefficiency in energy use because of overcrowding and obstructing the riverbed; and (3) they increased the frequency and destructiveness of the floods experienced in the two factory towns of Sora and Isola Liri.[14] Concerning the last observation, I will mention briefly that in the first half of the nineteenth century, the upper basin was suffering intense deforestation due to both political and demographic factors. In earlier decades, capitalism in its agrarian form had been spreading through the kingdom, leaving in its wake an intensification of environmental instability.[15] As a result, when it arrived in the factory towns of Sora and Isola Liri, the river already carried with it a huge quantity of deposits derived from increased soil erosion in the mountains and upper valleys. But in the valley, the river found industrial capitalism with its system of water enclosures—individual properties defined by weirs, stone walls, and tree branches located within the riverbed, which created an environment particularly favorable to obstructing the watercourse and overflowing. Dozens of major inundations were recorded in the nineteenth century, and ordinary floods occurred every year in the rainy season, so that the two towns, separated by a short five miles of river course, came to live in a permanent state of near disaster.[16]

This story of deforestation, water enclosures, and floods that took place over roughly a hundred years involved yet another story, albeit much less easily discernible: the shaping of a new ecological consciousness, dominated by the industrial capitalist vision of water. This new consciousness was itself the dialectic product of changing social relations and of a particular landscape, that of the river. My argument is that in the case of the

Liri Valley, the new ecological consciousness was shaped in important ways by the emergence of a narrative of the industrial landscape that hid the very existence of floods, a clear manifestation of capitalism's ecological contradictions.

Located along the road between Naples and Rome, not far from the Montecassino Abbey, and also being Cicero's birthplace, the Liri Valley was a popular destination for travelers, who left a series of descriptions sometimes accompanied by illustrations, or *vedute,* of the Isola Liri waterfalls. These were a major attraction to visitors, and they became the literary icon of the district of Sora. The Swiss naturalist Carl Ulisses von Salis-Marschlins, for example—who arrived in the valley in the very year of the French Revolution—depicted the local landscape as dominated by the feudal castle erected on a cliff between two waterfalls, one of which was vertical and the other inclined and both surrounded by nicely cultivated hills and deciduous woods. The Liri was described as completing the very beautiful scenery with the sinuosity of its course, and the surrounding countryside appeared as one of those delightful places whose beauty was rare even in Italy.[17] Regarding the local society, the traveler noted its quiet and idyllic life, complaining only about the missed opportunities that the poor road to Naples presented for the domestic wool industry. A similar veduta is the one that Abbot Domenico Romanelli received in 1819 from a local painter while traveling from Naples to Montecassino, which he noted as perhaps the most graceful image of the kingdom.

When this second traveler arrived in the Liri Valley, the area had already undergone fundamental political, social, and environmental changes. First, the duchy of Sora had been de-feudalized through a royal decree in 1796, with the express purpose of removing its waters from baronial control and developing an industrial district out of them.[18] At the same time and for the same purpose, the road to Naples was under construction. Waterpower had become a concession of the town corporation, which had rented the fulling mills to the wool merchants.[19] Within a few years, the French army entered the kingdom (in 1797), the Neapolitan Jacobins carried out a revolution and issued a glorious though short-lived republic (in 1799), the Bourbon monarchy was restored (and the Jacobins hanged), and then the French came again to rule over the country for ten years (from 1806 to 1815). In the meantime, being located at the northern border, the district of Sora went through an incredibly explosive period of both revolutionary and counterrevolutionary violence and environmental devastation.[20] Soon after, in 1809, the first mechanized paper mill started working in Isola Liri, followed quickly by many other wool and paper factories.

Abbot Romanelli's journey is in fact one of the earlier testimonies of the emerging industrial landscape in nineteenth-century Italy. After reaching the town of Sora, the abbot described an "active and industrious population, which makes an easy living from the manufacturing of wool and from agriculture." Nevertheless, his attention was mainly focused on "the greatest and most impressive sight" of the waterfall and, in general, on the beauty of the place, which appeared to him as an enchanted isle, with abundant gardens and citrus orchards, surrounded by a variegated landscape. He then visited the Fibreno River, in search of the ruins of Cicero's birthplace (stopping to contemplate scholarly questions about those ruins), but in walking on the road between Isola and Sora, along the Liri's eastern bank, the author was forced to stop and contemplate an unexpected landscape. Alongside the cultivated fields and orchards, he saw "many new houses built up for the woollen mills, canals and weirs, many factories of useful and sought-after arts." After coming to the site where the Liri and Fibreno rivers merge, he recorded a surprising discovery: before joining with the Liri, the Fibreno splits into two branches, one of which splits again to form two small islands. On one island stands the ancient monastery of San Domenico. This was Romanelli's original destination, as the monastery allegedly covers Cicero's villa, but the place now held a completely different attraction: "I stayed for a while contemplating more new wool mills which had been built up there"—the author writes—"and then headed to the other small island, called Carnello, where I first stayed to examine the paper- and fulling-mills which had been erected there, and then the ancient ruins."[21]

There, in the century's second decade, an industrial landscape was taking shape within and alongside the agrarian and the literary. The mills that the abbot saw at Carnello belonged to one of the earliest industrial complexes in the valley, a paper factory whose original 1812 location was inside a former convent (Santa Maria delle Forme), endowed with its own water rights from the Fibreno River, mostly at the service of the monks' grinding mills. A few years earlier, the original plant had been enlarged by adding some structures to the small isle located in the middle of the river. The woolen mills that the abbot visited on the isle of San Domenico were also once part of a monastery; the same can be said of another early factory in the valley, established in 1816 inside the former convent of San Francesco near Isola Liri.

The peculiar locations of some of the earliest factories in the valley provide a clue about something revolutionary that had occurred in the area, something that the abbot did not find necessary to remind his reader but that was nevertheless at the very origins of the Liri's early industrialization—namely, the suppression of several monastic orders that formerly had enjoyed the use of the waters to grind their grain and whose buildings, waterworks, and rights had been transferred to entrepreneurs. A major shift in water rights was thus at the origin of the Industrial Revolution in the Liri-Fibreno basin. Previously subject to the control of monastic orders and the town corporation, the valley's waters had—according to law—become "freely" accessible to the public, that is, to whomever could afford the necessary investments to make them a source of industrial power.

Despite Romanelli's representation of the mills as a natural feature of the landscape, industrial capitalism in the Liri Valley had indeed stemmed from violent and sudden changes, involving war and a revolutionary shift in law and institutions. It had been preceded by the passage of soldiers, foreign and domestic, and of bandits; it followed fights, death, and the devastation of landscape. This space had participated in the broader struggle of the Napoleonic Wars, and the result was a new imperial domain, whose main consequence for the local lifestyle was the introduction of economic liberties. Those liberties, however, which entailed the liberalization of land and water, had broad and revolutionary environmental consequences.

The importance of this shift for the economy of the area, and potentially of the nation, was anticipated and celebrated by the highest authorities in the Kingdom of Naples, well after the end of French rule, and it was

Fig. 12.1. Raffaele Carelli, "Cascata del Fibreno." From Domenico Cuciniello and Lorenzo Bianchi, *Viaggio pittorico nel Regno delle due Sicilie dedicato a Sua Maestà il re Francesco primo* (Naples: SEM 1971 [1829]), 35. Courtesy of Ministero per i beni e le attività culturali, Biblioteca Nazionale di Napoli, Sezione Lucchesi Palli

considered a progressive change by other contemporary observers. One eloquent testimony to this belief is a pictorial description of Isola Liri published in 1830. The authors of the description, commenting about an illustration of the town,[22] emphasized the wealth that falling water represented to "civilized nations, who, running those waters to their own benefit, take of them [. . .] as a power source for a thousand kinds of machines."[23] Progress, said the authors, was the very ability to harness a river's great potential to "increase industry and wealth and prosperity." The rising aura of energy, grounded in this particular Italian landscape, was well represented in a paragraph that followed: the authors depicted the Liri and Fibreno rivers as "spreading with their humours so much power and energy and prosperity" that it had become impossible to say if their fame was linked to their history and "the natural beauties of which they form such a great part" or to "the maximum utility they bring to the peoples that live along their banks."

The authors continued describing the course of the Liri down to the isle of Carnello, where, "running among gentle falls, it then narrows to a little pond, from where, splitting in several canals, it gives shape to very graceful small isles, joined by country bridges." The amenities of the place merited a careful description:

> All this place looks like a very precious garden, made from art less than from nature; and its main ornament is a long, twisty, delightful boulevard, offering one of those promenades that nowadays are called *romantic*. Thousands of variegated and pretty sights are enjoyed from it; but not one equals that of the so called *Cascatelle* [Little Falls]: before passing through the canal of Le Forme, as if announcing its big fall, here the Liri playfully breaks among declivous rocks, laying with peculiar irregularity in the shape of five stairs, among trees and leaved bushes. The water, pushed back and forth, rumbling, foaming and spreading in white flakes, finally merges in a large, short and regular fall.[24]

The authors were creating here an icon of the national path to industrialization, one in which art and nature, history and progress were completely merged and could not be separated:

> And, as if the beauty should never, in this lucky district, be separated from the useful, those falling waters have already been

moving the wheels and cylinders of the wool factory that currently honours the ancient palace of the Duchies of Sora, which sold it, along with all their possessions, to the Government, and the Government gave it to the nation's industry.[25]

In this concluding passage, we finally see reference to those changes in power that gave birth to the process of industrialization in the valley. What the authors called the "nation's industry" was in fact the factory owned by Gioacchino Manna, one of the first and more powerful industrialists in the valley. This narrative of the industrial landscape therefore acknowledged the play of social forces within the local environment. In its own way, it helped to legitimize the current assets of power by locating that power within a natural order that had been restored by politics. Rescued from feudal possession and redirected with governmental wisdom toward the best possible use, private industry, the Liri and Fibreno could realize their maximum beauty *and* utility, thereby contributing to the glory of the nation.

In this sense, the industrial landscape narrative was also one of political economy, since it appropriated the language of that discipline and translated it into a broader social discourse of economic and environmental change. In 1837, for example, the *Poliorama Pittoresco* (a popular journal of culture in the capital city) published a description of Isola Liri that was also a manifesto of economic liberalism. Inserted within a section devoted to travel reports from across the kingdom, the article started with the usual glorious account of the waterfall and the landscape, depicted as a "sunny valley of pleasant hills;" yet this description became merely a prelude to the "hollow and humdrum sound, which [was] the roar of the falling water and the incessant beating of fulling mills, processing paper, cloths and other works in this district." Perhaps for the first time in the century, the beauty of the waterfall was linked not so much to its bucolic and natural character as to its industrial and artificial one. Quoting Lord Byron to describe the cataract as a sublime "hell of waters," the author then depicted the falls as the natural backdrop for a "very commendable town with an extremely industrious and active population."[26]

The article drew rather contradictory images of memory and change, romantic ecstasy and industrialist production. In the workings of the paper and woolen mills, the author saw "the principles of political economy, *this sublime science* of the eighteenth century, accomplishing their sacred scope." Testimony to these changes was the "ancient tower" (or Ducal Palace), which was "not a stage for oppression anymore, but a sacred, honourable workshop, where industry and mechanical arts combine in the manufacture of paper and cloth." The author then wandered through the "labyrinth of stairs and rooms, under the dark and subterranean vaults where there are noisy splashes of water and echoes of the monotonous fulling machines." And then, to enjoy the contrast, he headed to the base of the second falls where the water, with "its fury and foam lost, flows through a bed of solitary and silent sand." There, at the end of this literary tour, Isola Liri became "one of the most romantic lands of our Kingdom."[27]

The language of political economy and the romantic sublime intermingled again in this text, to forge a new vision of the landscape that narrated a story of progress: from feudalism to industry, from the idyllic rural landscape of the past to the industrious town where capitalism could be finally celebrated within the factory walls. And yet, no real contradiction could be seen within this vision, beyond the aesthetic contrasts so attractive to a romantic sensibility. The beauty of nature was enhanced by its incorporation within the factory system, not by its association with an idealized past. The most striking feature of this account was its ability to "naturalize" both social and environmental changes that occurred in this place, hiding the oppressive character of industrialization toward nature and humans. The Ducal Palace, which once symbolized feudal power, was now a stage for a more modern form of oppression, that of industrial labor. This forced hundreds of women, men, and children to follow the rhythm of that same monotonous pounding of water-powered machines that our author found so enthralling. Furthermore, water itself was subjected to a process of increasing domination, since this palace was only one of dozens of mechanized sites concentrated along a short stretch of the river basin for taking advantage of the local availability of waterpower.

We can detect this vision of political economy through the quiet and reassuring language of the landscape narrative in numerous other secondary literary texts produced in the same period. In 1845, on the occasion of an international conference of scientists held in Naples, the economist Matteo De Augustinis took this process of transliteration to its apex, defining Isola Liri as "the Manchester of the Kingdom of the Two Siciles."[28] His description of the valley, for the benefit of his foreign colleagues, was a celebration of the industrial landscape in its most artificial form and a powerful exercise in environmental mystification: for him, the valley was simply "a huge and whole industry, so many are the buildings and workshops, and many are the mechanized factories." "Noise and sprinkling water, . . . the creaking of machines and wheels, the sight of exploited water, which has *become a thousand colours by the variety of dyes;* the encounter with endless wools and cloths, with rags, with piled up papers; the encumbrance of carts and barrows in all the streets, in all directions; everything you see shows that you are in *the valley of labor and industry, that once was of leisure, ease, and study.*"[29]

Here again, we recognize the development, though more advanced than the preceding one, of the progressive narrative of environmental and social transformation. In two powerful sentences, the author managed to transform the polluting effects of paper mills into a sign of increased ability to dominate nature, imbuing it with the colors of the new productive system and sanctioning the definitive closure of former leisure while replacing it with work.

In translating the ideas of political economy into the narrative of the industrial landscape, water was also subject to an increasing process of dematerialization, one that progressively transformed it into an abstract, mechanistic, and atomized commodity. The Liri and Fibreno rivers were now compared to the gold mines of the New World, being "in the scientific terms of economics" more valuable than the latter.[30] In the words of the German historian Ferdinand Gregorovius, who traveled through Italy in the late 1850s, the paper manufacturer Carlo Lefebvre arrived in town without means and "by carving pure gold from the force of water, transformed the Liri's riverbanks into an Eldorado," to gain the title of count and to leave his son Ernesto "factories and millions." The language of the industrial sublime was then employed again for describing the "magnificent and gracious buildings" of Lefebvre's two paper mills and the garden of his villa along the Liri riverbank. Enriched with canals and resembling "a little Tivoli and paradise of nymphs,"[31] this garden was in fact a celebration of the industrial mastering of water in its Edenic form.[32]

Gregorovius's depiction was probably the epitome of the industrial landscape narrative in the Liri Valley. The river basin was, to his eyes, an enchanted site, and the Liri "developing its green water amongst high poplars" was compared, "quiet and sleeping," to one of Germany's rivers. Its banks were "enchanting, melodic, sunny and dreamlike"; by contrast, the "quiet and idyllic" town of Sora, "now so modern," was described as "having a good road, an industrial life, an animated traffic."[33] Traveling along the Liri toward Isola, the author discovered the presence of an industrial elite, signified by the "delightful villas and their industrial workshops looking through the trees."[34] Although the traveler was mostly attracted by the beauty of the aquatic landscape, the sound of the waterfalls, the sight of innumerable canals brimming with water, and the "marvellous vegetation typical of southern countries," he nevertheless noted how the plentiful water running around Isola gave power to many industries, forming "a robust colony of factory workers," and thus producing a beneficent aura throughout the district. "Blessed by Nature, Isola will always be the first industrial town of the area."

Gregorovius's celebration of the place was likely the result of his romantic sensibility for contrasts, with which Isola Liri's industrial landscape was so well endowed. His enthusiasm about the place might as well have arisen by contrasting it with the desolate and malarial landscape of the Roman Campagna, which travelers had to pass when entering the Liri Valley from the north. Nevertheless, what matters here is the ideological perspective that Gregorovius shared with all other authors: the need to build an acceptable social space where history was not canceled, where nature was not denigrated but put to its appropriate use, where industry did not represent a satanic agency but a virtuous path toward public good. These landscapes had in common a pastoral ideal of industrialization that was in beautiful harmony with the cultural and natural life of Italy. Factories and agriculture were included in the same view of one river valley, in which ruins, poetry, and literary memories were all encompassed, and the observer could contemplate history as the passing of time from one form of civilization to the next. This was a place where there was no room for exploiting either human labor or the natural world and where not even the alienation of people from the environment that sustained them seemed to have yet occurred. This was a land in which the appropriation of rivers by mill owners was a wise achievement of modernity, conducive to prosperity for all.

WHILE INDUSTRIAL capitalism functioned by mechanizing both labor and nature, the Liri Valley's narrative followed the opposite path, attempting to close the circle between nature and technology. Through both literary and visual art, this narrative was a *naturalization* of the machine. It was the false consciousness of the valley's industrial capitalism that produced the discursive unity between human progress and natural endowment— between man and nature—at the very same time that industry was promoting the complete alienation of one from the other.

Industrial capitalism justified using nature for violent and potentially revolutionary social change while presenting itself as a mechanical manifestation of political economy's "natural" laws.[35] And yet, this water-powered, "organic" industrialization had its social costs. The archives are brimming with documents that explain destructive floods as the consequences of deforestation and the private appropriation of the river. The ecological contradiction of early industrial capitalism, with its ferocious denial of externalities, was thus clearly apparent in the valley at the same time that the narrative of the industrial landscape was being invented. It would produce, of course, a new narrative by exposing the negative effects of economic change on both the social and natural environments. The vision of the nature-society relationship would become dichotomized in two completely distinct and noncommunicating narratives: one of harmony and wealth, destined to legitimate economic progress that was also socially and politically acceptable; the other of misery and destruction, directed to solicit intervention by the public powers.

To understand the ecological consciousness of Italian industrialism, a key consideration must be the question of energy. Compared to the early English industrial landscape, the Italian equivalent similarly hosted water-powered mills, but it differed in many other respects. Insofar as there was no real Manchester in Italy, to find one there became a myth. Unlike the American locomotive in the garden, this Italian machine did not seem like a counterforce, resembling the violence of industry "as a memento of reality,"[36] but it was an enduring part of it, harmoniously inserted within the river as a sign of how humans can live with nature while using it, of how capitalism and nature can be unified by the pastoral-industrial landscape. Moreover, the machine belonged to a mill that was often a remnant of the past—as a feudal palace or a former monastery—symbolizing how work and nature can be harmonized with history as well.

Italian industrialization took place in riverscapes that did *not* resemble satanic places. Although this was initially true for England and other industrializing nations, the pastoral view of industrialization in Italy remained a definite possibility for a much longer time. Eventually, this image was broken by the hydroelectric plant, with its intrusive and highly disturbing technology of concrete dams and canals, its long and monotonous power lines, its dispossessing people from the land, submerging and transforming the landscape while requiring huge amounts of labor carried out under hard conditions and with risky materials.[37] This was a brave new world, one that required a new narrative and new poetry. From one of harmony and pastoralism, Italy's industrial landscape was reinvented to become one of conquest—the "conquest of power."[38]

Notes

1. The total area of the country is 301,338 square kilometers, 75 percent of which (nearly 225,000 square kilometers) comprises mountains and hills.

2. See Carlo Bardini, *Senza carbone nell'età del vapore* (Milan: Mondadori, 1998), and Andrea Giuntini, ed., "Fonti statistiche," in *Storia dell'industria elettrica in Italia*, vols. 1–3 (Rome: Laterza, 1992–95), 829–88, 805–70, and

1157–1258. A more recent calculation of energy consumption in Italy is available in Paolo Malanima, *Energy Consumption in Italy in the 19th and 20th Centuries: A Statistical Outline* (Naples: ISSM-CNR, 2006).

3. See Ornella Selvafolta, "La costruzione del paesaggio idroelettrico nelle regioni settentrionali," and Giovanni Bruno, "Paesaggi elettrici meridionali," both in *Paesaggi elettrici,* ed. Rosario Pavia (Venice: Marsilio, 1998), 41–71 and 73–95. On the initial phase of the hydroelectrical industry in Italy, see Giorgio Mori, ed., *Storia dell'industria elettrica in Italia,* vol. 1, *Le origini, 1882–1914* (Rome: Laterza 1992).

4. Most environmental histories of Italian industry focus on the twentieth century. See, for example, Simone Neri Serneri's essay in this volume. Among the studies devoted to the twentieth-century Italian industries, see: Simone Neri Serneri, ed., "Industria e ambiente," special issue of *I Frutti di Demetra: Bollettino di Storia e Ambiente* 15 (2007); Pier Paolo Poggio, ed., *Una storia ad alto rischio: L'ACNA e la Valle Bormida* (Turin: Gruppo Abele, 1996); Andrea F. Saba and Edgar H. Meyer, eds., *Storia ambientale: Una nuova frontiera storiografica* (Milan: Teti, 2001); Marino Ruzzenenti, *Un secolo di cloro e . . . PCB: Storia delle industrie Caffaro di Brescia* (Milan: Jaca Book, 2001); Simone Neri Serneri, *Incorporare la natura: Storie ambientali del Novecento* (Rome: Carocci, 2005); Salvo Ascione and Gabriella Corona, "Activités humaines et resources naturelle à Naples au XXe siècle: L'exemple du complexe industriel de Bagnoli," in *The Modern Demon: Pollution in Urban and Industrial European Societies,* eds. Christoph Bernhardt and Geneviève Massard-Guilbaud (Clermont-Ferrand, France: Presses Universitaires Blaise-Pascal, 2002), 351–76.

5. I use the expression *Industrial Revolution* as a synonym for *industrialization* in order to emphasize the revolutionary character of the transformation in terms of society-nature relations.

6. On industrialization as a new system of ecological relations, see Ted Steinberg, *Nature Incorporated: Industrialization and the Waters of New England* (New York: Cambridge University Press, 1991), 1–20.

7. A recent reformulation of this thesis is in Paolo Malanima, "Alle origini della crescita in Italia, 1820–1913," *Rivista di Storia Economica* 3 (December 2006): 307–30.

8. This image is inspired by Leo Marx's seminal work in technology and culture, *The Machine in the Garden: Technology and the Pastoral Ideal in America* (New York: Oxford University Press, 1964).

9. See, for example, David Nye, *America as Second Creation: Technology and Narratives of New Beginnings* (Cambridge, MA: MIT Press, 2005), 146. On the difference between water and coal landscapes in Britain, see also Barrie S. Trinder, *The Making of the Industrial Landscape* (London: J. M. Dent and Sons, 1982), 170–244.

10. The concept of "carboniferous capitalism" is in Lewis Mumford, *Technics and Civilizations* (New York: Harcourt, Brace, 1934), 156–58.

11. I use the concept as elaborated in Carolyn Merchant, *Ecological Revolutions: Nature, Gender and Science in New England* (Chapel Hill: University of North Carolina Press, 1989), 1–26.

12. For a discussion of this concept in relation to waterpower, see Stefania Barca, "Enclosing the River: Industrialisation and the 'Property Rights' Discourse in the Liri Valley (South of Italy), 1806–1916," *Environment and History* 13, no. 1 (2007): 3–23.

13. See *Bollettino delle sentenze della Commissione Feudale*, vol. 2, 611, Archivio di Stato di Napoli (hereafter ASN), Naples.

14. For a more detailed account, see Barca, "Enclosing the River," 14–15.

15. See Emilio Sereni, *Storia del paesaggio agrario italiano* (Rome: Laterza, 1962), translated by Robert Burr Litchfield as *History of the Italian Agricultural Landscape* (Princeton, NJ: Princeton University Press, 1997), 259–88; Piero Bevilacqua and Manlio Rossi Doria, *Le bonifiche in Italia dal '700 ad oggi* (Rome: Laterza, 1984), esp. the introduction; John R. McNeill, *The Mountains of the Mediterranean World: An Environmental History* (New York: Cambridge University Press, 1992), 236–59. On nineteenth-century deforestation in Abruzzo's mountains, upstream from the Liri Valley, see Marco Armiero, *Il territorio come risorsa: Comunità, economie e istituzioni nei boschi abruzzesi (1806–1860)* (Naples: Liguori, 1999), 110–20.

16. See ASN, Ministero dell'Interno (Ministry of the Interior), 2° Inv., 530; Archivio di Stato di Caserta (hereafter ASC), Intendenza Borbonica (hereafter IB), Affari comunali, 15; ASN, MI, Consigli Provinciali in Terra di Lavoro, 4054; ASC IB, Ponti e strade (bonifiche), 44, 183; ASC, Prefettura Prima Serie, 188, 2105; ASC, Prefettura Prima Serie, cat. XXII, 253, 2547; ASC, Prefettura Prima Serie, cat. XXII, 188, 2463; ASC, Prefettura Prima Serie, cat. XXII, 253, 2547; ASC IB, Ponti e strade (bonifiche), 44, 183.

17. Carl Ulysses von Salis Marschlins, *Travels through Various Provinces of the Kingdom of Naples in 1789* (London: T. Cadell, 1795), 294–97.

18. See Felicita De Negri, "La 'reintegra' al demanio dello Stato di Sora: Un momento del dibattito sulla feudalità nel regno di Napoli alla fine del '700," in Archivio di Stato di Frosinone, *Viabilità e territorio nel Lazio meridionale: Persistenze e mutamenti fra '700 e '800* (Frosinone: Archivio di Stato, 1992), 73–93. I am grateful to Ferdinando Corradini, who alerted me to this publication.

19. See ASC, IB, Ponti e strade, 44, 81 (1807?).

20. See Ferdinando Pistilli, *Descrizione storico-filologica delle antiche e moderne città e castelli esistenti accosto de' fiumi Liri e Fibreno* (Naples: Stamperia Francese 1824), 17–25.

21. See Domenico Romanelli, *Viaggio da Napoli a Montecassino ed alla celebre cascata d'acqua nell'isola di Sora* (Naples: A. Trani, 1819) , 122–23 (my translation).

22. Raffaele Carelli, "Cascata del Fibreno," in *Viaggio pittorico nel Regno delle due Sicilie dedicato a Sua Maestà il re Francesco primo,* ed. Domenico Cuciniello and Lorenzo Bianchi (Naples: SEM 1971 [1829]), 35.

23. Ibid., 34 (my translation).

24. Ibid., 36.

25. Ibid.

26. A[ntonio] Fazzini, "Isola di Sora," *Poliorama Pittoresco* 1 (1836): 91 (my translation).

27. Ibid.

28. Matteo de Augustinis, "Della valle del Liri e delle sue industrie," in Accademia Pontaniana, *Agli scienziati d'Italia del settimo congresso* (Naples: Stamperia e Cartiera del Fibreno, 1845), 73–75.

29. Ibid. (emphasis added).

30. R[affaele] Zarlenga, "Brevi considerazioni sul progetto di rendere navigabile il fiume Liri," *Poliorama Pittoresco* 15 (1854): 10–11 (my translation).

31. Ferdinand Gregorovius, *La campagna romana* (Rome: U. Carboni, 1906), quoted in Achille Lauri, *Sora, Isola Liri e dintorni* (Sora: Vincenzo D'Amico, 1914), 9–11(my translation).

32. On this aspect, see, for example, Myrna Santiago, *The Ecology of Oil: Environment, Labor, and the Mexican Revolution, 1900–1938* (New York: Cambridge University Press, 2006), 15–60; Steinberg, *Nature Incorporated,* 75–76. On the Italian villas and garden architecture, see Dianne Harris, *The Nature of Authority: Villa Culture, Landscape and Representation in Eighteenth-Century Lombardy* (University Park: Pennsylvania State University Press, 2003).

33. Gregorovius, *La campagna,* quoted in Lauri, *Sora,* 11.

34. Ibid., 108.

35. On this aspect, see Raymond Williams, "Ideas of Nature," in *Problems of Materialism and Culture,* ed. Raymond Williams (London: Verso, 1980), 67–85.

36. Marx, *Machine in the Garden,* 26.

37. For a beautiful narrative on these aspects of dam construction, see Richard White, *The Organic Machine* (New York: Hill and Wang, 1995), 59–63.

38. The expression is from Francesco Saverio Nitti, *La conquista della forza* (Turin: Roux e Viarengo, 1905). On this subject, see Stefania Barca, "Running Italian Waters: Hydraulics and Water Law in the Age of Industrialization," in *Views from the South: Environmental Stories from the Mediterranean World (19th–20th Centuries),* ed. Marco Armiero (Naples: ISSM-CNR, 2006), 23–36.

CHAPTER 13

Nationalizing the Mountains

Natural and Political Landscapes in World War I

Marco Armiero

> Here we are
> As leaves
> On the trees
> In autumn
>
> —Giuseppe Ungaretti, *Soldati*

Borders

One of the most emblematic images of the Alps is Hannibal leading his elephants across the mountains to descend upon Rome.[1] Since then, the Alpine mountain range has been crossed and contested many times. It has been celebrated as the sacred frontier of Italy and fortified as a rampart against invaders. The Italian nationalization of the mountains was not accomplished merely by the sportsmen and mountain climbers who conquered their slopes; it was also a military occupation undertaken to wrest them from the control of foreign occupiers or rebels. The geographic rhetoric of the Alps as the bastion of Italy developed smoothly into anthropological rhetoric about hardy mountaineers standing guard over the nation. This theme was especially popular in the early twentieth century, a time of confrontation between opposing nationalisms and patriotisms when the Alps ceased to be the playground of Europe and became a theater of World War I.[2]

In this essay, I argue that the war changed the Alpine landscape both with words and with bombs, creating a hybrid environment in which the nationalization of nature was particularly strong. By this, I do not mean to claim that there is no nature outside our world of words and discourses,[3] that there is no distinction between artifact and nature.[4] I share Donald Worster's preoccupation with the risks inherent in discursive reductionism. My point is not to deny the existence of a mountain nature. Monte Bianco and a forest, a cemetery and a glacier, a pasture and a monument represent very different combinations—and percentages—of nature and artifact. As Worster argues, nature is at once independent from us and created by us.[5] Rather than trying to measure how much of a given landscape is natural or artificial, I am interested in analyzing how nature and culture have interacted in shaping the landscape itself as well as the social practices of looking at it and using it. It seems to me that the experience of war, especially of the Great War, with its mobilization of masses of people, is an extraordinarily rich case study for understanding cultural perceptions of nature as collective attitudes and practices.[6] In other words, rather than looking at nature as discourse, I am intrigued by the opposite perspective, that is, by the fact that there has always been a lot of nature in the discourse about national identity and the practice of nationalizing space, memory, and people. One could say that in the pages that follow, I am striving to "materialize" discourses rather than to "dematerialize" nature.[7]

Memories

The nationalization and patriotic use of mountains was much more straightforward along the northern borders of Italy, in the Alps, where World War I catalyzed collective memory and modeled the landscape.

> Visitor, the mountain that you . . . are on the verge of piously ascending, was ravaged and mutilated by the war. Some of its forests burned down in terrifying fires sparked by exploding grenades, while others were sacrificed to provide wood for trenches and soldiers' shelters. Its beautiful and verdant fields were devastated, scarred by trenches, earthworks, and exploding shells . . . but like the face of a mutilated brother, the ravaged face of the mountain is even more beautiful.[8]

This description, taken from a Touring Club Italiano (TCI) guidebook,[9] contains all the main ingredients of the postwar rhetoric about mountains: nationalism, the merging of natural and internal landscapes, signs of destruction, and memories of a lost serenity. But what is even more interesting is that these considerations are voiced in the first of the TCI's six volumes dedicated to battlefields. The publication of this series was clearly a deliberate effort on the part of the TCI to recast Italy's mountains in a nationalistic and patriotic key, as a great natural sanctuary of Italian heroism. These books, published in the late 1920s and early 1930s, were hardly an isolated case in the European culture of the time. One has only to think of the *Guides illustrés Michelin des champs de bataille,* published in Paris in 1919,[10] or Thomas Cook and Sons's patriotic war site itineraries.[11] According to the historian George Mosse, Europe's modern rediscovery of its nature is directly connected with the experience of the Great War. Placing war and death within the natural space was a way to attenuate their emotional impact.[12] Naturalize death, nationalize mourning—this was the policy of European governments during the war and, especially, in the postwar period. What has often escaped notice, though, is that this strategy did not focus just on the perception of death and the management of collective mourning but also on the perception and "management" of nature itself. War—as I shall show further on—had indeed imposed itself on nature, leaving deep traces on the land, but the effects of the political organization of mourning and national memory on nature turned out to be as durable as those of explosions and fires.

The decade following the Great War has been called an age of memorials. In those years, more that thirty thousand war memorials were built in France alone.[13] Great Britain set up a special commission to honor fallen soldiers, the Imperial War Graves Commission, which in 1923 sent out four thousand headstones a week to supply five hundred war cemeteries in France and Great Britain.[14] In Germany, "heroes' groves" were planted across the countryside, a tradition going back to the Franco-Prussian wars of the 1870s.[15] In Italy, the memory of soldiers killed in battle was entrusted to Alpine memorials and, for a small part, to Parchi della Rimembranza (memorial parks) patterned after their German counterparts. In the Italian organization of the cult of fallen soldiers, it was not just mourning that was nationalized but also the places where the war had been fought. A network of war cemeteries, funerary monuments, and pilgrimages to battlefields turned into national sanctuaries redesigned what James M. Mayo defined as the "political landscape."[16] It was the war cemeteries especially that impregnated the landscape with meaning, transforming it into a new hybrid of nature and memory. The visible and unseen, words and silence, artificial and natural combined to give rise to a rhetorical landscape of war and its national memory. As Kathy E. Ferguson and Phyllis Turnbull write, war memorials are "national narratives . . . written directly onto material soil."[17] The organization of space becomes the organization of memory through

Fig. 13.1. War memorial (Lavaredo), G. Burloni, photographer. From TCI, *Sui campi di battaglia*. Courtesy of the Touring Club Italiano

the politicization of absence.[18] It is what one does not see—the remains of the fallen as well as the meanings and events they evoke—that informs the landscape, causing reality to merge with its representation.

Yet I do not think we should see this phenomenon as dematerializing the landscape, as reducing it to mere discourse. It would be very hard indeed to dematerialize the vast network of war memorials, cemeteries, monuments, gardens, and parks that, as Jay Winter has noted, dot European countries, from the big cities to rural villages, from the mountains to public buildings, giving visual testimony to the collective memory of war.[19] And it would be absurd to think of battlefields, such as the Alps, as immaterial. How could we regard as inconsequential the imposing war memorial of Redipuglia on the slopes of Mount Sei Busi in Friuli?[20] The architecture of the monument, the surrounding landscape, the relics on display there, and above all the deafening absence of a hundred thousand Italian soldiers buried there are at once a tangible reality made of stones, cypresses, and bones and a cultural medium that is a window onto a landscape behind the observers, a landscape that refers to personal and collective pasts, rather than to the one in front of them. When we look out from the observatory of Redipuglia today, it is actually difficult to recognize a war landscape, although everything in sight reminds one of it. The monument clouds the memory but not the cycle of nature and agency—or rather, the end of agency—of mountain communities that eventually led to reforestation. The contrast between the memorial, evoking a former landscape, and the newly rising forests, which tell another story—of a mountain depopulating—makes Redipuglia an emblematic hybrid of history and nature, of discourse and object so closely intertwined that it can be difficult to distinguish the natural from the artificial, the cultural from the ecological.

As we have seen, the "rearranging of memory," as the Italian historian Mario Isnenghi defines it, had a major impact on Italian mountains.[21] The natural spaces where the war had been fought were sanctified, and vast war cemeteries were created. These artificial spaces became, in a way, vehicles for meaning, capable of transferring perceptions and discourses along a triangular connection between individuals, the nation, and the landscape. The mountains had modified both war and the soldiers. Mountaineers had turned into heroic Alpini (members of the Italian Alpine Corps), and the wearisome and robotic war in the trenches had given way to bold deeds entrusted to the skill of individual soldiers.[22]

The geographic position of the Alps along the boundaries of Italy evoked a defensive conception of war, which went hand in hand with the celebration of the fallen. The Alps were the geographic sentinels of the nation, the keepers

Fig. 13.2. Redipuglia entrance, anonymous photographer. From TCI, *Sui campi di battaglia* (Milan: TCI, 1929). Courtesy of the Touring Club Italiano

of the memory of Italians rising in arms to defend their homeland. War and politics thus redrew the map of Italy. The names of insignificant, out-of-the-way places became universally known; formerly uninhabited peaks were populated with the ghosts of the fallen—at once present and absent—and the mountains became destinations of a whole nation's pilgrimage, visited by schoolchildren, families of fallen soldiers, and the authorities. Nature had transfigured warfare and the soldiers and then preserved the traces of war.[23] Politics organized and put an official stamp on that memory.

Alpine tourism gave a decisive boost to the mass diffusion of this dual cult of nature and memory. Both the Club Alpino Italiano (CAI) and the Touring Club hastened to organize guided tours, hikes, and pilgrimages to battlefields and war memorials.[24] Antonio Berti's guides to the eastern Alps and the TCI's previously mentioned guides to battlefields were more than collections of itineraries through the vestiges of a recent war.[25] They were true handbooks for the political and cultural use of the landscape, a landscape that had been reworked into an inseparable unity of memory and nature. The aim of the TCI, as well as that of several Alpine organizations, was to celebrate heroism and sacrifice, while placing a nationalistic stamp on recently acquired geographic spaces.[26]

What did these patriotic outdoorspeople, these nationalistic alpinists find in the mountains? First and foremost, of course, they found what they were looking for. The organized memory of war modeled the spiritual landscape of the beholders as well as the geographic landscapes they beheld. The rethinking of the war experience and its consolidation in the literary canon of memorial literature, all punctuated by the canon of war memorials, served to guide these pilgrims' quest and gaze.

Reinventing

However absurd it may seem, the Great War led to a discovery of the mountains.[27] The roads, mule tracks, and cableways that had carried thousands of soldiers into the mountains remained in use, and patriotic discourse encouraged Italians to explore their "redeemed" (or acquired) lands. At the same time, another vision of the mountains had taken hold alongside the celebration of the Alpini's heroism and of war as a challenge to nature. This was a bucolic vision, the very antithesis of the horrors of war. George Mosse has called our attention to German postcards from the front showing anticlimactic images of bucolic nature in the midst of the conflict. On these postcards, the battlefield was pictured as a field in bloom, with a rabbit peeking through the grass.[28] Likewise, descriptions of war in Italian mountains were also immersed in a surreal, bucolic scenery that seemed to take the edge off the harsh life in the trenches. In a report from the front lines in 1915, Mario Mariani, a journalist who authored several books on life in the trenches, wrote: "Oh peaceful townsmen who are discharging your own duty to your country on the scorching sidewalks of your cities, busy with the civil and industrial mobilization, none of our soldiers envies you. Here [in the mountains] life is healthy and the war gentle."[29]

Such descriptions, which we might collect under the heading "bucolic rediscovery and reinvention of mountain war," abound in World War I memoirs. The testimony of Ardengo Soffici, a writer and artist enlisted as a volunteer in the army, is a prime example of this kind of rhetoric. "Sometimes the trenches are idyllic," he unequivocally wrote in his diary, describing the blaze of wild flowers blooming over the trench parapets.

The military surgeon Angelo Malinverni, nicked by a bullet in the shoulder during the Sleme attack, found time as he fled to notice two spots in the grass, one red, the other white. One was a drop of his own blood, the other a lily: "I picked the lily, looked at it, smelled it. How strange that flower seemed to me in that instant! . . . If I had been killed then and there, with the flower in my hand, wouldn't that have been an elegant death?"[30]

Naturally, such memoirs were mainly written by a small elite of educated officers, who were often volunteers. They were rendering their experience of the war using the only cultural tools at their disposal, the classical high school culture of Arcadia and the "romantic" culture of weekend hikers and alpinists.[31] It goes without saying that this bucolic discourse about mountain nature had very little to do with the reality of high-altitude war.

The "elegy of the trenches," which made a violent, far-from-natural death banal and natural, was one of the filters through which the mountains came to be seen in the postwar period. Despite flowers, chirping birds, and snow-capped peaks, death never completely vanished from battle scenes. The pendant of the elegy was heroism, which war memorials transformed from image and discourse into monuments that became a permanent feature of the landscape. Heroism and elegy were closely connected, since both arose from the encounter with mountain nature. There was no room for poets or heroes in the trenches down in the plains. The historian Antonio Gibelli has stressed the role of the Alpine war theater in putting a heroic stamp on the conflict.[32] The pervasiveness of this heroic vision of war in the mountains is borne out by Achille Beltrame's illustrations for the most widely read illustrated weekly of the time, the *Domenica del Corriere*. As a historian of the Alpine Corps remarked, those drawings seem to show athletic feats and challenges to nature rather than war scenes.[33]

What I find interesting is that the discourse about mountain nature was transposed from nature to humans. In wartime and postwar mythology, the Alps became the repository of a valuable genetic and environmental heritage that produced a particular type of Italian—the Alpine mountaineer. It was certainly not the first time that the natural landscape was regarded as the mirror or even the very substance of the inner landscape, the character of its inhabitants. Friedrich Ratzel's anthropogeography had been influential, just as had been certain discourses on the presumed racial differences between the north and south of Italy.[34] Thus, the postwar nationalization of the mountain landscape produced at once a new Nature and a new Man—the masculine is the only genre of this rhetoric—and both epitomized the virtues of a nation that war had regenerated. Rhetoric about Italy's mountain soldiers, the Alpini played a central role in this reinvention of the landscape. It certainly

Fig. 13.3. Postcard: Fourth Alpine Corps Regiment. From Italo Cati, *Cara mamma ti scrivo: Le cartoline dei soldati della Grande Guerra* (Udine: Gaspari, 2006). Courtesy of Italo Cati's private archive

Figure 13.4. "The war of the prodigies. A 'corvée' of Alpini at three thousand meters," by Achille Beltrame. From *La Domenica del Corriere* 19, no. 4 (28 January–4 February 1917). Courtesy of Private Collection Marini, www.illustrated-history.org

changed the perception of mountain people as contrasted with city dwellers. The foolish and gullible mountaineer at the mercy of astute townspeople was replaced by the symbol of the healthy simplicity of the mountains as opposed to the unhealthy complications of the city.[35] "Mountaineers and mountains are one and the same. The land merges with its people. You can easily find a thousand plainsmen who have never paid any attention to the shape of the land or seen a foot of unpaved ground. But the mountaineer has a feeling for the mountains. He has a geographical sense of the area he lives in. . . . He feels and sees the geographic reality of his homeland.[36]

The author of this passage is Cesare Battisti, one of the symbols of Italian irredentism,[37] who was hanged by the Austrians in 1916. Battisti was also a geographer and hence ideally suited for the task of politicizing the natural landscape and its inhabitants. As the historian Marco Cuaz recently showed, he gave a decisive contribution to the building of the myth of the Great War as capable of transferring the virtues of the mountains from the materiality of places to the spirit of the mountaineers.[38]

The death of Cesare Battisti, who had himself fought as a volunteer in the Alpini, boosted the heroic image of the corps, which soon became the main symbol of the nation in arms, largely replacing in this role the *bersaglieri* (riflemen), whose popularity had risen dramatically during the wars of independence and the taking of Rome in 1871. The men of the Alpine

Corps differed from the bersaglieri, however, in that their military qualities depended strictly on the terrain they fought upon. They were recruited from mountain villages or at least among students or professionals who were members of the Club Alpino and had learned to love the mountains. The purpose, of course, was to take advantage of these soldiers' knowledge of the terrain, their knowledge of mountain-climbing techniques, and their being accustomed to living at high altitudes. But as Battisti made clear, it was more than that. In the rhetoric of war, the mountains had forged the character of the mountaineers, and in war, this perfect symbiosis of man and nature became apparent, as well as useful to the nation.

Now, it is indubitably true that mountaineers knew the mountains and their dangers better than anyone else. Even officers did not hesitate to turn to valley dwellers for advice about landslide risk before choosing their troops' camping site.[39] But in the perspective of nationalizing the mountain landscape—which included its inhabitants as well as its nature—this empirical lore was seen not so much as a social mediation between nature and culture but rather as a mediation between spiritual and material landscapes. In their nationalistic transfiguration, the multiple activities of mountain people were no longer viewed merely as an economic strategy for optimizing natural resources and work;[40] they became a metaphor of rural frugality as opposed to urban consumerism. The mountaineers' bowing to the ecological constraints imposed by the Alps was seen as reflecting an inclination to a resigned and conservative acceptance of hierarchies and power relations.[41]

Shaping

Bucolic elegies, hero-mountaineers, war memorials, and battlefields—these were the founding pillars of postwar mountain geography and of what the nation's pilgrims saw, not necessarily with their eyes, in what was now the national landscape. However, along with images and discourses, other things had been settling into the landscape. Although the mountains had reconfigured war and, above all, the soldiers, exalting their courage and abnegation, the reverse was also true. The mountains could not remain the same after the fury of the conflict had swept over them. The antithesis to bucolic elegies about war in the mountains was the description of deep scars left by the war in the Alpine landscape. In a book published in 1929, one can read this description: "War has left conspicuous traces here [in Venetian Tridentina] and the Alpine landscape bears its perturbing stamp: *chevaux de frise*, barbed wire, heaps of crushed bags arranged along the edges of trenches, and a regular little village former Austrian barracks."[42]

The same kind of descriptions can be found for all the Alpine battle-fields. "Everything speaks of death on the Sabotino," wrote the Italian war reporter Luigi Barzini in 1917. According to his descriptions, the Trentino mountains were devastated by trenches, dugouts, and explosives, to become a huge ossuary where even the soil had acquired the red tint of blood.[43] In 1925, a montane writer depicted the Marmolada area as an immense ruin, still carrying the stigmas of war: "tattered remnants of clothing, shell cases and shrapnel, battered wooden beams, rusted bayonets, stockless rifles, petards, bomb shells, crushed canteens, harpoons, loaders, cartridges."[44] More or less with the same words, Mario Rigoni Stern, one of Italy's few mountain writers,[45] depicted the landscape that confronted refugees of Asiago upon their return at the end of the war: "Even the most remote woods bore the signs of war: cut down or uprooted trees, sheds, artillery emplacements with their cannons still pointed towards the Val di Nos and Val d'Assa, ammunition deposits, dugouts, trenches, barbed wire. . . . The smell of iodine tincture, rotted wood, and explosives still hung on the air."[46]

The conflict had left deep scars in the Alpine landscape. Immediately after the end of the war, Meuccio Ruini, an Italian politician particularly attentive to mountains and their problems,[47] spoke of the destructive axe that had swung down on Italian forests, especially after the defeat of Caporetto.[48] The botanist Lino Vaccari estimated that war had robbed Italian forests of at least two million cubic meters of timber.[49] According to statistics of the Istituto Nazionale di Economia Agraria, the mountains of Vicenza lost 4,680 hectares of forests, and over 5,700 hectares were severely damaged.[50] As is usual in such surveys, these figures are tentative; other sources speak of a nationwide loss of 15,000 hectares of forests and severe damage to 25,000 hectares.[51]

Wars often affect forests,[52] but the impact of the Great War was especially dramatic, mainly because wood was one of the most essential materials used for military purposes. There would not have been trenches, barracks, telegraph poles, or ammunition without the contribution of forests. One could say that the whole front was built on the roots of trees.[53] Significantly, Colonel William B. Parsons of the U.S. Eleventh Engineers said that lumber had to be considered war munitions.[54] In Britain,[55] in France,[56] in the countries occupied by the German Army,[57] and in the rest of Europe, World War I had a double impact on forest ecosystems: along the front, it was the fury of the battle that dramatically changed forests,[58] but forests situated far from the front were also deeply affected. For example, Italy's Fontana Forest in the former hunting grounds of the Gonzaga family near Mantua witnessed intensive timbering for the construction of bridges over the Piave River.[59] In the Altipiano dei Sette Comuni (Seven Towns Plateau) in the province of Vicenza, 35 percent of the forests were destroyed and 50 percent seriously damaged.[60]

The Italian forests suffered additional stress because they had to make up for the huge amount of lumber that Italy had been importing before the war; ironically, many of Italy's forest resources came from the Austro-Hungarian Empire, that is, from the other side of the battlefront. Considering both the higher demand for wood for military purposes and the decrease in imported lumber, Italian forests would need to have produced about four times more than they did before the war. It seems to me that looking at the war "as if nature existed" reveals how closely intertwined ecology, economy, and politics were.

The fact that the Great War, like all wars, significantly modified nature is indisputable and possibly obvious, although it seems less obvious when we look at the ways in which historians have generally dealt with this subject. Yet one might still be wondering how durable these war scars were. Just how deep down did these scars go?

Speaking of battlefields in Flanders, Voltaire remarked that after only a few years, nature had already obliterated all traces of the war.[61] Of course, because of the technological potential deployed, the Great War had deeper

Fig. 13.5. Forest after an explosion, anonymous photographer. From TCI, *Sui campi di battaglia.* Courtesy of the Touring Club Italiano

and longer-lasting effects than previous conflicts, both on the contingent and the structural plane. According to Pietro Piussi, a leading Italian forestry expert, in many areas of the Alps lumber was checked with metal detectors before being processed in sawmills for decades after the war. This precaution was made necessary by the frequent incidents caused by dangerous war fragments impregnated in the wood.[62] A similar situation existed in France, where studies on the forests of Lorraine, Marne, and Aisne, which French scholars appropriately called *bois mitraillés* (machine-gunned forests), demonstrated that the associated wood products were laced with huge quantities of metals and war materials.[63] Then there are the indirect ecological consequences of war, such as infestations of xylophagous insects attracted by the huge amounts of wood damaged in the fighting, which had been impossible to remove. Such was the case for the forests of the Altipiano dei Sette Comuni, where fourteen thousand hectares of forest were infested by *Scolytid coleoptera.* Three hundred thousand firs were cut down to save the remaining trees, and ninety thousand more were sacrificed and used as bait to eliminate the infestation.[64] Something similar occurred in the Panaveggio Forest in the Trentino region, where a study of tree age structure and variations in tree-ring width has shown a high concentration of disturbances around the time of World War I.[65] Direct military operations were certainly responsible for a large part of these disturbances, but the invasion of *Ips typographus* and subsequent intensive cutting in the immediate postwar years were also war consequences.[66] In those same years, an infestation of *Tortricide tortix* was the pretext for razing three hundred hectares of forest in the Venetian Province.[67] In the Piedmont Alps, the destruction of forests in the Toce, Sesia, Mastellone, and Tessera watersheds severely compromised the hydrographical regime of the whole area.[68]

Some of the war's alterations were even more dramatic. On 11 July 1915, Italians set off the most powerful mine of World War I, shaking Mount Tofana like an earthquake tremor.[69] In the case of the southwest cliff of Mount Piccolo Lagazuoi, a series of exploding Austrian mines repositioned an entire rock face during 1916 and 1917. Perhaps the most long-lasting traces, though, were left by the war machine's array of technological innovations used for coping with the difficulties of the mountain environment. Cableways, mule tracks, and carriage roads took thousands of men to high altitudes, and in many cases, these tools of Mars are still visible.[70] And wherever soldiers went, the forests shrank further.[71]

Epilogue

The war remodeled the mountains. These formerly poor, cursed, and peripheral areas came to epitomize the Italian identity more than any of the country's other geographic features. Alpine war memorials and cemeteries, as well as places made famous by bloody battles, became destinations of pilgrimages, both material and literary. Alpine and tourist organizations such as the CAI and TCI played a crucial role in consolidating this heritage of memory and in making it accessible. The political use of the mountains actually predated the war. The bylaws of both the CAI and the TCI committed these groups to helping Italians discover Italy and, in the case of the alpine organizations, their mountains. That this pedagogic objective was amalgamated to nationalistic concerns was especially clear in the regions along the Alpine border, where the promotion of Italian tourism went hand in hand with military espionage and competition with Austrian alpinists. It is significant that in 1915, the Austrian government abolished the Alpine Society of Trentino.[72] Even before the true war began, a bloodless battle was already being fought on the mountains as Austrian and Italian alpinists rivaled one another for the conquest of peaks and the control of shelters.[73]

The Great War gave the Alps a central role in Italy's nationalistic discourse. However, the stratification of meaning and memory onto a "nationalized" mountain landscape lived on beyond the war and the postwar period. The political landscape of Monte Grappa, intelligently analyzed by Livio Vanzetto,[74] offers keen insight into this persisting image. Here, memories and meanings are juxtaposed to form an extraordinary national landscape that is at once natural and artifactual. The mountain stands guard over an ossuary of fallen soldiers of the Great War, a monument to the partisans, a mule track built by military engineers in 1917, a chapel dedicated to the Virgin Mary, and two enormous letters, W and M, written with living trees along its slopes. This acronym has been variously read as *Viva Maria* (Long Live Mary; Italians use "W" as an abbreviation for "Viva"), *Viva Mussolini,* and, by revolutionary students in the 1960s and 1970s, *Viva Mao.* Italy's history is quite literally inscribed on its mountains.

Notes

This essay is a sample of my forthcoming book on mountains and nation in modern Italy. I would like to thank the many friends and colleagues who have read and discussed this essay, including Stefania Barca, Piero Bevilacqua, Gia Caglioti, Giuseppe Civile, and Duccio Scotto di Luzio. I owe a special debt to Paolo Macry, whose example led me to become a historian. Thanks to the Department of Italian Studies at the University of California–Berkeley for comments received on a first version of this paper. Special thanks also to Pietro Piussi and Antonio Gabbrielli for helping to find sources and information on the ecological effects of war on Italian forests.

1. On Hannibal and the Alps in the Romantic imagination, see Simon Schama, *Landscape and Memory* (New York: Knopf, 1995), translated by Paola Mazzarelli as *Paesaggio e memoria* (Milan: Arnoldo Mondadori, 1997), 468–69.

2. Leslie Stephen, *The Playground of Europe* (London: Longmans, Green, 1871) is the Bible of this vision.

3. "Say the Word, and whole planets, solar systems, galaxies—light itself—spring forth out of the darkness. Say something else and they vanish. It is our genesis illusion: God spoke and the thunder rolled, lightning flashed, matter was born." Donald Worster, *Nature's Economy: The Roots of Ecology* (San Francisco: Sierra Club, 1977), 191.

4. "A cutover land can be seen as good ecologically as a forested one. A landscape riddled with opencast coal mines, bleeding acid into streams, is as 'natural' as any other. Only human subjectivity can decide which state of the earth is preferable to another." Donald Worster, *The Wealth of Nature: Environmental History and Ecological Imagination* (New York: Oxford University Press, 1993), 176.

5. Donald Worster, "Doing Environmental History," in *The Ends of the Earth: Perspectives on Modern Environmental History,* ed. Donald Worster (New York: Cambridge University Press, 1988), translated as "Studiare la storia dell'ambiente," in *I confini della Terra: Problemi e prospettive di storia dell'ambiente* (Milan: Franco Angeli, 1991), 252.

6. Ibid.

7. From this point of view, I completely share the approach proposed by Linda Nash, who has expressed this idea better than I can: "Any environmental history must confront the idea that the environment about which we write is, inevitably, something that we always understand through language and certain cultural practices. . . . But like most environmental historians, I remain committed to a materialistic view of the world. I am interested not only in how people talked about environment and disease, but also in what happened on the ground, the changing pattern of disease, the changing use of the land, the changing qualities of air, water, and soil. Consequently, I do not hew to either a materialistic or a cultural approach, nor have I tried to separate out the two. That is precisely the point. Our understandings of environment and disease are shaped simultaneously by culture and by material realities of the world. These stories need to be told together." See Linda Nash, *Inescapable Ecologies:*

A History of Environment, Disease, and Knowledge (Berkeley: University of California Press, 2006), 10.

8. Touring Club Italiano, *Sui campi di battaglia: Il Monte Grappa* (Milan: Presso il TCI, 1928), 1.

9. The Touring Club Italiano was founded in Milan in 1894, initially under the name Touring Club Ciclistico Italiano (TCCI, or Italian Bicycle Touring Club), by a group of fifty-seven cycling enthusiasts. In 1900, it became the Touring Club Italiano, and it was briefly known as Consociazione Turistica Italiana from 1937 to 1945. Though the aim of the TCI was to promote tourism, the organization's cultural politics placed this objective in the service of the complete nationalization, or cultural appropriation, of the Italian landscape. On the TCI and nature protection, besides Luigi Piccioni's essay in this volume, see Richard James Boon Bosworth, "The Touring Club Italiano and the Nationalization of the Italian Bourgeoisie," *European History Quarterly* 27, no. 3 (1997): 371–410, and Luigi Piccioni, *Il volto amato della Patria* (Camerino: Università di Camerino, 1999), 58–68.

10. On Michelin guides, see David G. Troyansky, "Monumental Politics: National History and Local Memory," *French Historical Studies* 15, no. 1 (1987): 131–33.

11. George L. Mosse, "National Cemeteries and National Revival: The Cult of the Fallen Soldiers in Germany," *Journal of Contemporary History* 14, no. 1 (1979): 12.

12. George L. Mosse, *Fallen Soldiers: Reshaping the Memory of the World Wars* (New York: Oxford University Press, 1990), esp. 107–25.

13. Paul Gouch, "From Heroes' Grove to Parks of Peace: Landscapes of Remembrance, Protest and Peace," *Landscape Research* 25, no. 2 (2000): 214.

14. Ibid.

15. Mosse, "National Cemeteries," 13.

16. James M. Mayo, "War Memorials as Political Memory," *Geographical Review* 78, no. 1 (1988): 62.

17. Kathy E. Ferguson and Phyllis Turnbull, "Narratives of History, Nature, and Death at the National Memorial Cemetery," *Frontiers: A Journal of Women Studies* 16, nos. 2–3 (1996): 1.

18. Ibid., 7.

19. Jay Winter, *Sites of Memory, Sites of Mourning: The Great War in European Cultural History* (New York: Cambridge University Press, 1995), 1.

20. On Redipuglia, see Patrizia Dogliani, "Redipuglia," in *I luoghi della memoria: Simboli e miti dell'Italia unita,* ed. Mario Isnenghi (Rome: Laterza, 1996), 375–90.

21. Mario Isnenghi and Giorgio Rochat, *La grande guerra, 1914–1918* (Milan: RCS Libri, 2000), 498.

22. Antonio Gibelli, *La grande guerra degli italiani* (Milan: RCS Libri, 1998), 101–2.

23. One could say that mountains have created and preserved a distinctive war landscape. Of course, it is hardly surprising that the traces of the war have survived more easily in high mountains or, more generally, in less frequented places. However, politics also had a role in preserving those traces. On this subject, see Luca Valente and Giorgio Dall'Igna, eds., *La tutela del patrimonio storico della Grande Guerra* (Schio: Tipografia Operaia Menin, 2002).

24. The CAI, founded in 1863, contributed greatly to the nationalization of Italian mountains, both politically, through its role in the appropriation of disputed spaces (CAI members played an important part in the Alpine Corps), and culturally, by helping to construct the discourse on Italy's nature. On the history of the CAI, see Alessandro Pastore, *Alpinismo e storia d'Italia* (Bologna: Il Mulino, 2003).

25. On Berti's guidebooks, see Isnenghi and Rochat, *La grande guerra,* 499–500, and Marco Cuaz, *Le Alpi* (Bologna: Il Mulino, 2005), 91–92.

26. After World War I, Italy obtained territory on its northeastern borders (Trentino, Venezia Giulia, and Istria) from the Austro-Hungarian Empire. On patriotic efforts to make these areas known to Italians, see Gibelli, *La grande guerra,* 345.

27. Of course, the use of the word *discovery* is rather disputable here. It is not only true that alpinists from several countries had already "discovered" the Alps, at least from the eighteenth century; one should remember that smugglers, poachers, herders, and mountaineers generally did not need the invention of hiking or climbing to be familiar with *their* mountains. In this case, what I mean by *discovery* is the encounter between the whole nation and the Alps through the war experience.

28. Mosse, *Fallen Soldiers,* 126–36.

29. Mario Mariani, *Sulle Alpi e sull'Isonzo* (Milan: Società Editrice Italiana, 1915), 41.

30. Angelo Malinverni, *"O Luna, o luna tu me lo dicevi . . ."* (Turin: Edizioni Montes, 1942), reprinted in Marco Balbi and Luciano Viazzi, *Spunta l'alba del sedici giugno* (Milan: Mursia, 2000), 90.

31. On this subject, see Adolfo Scotto di Luzio, *Il liceo classico* (Bologna: Il Mulino, 1999), 110–11.

32. Gibelli, *La grande guerra,* 101–2.

33. Gianni Oliva, *Storia degli Alpini* (Milan: Rizzoli, 1985), 108–10. Cuaz, *Alpi,* 85–86, had similar considerations.

34. Claudia Petraccone, *Le due Italie: La questione meridionale tra realtà e rappresentazione* (Rome: Laterza, 2005), esp. chaps. 1 and 4.

35. On the Italian cultural representation of townspeople versus peasants, see Giulio Bollati, *L'italiano: Il carattere nazionale come storia e come invenzione* (Turin: Einaudi, 1983), 48–63.

36. Cesare Battisti, *Gli alpini* (Milan: Fratelli Treves Editori, 1918), 30–31.

37. Irrendentism was a nationalistic movement to incorporate into Italy the eastern provinces that were under Austrian control (Venetian, Trentino, Alto Adige, Friuli, Istria, and Dalmatia).

38. Cuaz, *Alpi*, 83–84.

39. Luigi Cognetti De Martiis, "Neve e fiori nell'Alta Carnia," in *Ricordi di guerra alpina: Testimonianze dei combattenti sul fronte italiano, 1915–1918*, ed. Marino and Francesca Michieli (Trento: Casa Editrice Panorama, 2001), 256.

40. On pluriactivity in the Italian mountains, see Gauro Coppola, "La montagna alpina: Vocazioni originarie e trasformazioni funzionali," and Pietro Tino, "La montagna meridionale: Boschi, uomini, economie tra Otto e Novecento," both in *Storia dell'agricoltura italiana in età contemporanea*, vol. 1, *Spazi e paesaggi*, ed. Piero Bevilacqua (Venice: Marsilio, 1989), 495–530 and 677–754; Marco Armiero, "Italian Mountains," in *Views from the South: Environmental Stories from the Mediterranean World (19th–20th Centuries)*, ed. Marco Armiero (Naples: ISSM-CNR, 2006), 141–58.

41. "[Mountaineers are so disciplined] because the mountain is their master and absolute lord. . . . In cities you go on strike to improve your lot. But it is up to the mountain to improve your lot, if it so feels inclined. . . . [Mountaineers are so acquiescent] because they regard social evils in the same way they regard natural evils. . . . You do not rebel when rocks wipe out your field in an instant, or when you arrive with your sled to find that a landslide has swept away your winter stock of fascines. . . . Your task is to preserve and repair." See Piero Jahier, *Con me e con gli alpine* (Turin: Einaudi, 1934), 121–22, 125 (my translation).

42. Attilio Virgilio, *A fil di cielo, impressioni di vita e ambiente alpini* (Turin: Alfredo Fornica, 1929), 14.

43. Luigi Barzini, *Dal Trentino al Carso* (Milan: Fratelli Treves, 1917), 109, 147, and 182.

44. Ibid., 106.

45. On Mario Rigoni Stern, see (in English) Felix Siddel, "Sette volte bosco, sette volte prato: An Interview with Mario Rigoni Stern," *MNL* 113, no. 1 (1998): 23143.

46. Mario Rigoni Stern, "La ricostruzione (1919–21)," in *Storia dell'altipiano dei Sette Comuni* (Vicenza: La Grafica e Stampa, 1994), 553–54.

47. He was among the founders of the Parliamentary Committee "Amici della Montagna (Friends of the Mountain) devoted to the promotion of any kind of activities in favor of mountains and their people." On Ruini's commitment to mountains, see Oscar Gaspari, *Il segretariato per la montagna*

(1919–1965): *Ruini, Serpieri e Sturzo per la bonifica d'alta quota* (Rome: Presidenza del Consiglio dei Ministri, Dipartimento per l'Informazione e l'Editoria, 1994), 8–14, 45–46.

48. Meuccio Ruini, *La montagna in guerra e dopo la guerra* (Rome: Athenaeum, 1918), 34.

49. Bruno Vecchio, Pietro Piussi, and Marco Armiero, "L'uso dei boschi e degli incolti," in *Storia dell'agricoltura italiana,* vol. 3, *L'età contemporanea,* ed. Reginaldo Ciamferoni, Zeffiro Ciuffocetti, and Leonardo Rombai (Florence: Polistampa, 2003), 182.

50. G. Pittoni, "Montagna vicentina," in INEA, *Lo spopolamento montano in Italia,* vol. 4, *Le Alpi venete* (Rome: Tipografia Failli, 1938), 141.

51. Antonio Gabbrielli, "La prima guerra mondiale e i nostri boschi," *Linea Ecologica* 26, no. 5 (1994): 3.

52. John Robert McNeill, "Woods and Warfare in World History," *Environmental History* 9, no. 3 (2004): 388–410.

53. Frank N. Schubert, "All Wooden on the Western Front," *Journal of Forest History* 22, no. 4 (1978): 180.

54. Ibid., 181.

55. According to John McNeill, half of Britain's productive forests were felled in three years (from 1916 to 1918). See McNeill, "Woods and Warfare in World History," 388–410.

56. In France, by the close of operations in May 1919, the American forestry troops had produced 218,211,000 feet of lumber; 3,051,137 standard-gauge railroad ties; 954,667 small ties; 1,926,603 miscellaneous round products; 39,065 pieces of piling; 4,669 fagots and fascines; and 534,000 cords of fuelwood. See David A. Clary, "The Biggest Regiment in the Army," *Journal of Forest History* 22, no. 4 (1978): 184.

57. The best-known example is the forest of Białowieża in Lithuania, 5 percent of which was cleared by the Germans after the battle of Tannenberg. See Schama, *Paesaggio e memoria,* 65–66.

58. The most detailed work on the ecological consequences of World War I on the forests is Andrée Corvol and Jean-Paul Amat, eds., *Forêt et guerre* (Paris: Harmattan, 1994).

59. Ibid., 162.

60. Andrea Battisti, "I boschi," in *Storia dell'altipiano dei sette comuni,* 65.

61. Quoted in Troyansky, "Monumental Politics," 121.

62. Pietro Piussi, e-mail message to the author, 8 March 2007.

63. Maurice Bach, "La convalescence et la guérison des Forêt lorraines," in *Forêt et guerre,* 183–89; Francis Gaudemard, "*Les bois mitraillés dans le département de la Marne,*" ibid., 193–96; Paul Arnould and Laurent Simon, "*Forêt, guerre, après-guerre autour du Chemin-des-Dames,*" ibid., 251–69.

64. Battisti, "I boschi," 65.

65. Renzo Motta, Roberta Berretti, Emanuele Lingua, and Pietro Piussi, "Coarse Woody Debris, Forest Structure and Regeneration in the Valbona Forest Riserve, Panaveggio, Italian Alps," *Forest and Ecology Management* 235, nos. 1–3 (2006): 157.

66. Renzo Motta, Paola Nola, and Pietro Piussi, "Long-Term Investigations in a Strict Forest Reserve in the Eastern Italian Alps: Spatio-temporal Origin and Development in Two Multi-layered Subalpine Stands," *Journal of Ecology* 90, no. 3 (2002): 495–507.

67. Gabbrielli, "La prima guerra mondiale," 4.

68. Ibid., 5.

69. Tullio Vidulich and Corrado Pasquali, *Alpini in guerra: Storie di uomini atti di leggenda* (Bolzano: Società Storica della Grande Guerra, 2000), 115 and 127.

70. For example, in his history of the Italian Alpine Corps, Gianni Oliva mentions the cableways of Mount Adamello and Mount Cavento and the roads running through the Avio Valley. See Oliva, *Storia degli alpini,* 116–17.

71. As in the case of the Seven Village Plateau analyzed in Giulio Vescovi, "Dal fascismo alla resistenza," in *Storia dell'altipiano dei sette comuni,* 580.

72. Mauro Nequirito, "Alpinismo e politica: La società degli alpinisti tridentini, 1872–1931," *Cheiron* 9–10 (1988): 257–58.

73. Michael Wedekind, "La politicizzazione della montagna: Borghesia, alpinismo e nazionalismo tra otto e novecento," in *L'invenzione di un cosmo borghese: Valori sociali e simboli culturali dell'alpinismo nei secoli XIX e XX,* ed. Claudio Ambrosi and Michael Wedekind (Trento: Museo Storico, 2000), 28.

74. Livio Vanzetto, "Monte Grappa," in *I luoghi della memoria: Simboli e miti dell'Italia unita,* 391–402.

CHAPTER 14

Nature Preservation and Protection in Nineteenth- and Twentieth-Century Italy, 1880–1950

Luigi Piccioni

Anticipation, Censorship, Regression, Revival

Italian environmental cultures of preservation and protection have a dramatic and erratic history. The beginning of this history coincides with the first wave of European environmentalism, in the years bridging the nineteenth and twentieth centuries. The accomplishments of this phase led to several successes that by the early 1920s were putting Italy in the vanguard of European policies for environmental protection. However, the continental crisis of preservation that followed World War I proved more serious in Italy than elsewhere, with the Fascist regime suffocating special interest groups and bureaucratizing institutions of environmental protection to the point of paralysis. The Fascist decades would in turn influence the culture and politics of the post–World War II period to the extent that, even as most European nations were making up for their earlier tardiness, Italy went through another two decades of political and institutional negligence. A true revival came about only after the mid-1960s in a context marked by such complex events as the so-called economic miracle, the reform of

Center-Left governments, the penetration and rapid diffusion of Anglo-Saxon environmental culture, the emergence of mass movements sensitive to quality-of-life issues, and the establishment of twenty semiautonomous "regions" within Italy. Unlike most northern European countries, Italy's experience with preservation at the end of the twentieth century began reflecting structural weakness and fragility.[1]

A Cosmopolitan Dimension

The history of environmental preservation and protection in Italy cannot be correctly understood if it is not set, from the start, in both European and worldwide contexts. The modern culture of environmental protection started in the second half of the nineteenth century, in the United States and Europe, but with cultural connotations that differed from area to area and that took very independent paths on the two sides of the Atlantic. In the United States of the mid-nineteenth century, environmental concern was embedded in an idealized vision of pristine nature, which ended up constituting a fundamental element of the young nation's identity. European colonists in the Americas came to believe they were confronting enormous, seemingly uncontaminated spaces, thereby contributing to a collective imagination in which large land expanses became fixed in the national psyche.

But in the case of environmental protection in western Europe, especially of industrializing north-central countries (which also enjoyed the political and cultural leadership in the Old World), modern Italian environmentalism started from an extremely old, anthropocentric attitude toward nature that was much less willing to confront indomitable, powerful natures, either real or imaginary. As a result, various forms of nature appreciation and subsequent efforts for its protection followed different channels and displayed different manifestations. One of these was the cult of country life, typified by English society, which became even stronger when faced by the dramatic social and environmental consequences of nineteenth-century urban trends involving the middle and urban working classes. Aesthetic appreciation of nature—such as the beauty of landscapes, picturesque places, and national monuments—was likewise a central theme of environmental awareness in Europe. Another popular trait prevalent in Great Britain was sympathy for nonhuman forms of life.[2] The sense of sight was rather fundamental in all these concepts of nature, but it must be emphasized that they all involved natures transformed by centuries of human labor, according to the individual needs, habits, intellects, and artistries of local communities and their genius loci. The concept of a national monument, also popular with U.S. preservationists, located its European distinctiveness in human-made objects bathed with historical significance.

The preceding distinctions delineate a European system of categories whereby cultural and natural phenomena blended together, representing values that were simultaneously aesthetic, atemporal, and patriotic in a very broad sense. John Ruskin's idea that landscape is the "beloved face of the homeland" referred precisely to its constituent dimension, which rendered it the fruit of ancient wisdom and of the people's spirit molded by collective identity. Landscapes, natural attractions, picturesque places, and monuments became integral to the French romantic concept of *patrimoine*, the great heritage that centuries of civilization left on the land and in which each country reflected and nourished itself. Patrimoine had as its core the masterpieces of visual, sculptural, and monumental art, but it gradually came to include a wider range of objects, both cultural and natural, as long as they were imbued with the spirit of a national civilization.[3]

This complex system of cultural cross-references at the turn of the nineteenth century was the stage on which European preservationism would be carried out. Within this system, a handful of environmentally conscious thinkers, often buttressed by nascent ecological concepts, began to lobby for concrete measures of preservation. Italy was no exception in this regard.

The First, Difficult Steps

The first sustained evidence of an interest in environmental protection in Italy dated to the mid-1880s and coincided with the formation of scientific societies that were being integrated into international contexts. Beyond earlier widespread British associationism, which appears to have been a special case in Europe,[4] it was mostly small academic groups such as the Association pour la Protection des Plantes, founded by the botanist Henri Correvon in Geneva in 1883, that contributed to the creation of a cosmopolitan climate favorable to nature protection. Several members of the newly formed Società Botanica Italiana, founded in Florence in 1888, joined the Association, and it was occasionally Correvon himself who convinced the Società to take a position on this or that problem or persuaded authorities to find a positive solution. From 1891, sporadic and individual crusades, such as Oreste Mattirolo's efforts to save medicinal Alpine plants and Bardo Corsi Salviati's calls for saving the remains of a historical chestnut tree in the Casentino area, became frequent motions to address the responsible parties.[5] The 1890s represented a general period of consolidation and articulation of protectionist sensibilities in which nonscientific societies began to add their voices. Such was the case with the venerable Club Alpino Italiano (CAI), which was heavily influenced, especially in Piedmont and Valle d'Aosta, by French and Swiss Alpine clubs.[6] Even though there were many attempts to set up an interest group for protecting Alpine flora within the CAI, only in 1897 did Pro Montibus, as an offshoot of CAI, become the first Italian association established specifically with a protectionist mission, in part due to the contribution of Correvon.

The people who established this group were all linked to the CAI and to the scientific world and were all based geographically around the Alps; they included Giulio Grünwald, Lino Vaccari, and Pietro Chanoux. Meanwhile, conditions were right for the formation of a second protectionist body, linked especially to the large cities of central Italy and focusing mostly on historic-artistic-literary values. Indeed, an alienation toward positivism had developed in those years, mainly with young intellectuals, and Italian periodicals and clubs were being founded under a "revival of idealism" that was then sweeping Europe.[7] Within this scenario at the turn of the century, a renewed, neoromantic interest was emerging in the arts, in ethnic and national roots, and in the rapport between people and nature.

The Predominance of the Aesthetic-National Dimension

The combined Italian sensitivities toward aesthetics and nationalism attracted increasing numbers of followers, especially in artistic circles. The critic Ugo Ojetti, an important player in the cultural renewal of that period, introduced John Ruskin to the Italian public by reviewing his work in 1897; in 1904, Ojetti was also one of the first intellectuals to come out in favor of the Italian landscape in the prestigious and widely read periodical *Nuova Antologia*.[8] A prominent place for writings on the landscape and its protection was the Florentine review *Il Marzocco*, which counted among its contributors such well-known men of letters and government officials as Gabriele D'Annunzio, Pompeo Molmenti, Giovanni Rosadi, Angelo Conti, and Corrado Ricci. Although young intellectuals were intermittently interested in such matters as cultural and landscape heritage, greater attention was paid to these issues by a core of highly trained managers, officers, and consultants from the Department of Antiquities and Fine Arts at the Ministry of Public Instruction, including Corrado Ricci, Gustavo Giovannoni, Giacomo Boni, and Luigi Parpagliolo. In some years, these men worked under the management of ministers and undersecretaries, such as Luigi Rava, Pompeo Molmenti, and Giovanni Rosadi, who were also directly involved in the protectionist movement.

Beginning in the period 1904 to 1906, the pace quickened in the field of European nature protection. In Dresden in 1904, the Federation for Heimat

Protection (Bund für Heimatschutz) was founded, growing to fifteen thousand members within seven years.[9] One might mention the preservationist writings of German naturalist Hugo Wilhelm Conwentz, which were influential well beyond German borders; Conwentz was invited in 1906 to set up and manage Europe's first public agency for nature protection, the Prussian Central Institute for Natural Monument Protection (Staatliche Stelle für Naturdenkmalpflege).[10] Switzerland's Carl Schröter and Jean Coaz suggested in 1905 the possibility of establishing a strict nature reserve based on the U.S. model in the S-charl Valley within the Engadin region.[11] In 1906, the Schweizerische Vereinung für Heimatschutz was established, and this too acquired a remarkable number of followers in just a few years.[12] Also in 1906, France developed the theoretical coordinates for an important law on the protection of monuments and natural sites of historical interest.

Italian preservationism during these years was in tune with the rest of Europe. Reflections, proposals, and propaganda about nature conservation intensified in Italy, and beyond that, a marked improvement was made on the institutional level. One might mention Ugo Ojetti's pioneering 1904 article in the widely read periodical *Illustrazione Italiana* calling for a survey and listing of Italian natural sites. This article was immediately reprinted in the *Monthly Review* of the Touring Club Italiano. Between February and July 1905, two controversial campaigns were initiated for preventing the opening of a passage through the city walls of the Tuscan city of Lucca and for protecting the pinewood along the Adriatic at Ravenna; this involved many members of the intelligentsia and led to a remarkable article by Corrado Ricci in the *Emporium*. The result was the first Italian parliamentary measure in environmental preservation: a law for protecting Ravenna's pinewood.[13] In September 1905, an influential officer in the Ministry of Public Instruction, Luigi Parpagliolo, published a dense essay in two installments in the *Fanfulla della Domenica* that described the situation of European and American nature conservation, while summarizing the Italian situation and making detailed propositions well grounded in theory.[14] Meanwhile, a motion was introduced in Parliament calling for a law "for the protection of natural attractions connected with literature, art and Italian history" modeled after the French law, and in 1906, a general move against the disfigurement of Rome's Villa Borghese park ended successfully. Corrado Ricci, by then a prominent player in Italian protectionism, was appointed manager of the Department of Antiquities and Fine Arts, a post he held until 1919. In that same year, the Italian National Association for Picturesque Landscapes and Monuments (Associazione Nazionale per i Paesaggi e i Monumenti Pittoreschi d'Italia) was founded in Florence,

N. A. FALCONE

IL PAESAGGIO ITALICO

E

LA SUA DIFESA

LE FONTI DEL CLITUNNO

A più dei monti e de le querole a l'ombra
co' fiumi, o Italia, è de' tuoi carmi il fonte.
CARDUCCI, *Alle Fonti del Clitunno.*

**FIRENZE
FRATELLI ALINARI, EDITORI
1914**

Fig. 14.1. Cover illustration of N. A. Falcone's *Il paesaggio italico e la sua difesa: Studio giuridico-estetico* (Florence: Alinari, 1914)

becoming the first Italian association established explicitly for protecting the countryside.

The Elitism of the Post–World War I Period

From that moment, scientific and patriotic protectionism became well integrated into Italian society, producing real and effective results. The successes and novelty of the years 1904 to 1906 brought optimism, activism, and a certain enthusiasm. Organizations multiplied, as the hope spread for involving great numbers of people from all areas of the country and from all social classes via public education and popular publications. Politicians and statesmen began to accept the movement's ideas, and several objectives were set. Prominent among them were the creation of a list (or "catalog") of natural beauties,[15] the approval of a general law on landscape protection, and the establishment of national parks based on U.S. and Swiss precedents.[16] Between 1907 and 1913, this movement progressed rapidly on all fronts, except perhaps in enlisting members from the working class, which did not respond as strongly as its counterparts in England, Germany, and Switzerland.

A testimony to this growing influence and efficacy was given by the protectionist interests of the Touring Club Italiano (TCI) and its main leader, Luigi Vittorio Bertarelli. The TCI was not only the biggest Italian association in terms of members (fifty thousand in 1905), it was also, at the end of the 1890s, successfully educating Italians in tourism and in the appreciation of their country's artistic and environmental values through its activities and publications. It was often called in to compensate for the shortcomings and delays of public administration in various fields that went beyond tourism.[17] The approach of Bertarelli and the TCI to themes of landscape and nature protection was always very pragmatic, if not politically expedient. Apart from occasional early notes in its *Monthly Review,* the TCI's first concrete signs of interest in the environment appeared between 1909 and 1911 when Bertarelli promoted a coalition of associations, private companies, and governmental bodies that supported the complex line of public intervention called *bonifica integrale* (integral land reclamation). This great national plan aimed to consolidate and combine reforestation, river management, and land reclamation across the country.[18] It should be emphasized that bonifica integrale did not focus on strict environmental preservation but rather on rationalizing and improving land resources with an emphasis on agricultural production, flood safety, and water-borne disease, all considered serious national issues at the time. This ambitious plan brought together organizations, politicians, administrators, and scholars (most of whom were also interested in the emerging protectionist matters); it would be a model for successive coordination and propaganda through the efforts of the TCI, which was becoming intensely interested in landscape protection.

This interest by the Touring Club was reflected in several articles in its *Monthly Review* appearing after December 1912, and it found expression through two initiatives: the establishment of a national group of protectionist associations and a national survey of key natural sites in a catalog like the one proposed by Ojetti in 1904. The Ministry of Foreign Affairs asked the TCI in 1911 to promote a national coalition of landscape concerns, and two years later, Bertarelli succeeded in establishing the Italian National Committee for the Defense of Landscape and Monuments (Comitato Nazionale per la Difesa del Paesaggio e dei Monumenti Italici). This committee consisted of thirty-one members: six representing the TCI, six representing the ministries, two from the Department of Antiquities and Fine Arts, two members of Parliament, one representing the academic world, and fourteen representing ten protectionist organizations. Bologna's Associazione Nazionale per i Paesaggi e i Monumenti Pittoreschi d'Italia took the lion's share of these places, to the point that the Comitato Nazionale could be considered composed of the Touring Club Italiano and the Associazione per i Paesaggi.[19]

Mostly because of Bertarelli's political sensibilities, the Comitato Nazionale did not advocate ambitious objectives such as nominating national parks, despite the presence of naturalists who had been devoted to this project for years. Bertarelli's conservative strategy made it clear to zoologists and botanists that there was a need to found another organization that would be more attentive to the scientific dimensions of nature protection. As a result, the Lega Nazionale per la Protezione dei Monumenti Naturali in Italia was founded in 1913 in Rome, to include many members of the Comitato Nazionale in Milan; there was no competitive intention, however, only an awareness of the committee's theoretical and operational limits.[20]

The outbreak of the war interrupted the activities of both organizations (bringing the Lega Nazionale to an end) and shut down rather promising efforts for enacting parliamentary legislation on natural beauties and creating national parks. Although some nature protection advocates maintained hope,[21] the start of the war brought the curtain down on the chance of consolidating a deep-rooted, mass-protectionist conscience that would generate dynamic influence in the political and institutional worlds. The public attention on military efforts diminished appreciation for cultural matters, deepened social conflicts, worsened the plight of the middle classes, drained the coffers of the state, and broke the international solidarity that had been so important during the Belle Époque for convincing so many people to cherish their country's landscapes and natural attractions.[22] In Italy perhaps even more than other places, war contributed to a dramatic weakening of the preservation movement that only a few years earlier had been showing signs of significant growth.[23] After the war, efforts at nature preservation would face a new, difficult reality while demonstrating a remarkable adaptability.

Advanced Fulfillments Realized by an Avant-Garde

The first and most important form of this adaptation was the awareness that pursuing a few concrete, specialized objectives was more important than attempting to construct a mass sensibility and that, in order to achieve these goals, targeted support was needed from an elite with access to places of power. From that point of view, the decisive nuclei of Italian protectionism were basically three in number: the Department of Antiquities and Fine Arts, the TCI, and Pro Montibus. Other institutions continued, with more or less success and with more or less continuity, the work that had been started before the war, but their incisiveness turned out to be very limited, if not marginal. In those years, managers and officers of the Department of Antiquities and Fine Arts, the TCI with its renewed National Committee for the Protection of Italian Landscape, and the Pro Montibus with its various commissions combined people and activities into a generally cooperative group that centered on three basic objectives: the institution of a network of national parks, the creation of a national catalog of natural beauties, and the approval of a law for the protection of these beauties.

If the preservationists' ability to maneuver within Italian society and culture seemed less than it was before the Great War, their influence within the institutions had definitely grown. For example, the network of sympathetic senators and deputies, who all belonged to the traditional liberal world, expanded significantly, and many of them were appointed to important governmental positions between 1918 and 1922. A fine example of this was Giovanni Rosadi, who from 1905 lobbied tenaciously for the law protecting natural beauties; he was appointed undersecretary for fine arts in May 1920, succeeding the equally prominent figure of Pompeo Molmenti, who had become the first to hold the post the previous year. In spite of this success, the task of achieving established objectives was far from easy. Most organizations were dwindling in numbers, including the traditionally popular Touring Club Italiano. Preservationist interest groups had become marginal in both the Parliament and the ministries. This dissipating protectionist sensibility often made the requests posed by the movement seem superfluous, and there was no lack of hostility from the many who considered the proposed projects to be excessively binding. It was only the foresight, ability, and tenacity of the movement's leaders that guaranteed the enactment of the law on natural beauties in June 1922 and then the institution of two national parks in 1922 and 1923, Abruzzo and Gran Paradiso.

The law was entitled "For the Protection of Natural Beauties and Buildings of Special Historic Interest," and it was the result of seventeen years of pressure and study since it had first been proposed in 1905.[24] The underlying philosophy of this legislation was much like that of the French law of 1906. It gave legislators authority to designate the sites or objects to protect, obliged owners to inform authorities about the presence of remarkable objects, included measures of protection within urban development plans and building codes, and made law enforcement the responsibility of several governmental departments. Because of great political resistance, the wording of the law was quite substantially watered down compared with the original proposal. Nonetheless, a wide range of objects considered to be of natural or cultural heritage were managed or protected for the first time, objects that had formerly survived only under tenuous, ad hoc solutions. This Italian law also represented an achievement in that it was passed during a general period of environmental apathy in Europe. Moreover, it avoided some of the contradictions present in its French counterpart and offered such innovative measures as requiring ministerial authorization to modify places of natural beauty and enforcing the drawing up of borders and other rules to avoid damaging the landscape. It should also be pointed out that this 1922 law was, in its slightly modified version of 1939, the only broad measure for nature protection passed in Italy until 1975.

Not even the creation of Italy's first two national parks was due to rigid government mandate. Rather, the parks resulted from a laboriously won conquest achieved through the persistent efforts of an active minority.[25] The Gran Paradiso park had a less dramatic genesis, since King Vittorio Emanuele II, in abolishing the royal hunting preserve in the Graian Alps in 1919, asked in no uncertain terms that it be converted into a national park. For Abruzzo park, by contrast, it took two years of frenetic activity and risk-taking by a local young deputy together with the Pro Montibus Federation to convince Parliament and the king to yield. Even though these measures did not fit into a coherent governmental policy but rather emerged from many difficulties and struggles, such laws ushered Italy to the forefront of European countries enacting progressive environmental protection measures in the 1920s. Few other countries had a systematic law for the protection of places of natural beauty. And even among the wealthiest nations, only a handful had national parks.[26]

Fascism: Crisis, Repression, Inheritance

The reconstitution of the National Committee for Protection of Italian Landscape, the law on natural beauties, and the establishment of the national parks of Abruzzo and Gran Paradiso happened between 1921 and 1923. This concentrated phase of activity and achievement seemed to portend a new and promising period of Italian environmental protection, but this would not be the case. In fact, after 1923, the movement began to unravel, as was happening in the rest of Europe, while the looming Fascist regime further smothered these protectionist initiatives. Benito Mussolini's rise to power delivered a double blow to Italian nature protection: first, it marginalized

Fig. 14.2. Giambattista Conti's illustration (1928) for Erminio Sipari's *Il parco nazionale d'Abruzzo*. Courtesy of the Archivio Storico Ente Autonomo Parco Nazionale d'Abruzzo, Lazio e Molise

and silenced the political class along with the liberal cultural leaders who were so important to protectionist sensibility; second, it progressively suppressed all organizations and institutions connected to the subject of natural beauty or else reduced them to administrative arms of the regime, devoid of any autonomy. Two examples illustrate these developments. In 1927, the Pro Montibus Federation was disbanded and absorbed by the regime's forestry organization, the Opera Nazionale Forestale, and in 1933, the independent bodies responsible for managing the two national parks for a decade were dissolved, with the reserves becoming entrusted to the Milizia Forestale (National Forestry Militia). During this period, with the regime showing no interest in environmental protection, the Club Alpino and the Touring Club were also being rendered largely, if not completely, Fascist, and their activities for protecting natural beauty ceased. The last stronghold of the first Italian preservationist season remained the Department of Antiquities and Fine Arts, which was responsible for overseeing the 1922 law and served as the operational home of the movement's major figures, from Gustavo Giovannoni to Luigi Parpagliolo.

It was not by accident that these men and the Department of Antiquities and Fine Arts represented the most important, if not the only, connection between the first season of Italian protectionism and the history of environmental protection in the Italian Republic after 1946. Giuseppe Bottai, the only leading figure in the Fascist regime showing sensitivity toward landscape matters and land management, was a key figure in the wording of the 1922 law, which would become the fundamental coordinates for preparing Article 9 of the Republican Constitution, which remained the only legal framework on the Italian environment until 1975.[27]

After World War II

After World War II, despite the end of Fascism and the new cultural and institutional climate ushered in by the republican experience, there were only limited successes in resurrecting a sensitivity toward protecting nature and preserving and consolidating the scattered conquests made during the earlier Liberal period. In the decade after the war, we might at least remember the experience of Movimento Italiano per la Protezione della Natura (Italian Movement for the Protection of Nature) founded in 1948 and then transforming into Pro Natura. Or we might recall the new energies collected by Italia Nostra, founded in 1955 but with mostly artistic-cultural interests.[28] Yet these and other nature protection groups were facing what appeared to be new political parties and a new political culture—all of which shared with Fascism a complete disinterest in natural beauty in its various meanings and manifestations.[29]

Italy's environmental interests were confronting, above all, a new phase of aggressive economic development that was destined, over the next few years, to radically transform the country's social landscape as well as its

Movimento Italiano Protezione della Natura

Sede Centrale:

Torino - Via Maria Vittoria, 12

O Natura! Tutto viene da te, tutto è in te, tutto rientra in te..
Imperatore Marco Aurelio.

Laudatu si, mi' signore, cum tucte le tue creature.
San Francesco d'Assisi.

TESSERA RICONOSCIMENTO

Sezione di ....

n. ....

Fig. 14.3. Membership card, Movimento Italiano Protezione Natura (1948), designed by writer and alpinist Domenico Rudatis. Courtesy of Franco Pedrotti

territory. Only in the mid-1960s did the situation begin to change due to the growing influence of Anglo-Saxon-inspired environmentalism that found a wider appeal among a new urban middle class that had arisen with the economic miracle.[30] The social struggles that emerged in 1968 and 1969 would fuel greater attention to environmental issues among the working classes too. At that point in time, Italy's first mass environmental movement began, and environmental politics, though never lacking contrasts or contradictions, entered into the thinking and planning of the Italian government.[31]

Notes

This essay represents a synthesis of my more ample study, entitled *Il volto amato della Patria: Il primo movimento per la protezione della natura in Italia, 1880–1934* (Camerino: Università di Camerino, 1999).

1. On the history of Italian environmentalism over a longer period, see James Sievert, *The Origins of Nature Conservation in Italy* (Bern: Peter Lang, 2000); Franco Pedrotti, *Il fervore dei pochi: Il movimento protezionistico italiano dal 1943 ad oggi* (Trent: Temi, 1998); and Edgar Meyer, *I pionieri dell'ambiente: L'avventura del movimento ecologista italiano—Cento anni di storia* (Milan: Carabà, 1995). To date, there does not appear to be any comprehensive reconstruction of European environmentalism, even though contemporaries seemed completely aware of the importance of the movement's international dimension. Among the many writings available, see Luigi Parpagliolo, "La protezione del paesaggio," *Fanfulla della Domenica* 27 (1905), 36:2–3, 37:2–3; Jean Astié, *La protection des paysages* (Lyon: Imprimerie Paul Legendre, 1912); Nicola A. Falcone, *Il paesaggio italico e la sua difesa: Studio giuridico-estetico* (Florence: Alinari, 1914); Hugo Wilhelm Conwentz, "On National and International Protection of Nature," *Journal of Ecology* 2, no. 2 (1914): 109–22.

2. With regard to English sensibility to nature between the sixteenth and seventeenth centuries, see the classic work by Keith Thomas, *Man and the Natural World: A History of the Modern Sensibility* (New York: Pantheon, 1983).

3. For a quick introduction to patrimoine, see Dominique Audrerie, *La notion et la protection du patrimoine* (Paris: Presses Universitaires de France, 1997).

4. David Evans, *A History of Nature Conservation in Britain* (London: Routledge, 1992), 41–59.

5. Franco Pedrotti, ed., *La Società Botanica Italiana per la protezione della natura (1888–1990)* (Camerino: Università degli Studi, 1992), 84–95.

6. Club Alpino Italiano, Head Office and Turin Section, *L'opera del Club Alpino Italiano nel suo primo cinquantennio* (Turin: Club Alpino Italiano, 1913), 116. On CAI, see also Marco Armiero's essay in this volume.

7. For a quick introduction to the subject, see Stuart H. Hughes, *Consciousness and Society* (New York: Knopf, 1958), esp. chap. 6, and George L. Mosse, *The Culture of Western Europe: The Nineteenth and Twentieth Centuries* (Chicago: Rand McNally, 1961), esp. 147–58.

8. Ugo Ojetti, "Notizia letteraria: *Ruskin et la religione de la beauté* par Robert de la Sizeranne," *La Nuova Antologia di Lettere Scienze e Arti* 32 (16 July 1897): 368–76; Il Conte Ottavio (Ugo Ojetti), "In difesa dei nostri paesaggi," *L'Illustrazione Italiana* 30 (12 June 1904): 467.

9. Christian F. Otto, "Modern Environment and Historical Continuity: The Heimatschutz Discourse in Germany," *Art Journal* 43, no. 2 (1983): 148–57.

10. See Hugo Wilhelm Conwentz, *Die Gefährdung der Naturdenkmäler und Vorschläge zu ihrer Erhaltung* (Berlin: Gebrüder Borntraeger, 1904). Five years later, a short edition appeared for the English-speaking world, entitled *The Care of Natural Monuments, with Special Reference to Great Britain and Germany* (New York: Cambridge University Press, 1909).

11. Johann Coaz and Carl Schröter, *Ein Besuch im Val Scarl* (Bern: Stämpfli, 1905).

12. There were seven thousand members in 1911. Stephan Bachmann, "Heimatschutz," in *Historical Dictionary of Switzerland*, available at http://www.hls-dhs-dss.ch/textes/i/I16450.php, version of 3 July 2008 (accessed 5 May 2009).

13. Corrado Ricci, "Per la bellezza artistica d'Italia," *Emporium* 21, no. 124 (1905): 294–309, and 22, no. 127 (1905): 34–44.

14. Parpagliolo, "La protezione del paesaggio."

15. Luigi Parpagliolo, *Il catalogo delle bellezze naturali d'Italia e la legislazione estera in materia di tutela delle bellezze naturali e del paesaggio* (Milan: Touring Club Italiano-Comitato Nazionale per la Difesa dei Monumenti e dei Paesaggi Italici, 1922).

16. The maturity of scientific societies is very important in this context, as testified to by two wonderful reports given a few months apart by Renato Pampanini and Lino Vaccari. See Pampanini, *Per la protezione della flora italiana: Relazione presentata alla riunione generale della Società Botanica Italiana in Roma (12–16 ottobre 1911)* (Florence: Pellas, 1911), and Vaccari, *Per la protezione della fauna italiana: Comunicazione alla Società Zoologica Italiana* (Perugia: Tipografia Bartelli, 1912).

17. A recent synthesis of the history of the association is Stefano Pivato, *Il Touring Club Italiano* (Bologna: Il Mulino, 2006).

18. Luigi Piccioni, "La tutela del bosco e dell'albero nell'associazionismo protezionistico di inizio Novecento," in *Diboscamento montano e politiche territoriali: Alpi e Appennini dal Settecento al Duemila*, ed. Antonio Lazzarini (Milan: Franco Angeli, 2002), 330–46.

19. In successive versions, the Comitato Nazionale published a good deal of material, which is very useful for the reconstruction of events and characters from the first phase of Italian protectionism. See Touring Club Italiano—Comitato Nazionale per la Difesa del Paesaggio e dei Monumenti Italici, *Per la difesa del paesaggio e dei monumenti italici* (Milan: Touring Club Italiano, 1914); Touring Club Italiano, *Comitato nazionale e comitati locali per la difesa dei monumenti e dei paesaggi italici* (Milan: Touring Club Italiano, 1921); Luigi Vittorio Bertarelli, Giovanni Bognetti, and Doro Rosetti, *I parchi nazionali: Deturpazioni di monumenti in periodi elettorali—Le cartoline illustrate di paese* (Milan: Touring Club Italiano—Comitato Nazionale per la Difesa dei Monumenti e dei Paesaggi Italici, 1923).

20. On the vicissitudes of the Lega Nazionale, see C[?]. Paladini, "Per la difesa del paesaggio, degli animali e delle piante: La Lega Nazionale per la protezione delle bellezze naturali—La istituzione dei Parchi Nazionali," *La Nazione*, 2 January 1914, 3; Renato Pampanini, "La protezione della natura in Italia," *Bollettino della Sezione Fiorentina del C.A.I.* 2 (1918): 63–77; Pampanini, "Gli esponenti più rimarchevoli e più rari della flora toscana nel censimento dei monumenti naturali d'Italia," *Nuovo Giornale Botanico Italiano* 32, no. 1 (1925): 5–35.

21. Still in 1918, Luigi Parpagliolo believed it would be possible to create a park in Abruzzo that would attract tens, if not hundreds, of thousands of people. See Parpagliolo, "Un parco nazionale in Abruzzo," *La Nuova Antologia di Scienze Lettere ed Arti* 19 (16 May 1918): 146–59.

22. This solidarity had led to, among other things, the organization of various international meetings on the protection of nature, the most important of which was in Bern in 1914. See *Récueil des procès-verbaux de la Conférence internationale pour la protection de la nature: Berne 17–19 nov. 1913* (Bern: Imprimerie K. J. Wyss, 1914).

23. On the effects of war on the national appreciation of landscape, see Marco Armiero's essay in this volume.

24. A brilliant illustration of the law and its procedural process by one of its main inspirations is Luigi Parpagliolo, *La difesa delle bellezze naturali d'Italia* (Rome: Società Editrice d'Arte Illustrata, 1923).

25. Still fundamental with regard to the Abruzzo park is Erminio Sipari, *Relazione del Presidente dell'Ente Autonomo del Parco Nazionale d'Abruzzo alla Commissione Amministratrice dell'Ente stesso, nominata con regio decreto 25 marzo 1923* (Tivoli: Tipografia Maiella, 1926); see also Luigi Piccioni, "La natura come posta in gioco: La dialettica tutela ambientale-sviluppo turistico nella storia della 'regione dei parchi,'" in *Storia d'Italia: Le regioni*, vol. 15, *Abruzzo*, ed. Massimo Costantini and Costantino Felice (Turin: Einaudi, 2000), 921–1074.

Still important today with regard to the Alpine park is *Il Parco Nazionale del Gran Paradiso,* 3 vols. (Turin: Ente Autonomo del Parco Nazionale del Gran Paradiso, 1925–33, repr., 1951); see also Bruno Bassano, *70 anni di storia, di cultura e di ricerca scientifica nel Parco Nazionale Gran Paradiso* (Turin: Ente Parco Nazionale del Gran Paradiso, 1995). On Gran Paradiso National Park, see also Wilko Graf von Hardenberg's essay in this volume.

26. In 1923, Italy was the fourth European country to create national parks, after Sweden (1909), Switzerland (1914), and Spain (1918). The great industrialized nations did not create national parks until much later: Great Britain (1951), France (1963), and Germany (1970).

27. Article 9 of the Constitution of the Republic of Italy reads: "The Republic promotes the development of culture and scientific and technical research. It protects the landscape and the historic and artistic patrimony of the Nation." See *Gazzetta Ufficiale,* no. 298 (27 December 1947).

28. Regarding the history of these two organizations, see Meyer, *I pionieri,* 41–45 and 133–43, and Pedrotti, *Il fervore dei pochi,* i–xiii.

29. Probably the most important result obtained by Italian preservationists in the 1950s and 1960s was the return of Gran Paradiso and Abruzzo national parks to autonomous management, thereby removing the control of forestry agencies. Gran Paradiso was managed competently and passionately by Renzo Videsott between 1948 and 1970, but the story was very different in Abruzzo park, which suffered from violent local attacks after the mid-1950s.

30. This changing environmental sensitivity did not take long to manifest itself. For example, in 1966, the first Italian law against pollution was passed; in 1968, the first national park of the republican period was created, the Calabria National Park (the previous national park established was Stelvio in 1935); in 1969, the administration of Abruzzo National Park was revamped after many years of speculative abuse; and in 1970, the environment was given wide attention in the planning document entitled *Progetto 80.*

31. For surveys of recent Italian environmentalism, see Simone Neri Serneri, "Culture politiche del movimento ambientalista," in *L'Italia repubblicana nella crisi degli anni settanta,* vol. 2, *Culture, nuovi soggetti, identità,* ed. Fiamma Lussana and Giacomo Marramao (Soveria Mannelli: Rubbettino, 2003): 367–99. For a more general look at this movement, along with the testimony of one of the period's leading players, see Giorgio Nebbia, "Limiti alla crescita e lotte per l'ambiente," in *Le radici della crisi: L'Italia tra gli anni sessanta e settanta,* ed. Luca Baldissara (Rome: Carocci, 2001), 211–38.

Selected Bibliography

The following list of books and articles is by no means exhaustive and does not substitute for the references related to specific topics addressed in the essays of this volume. This list has been compiled as a tool to help readers who are interested in continuing their journey through Italian history and nature. The subject is further explored in the journal *I frutti di Demetra: Bolletino di storia e ambiente*, available at http://www.issm.cnr.it.

Adorno, Salvatore. *La produzione di uno spazio urbano: Siracusa tra ottocento e novecento*. Venice: Marsilio, 2004.

———, ed. *Professionisti, città e territorio: Percorsi di ricerca tra storia del'urbanistica e storia della città*. Rome: Gangemi, 2002.

Adorno, Salvatore, and Simone Neri Serneri, eds. *Industria, ambiente e territorio: Per una storia ambientale delle aree industriali in Italia*. Bologna: Il Mulino, 2009.

Agnoletti, Mauro. "Osservazioni sulle dinamiche dei boschi e del paesaggio forestale italiano fra il 1862 e la fine del secolo XX." *Società e Storia* 28, no. 108 (2005): 377–96.

———. *Segherie e foreste nel Trentino, dal Medioevo ai giorni nostri*. San Michele all'Adige: Museo degli Usi e Costumi della Gente Trentina, 1998.

———, ed. *Storia e risorse forestali*. Florence: Accademia italiana di scienze forestali, 2001.

Agnoletti, Mauro, and Steve Anderson, eds. *Forest History: International Studies on Socio-economic and Forest Ecosystem Change*. Wallingford: CABI Publishing, 2000.

Ambrosi, Claudio, and Michael Wedekind, eds. *L'invenzione di un cosmo borghese: Valori sociali e simboli culturali dell'alpinismo nei secoli XIX e XX*. Trento: Museo Storico in Trento, 2000.

Amendola, Gianfranco. *In nome del popolo inquinato*. Milan: Franco Angeli, 1985.

Armiero, Marco. "L'ambiente nelle riviste storiche italiane (1976–1996)." *Società e Storia* 83 (1999): 145–85.

————. "Seeing Like a Protester: Nature, Power, and Environmental Struggles." *Left History* 13, no. 1 (2008): 59–76.

————. *Il territorio come risorsa: Comunità, economie e istituzioni nei boschi abruzzesi (1806–1860)*. Naples: Liguori, 1999.

————. *Views from the South: Environmental Stories from the Mediterranean World (19th–20th Centuries)*. Naples: ISSM-CNR, 2006.

Armiero, Marco, and Stefania Barca. *Storia dell'ambiente: Una introduzione*. Rome: Carocci, 2004.

Armiero, Marco, and Marcus Hall. "Italy." In *Encyclopedia of World Environmental History*, edited by Shepard Krech III, J. R. McNeill, and C. Merchant. New York: Berkshire Publishing Group and Routledge, 2003.

Armiero, Marco, Pietro Piussi, and Bruno Vecchio. "L'uso del bosco e degli incolti." In Accademia dei Georgofili di Firenze, *L'Italia agricola dalle origini ad oggi*. Florence: Polistampa, 2003.

Barbera, Giuseppe. *L'orto di Pomona: Sistemi tradizionali dell'arboricoltura da frutto in Sicilia*. Palermo: L'Epos, 2000.

Barca, Stefania. "Le acque urbane in età contemporanea." In *La natura e la città: Per una storia ambientale di Napoli fra '800 e '900*, edited by Ilaria Zilli. Naples: Edizioni Scientifiche Italiane, 2004.

————. "Il capitale naturale: Acque e rivoluzione industriale in valle del Liri." *Memoria e Ricerca* 15 (2004): 151–66.

————. "Enclosing the River: Industrialisation and the 'Property Rights' Discourse in the Liri Valley (South of Italy), 1806–1916." *Environment and History* 13, no. 1 (2007): 3–23.

————. *Enclosing Water: Nature and Political Economy in a Mediterranean Valley, 1796–1916*. Cambridge, UK: White Horse Press, 2010.

Benevolo, Leonardo. *Storia dell'architettura nell'Italia contemporanea*. Bari: Laterza, 1998.

Betri, Maria Luisa, and A. Gigli Marchetti, eds. *Salute e classi lavoratrici in Italia dall'Unità al fascismo*. Milan: Franco Angeli, 1982.

Bettin, Gianfranco, and Maurizio Danese. *Petrolkiller*. Milan: Feltrinelli, 2002.

Bevilacqua, Piero. *Demetra e Clio: Uomini e ambiente nella storia*. Rome: Donzelli, 2001.

————, ed. "Montagna." *Meridiana: Rivista di Storia e Scienze Sociali* 44 (2002), numero monografico.

————. *Il paesaggio italiano nelle fotografie dell'Istituto Luce*. Rome: Editori Riuniti, 2002.

————. "Le rivoluzioni dell'acqua: Irrigazioni e trasformazioni dell'agricoltura tra Sette e Novecento." In *Storia dell'agricoltura italiana in età contemporanea*, vol. 1, *Spazi e paesaggi*, edited by Piero Bevilacqua. Venice: Marsilio, 1989.

————, ed. *Storia dell'agricoltura italiana in età contemporanea*. Vol. 1, *Spazi e paesaggi*. Venice: Marsilio, 1989.

————. *Tra natura e storia: Ambiente, economie, risorse in Italia*. Rome: Donzelli, 1996.

————. *Venezia e le acque: Una metafora planetaria*. Rome: Donzelli, 2000. Translated as *Venice and the Water: A Model for Our Planet*, by Charles A. Ferguson; with an afterword by Massimo Cacciari. Solon, ME: Polar Bear, 2009.

Bevilacqua, Piero, and Manlio Rossi Doria. *Le bonifiche in Italia dal '700 a oggi*. Rome: Laterza, 1984.

Biacchessi, Daniele. *L'ambiente negato: Viaggio nell'Italia dei dissesti*. Rome: Editori Riuniti, 1999.

————. *La fabbrica dei profumi: La verità su Seveso, l'ICMESA, la diossina*. Milan: Baldini & Castoldi, 1995.

Bianco, Furio, and Antonio Lazzarini. *Forestali, mercanti di legname e boschi pubblici: Candido Morassi e i progetti di riforma boschiva nelle Alpi Carniche tra Settecento e Ottocento*. Udine: Forum, 2003.

Bigatti, Giorgio. *La provincia delle acque: Ambiente, istituzioni e tecnici in Lombardia tra Sette e Ottocento*. Milan: Franco Angeli, 1995.

————. *Uomini e acque: Il territorio lodigiano tra passato e presente*. Lodi: Giona, 2000.

Bonelli, Franco. "La malaria nella storia demografica ed economica d'Italia." *Studi Storici* 7, no. 4 (1966): 659–87.

Boscacci, Flavio, and Roberto Camagni, eds. *Tra città e campagna, periurbanizzazione e politiche territoriali*. Bologna: Il Mulino, 1994.

Boschi, Enzo, et al. *Catalogo dei Forti Terremoti in Italia dal 461 A.C. al 1980*. Bologna: Istituto Nazionale di Geofisica, 1995.

Caffiero, Marina. *L'erba dei poveri: Comunità rurale e soppressione degli usi collettivi nel Lazio (secoli XVIII–XIX)*. Rome: Edizioni dell'Ateneo, 1982.

Caracciolo, Alberto. *L'ambiente come storia*. Bologna: Il Mulino, 1988.

Caracciolo, Alberto, and Gabriella Bonacchi, eds. *Il declino degli elementi: Ambiente naturale e rigenerazione delle risorse*. Bologna: Il Mulino, 1990.

Cazzola, Franco, ed. *Acque di frontiera: Principi, comunità e governo del territorio nelle terre basse tra Enza e Reno (secoli XIII–XVIII)*. Bologna: CLUEB, 2000.

————. *Storia delle campagne padane dall'Ottocento a oggi*. Milan: Bruno Mondadori, 1996.

————. "Tra conflitto e solidarietà: Considerazioni sull'esperienza storica delle partecipanze agrarie dell'Emilia Romagna." *Cheiron* 14–15 (1990–91).

Cederna, Antonio. *La distruzione della natura in Italia.* Turin: Einaudi, 1975.

————. *I vandali in casa.* Bari: Laterza, 1956.

Centemeri, Laura. *Ritorno a Seveso: Il danno ambientale, il suo riconoscimento, la sua riparazione.* Milan: Bruno Mondadori, 2006.

Cibotto, Gian Antonio. *Cronache dell'alluvione: Polesine 1951.* Venice: Marsilio, 1998.

Ciriacono, Salvatore. *Acque e agricoltura: Venezia, l'Olanda e la bonifica europea nell'età moderna.* Milan: Franco Angeli, 1994.

Ciuffetti, Augusto. *Condizioni materiali di vita, sanità e malattie in un centro industriale: Terni 1880–1940.* Naples: Edizioni Scientifiche Italiane, 1996.

Club of Rome. *Il rapporto sui limiti dello sviluppo.* Milan: Mondadori, 1974.

Conti, Laura. *Questo pianeta.* Rome: Editori Riuniti, 1988.

————. *Visto da Seveso: L'evento straordinario e l'ordinaria amministrazione.* Milan: Feltrinelli, 1977.

Coppola, Gauro. "La montagna alpina: Vocazioni originarie e trasformazioni funzionali." In *Storia dell'agricoltura italiana in età contemporanea,* vol. 1, *Spazi e paesaggi,* edited by Piero Bevilacqua. Venice: Marsilio, 1989.

Corona, Gabriella. *Demani ed individualismo agrario nel regno di Napoli (1780–1806).* Naples: Edizioni Scientifiche Italiane, 1995.

————. *I ragazzi del Piano: Napoli e le ragioni dell'ambientalismo urbano.* Rome: Donzelli, 2007.

————. "La sostenibilità urbana a Napoli: Caratteri strutturali e dinamiche storiche." *Meridiana* 42 (2001): 45–52.

Corona, Gabriella, and Simone Neri Serneri, eds. *Storia e ambiente: Città, risorse e territori nell'Italia contemporanea.* Rome: Carocci, 2007.

Cosmacini, Giorgio. *Medicina e sanità in Italia nel ventesimo secolo: Dalla "spagnola" alla II guerra mondiale.* Rome: Laterza, 1989.

Cuaz, Marco. *Le Alpi.* Bologna: Il Mulino, 2005.

D'Antone, Leandra. *Scienza e governo del territorio: Medici, ingegneri, agronomi e urbanisti nel Tavoliere di Puglia (1865–1965).* Milan: Franco Angeli, 1990.

Della Porta, Donatella, and Mario Diani. *Movimenti senza protesta? L'ambientalismo in Italia.* Bologna: Il Mulino, 2004.

Della Porta, Donatella, and Gianni Piazza. *Voices of the Valley, Voices of the Straits: How Protest Creates Communities.* New York: Berghahn Books, 2008.

Della Seta, Roberto. *La difesa dell'ambiente in Italia: Storia e cultura del movimento ecologista.* Milan: Franco Angeli, 2000.

De Lucia, Vezio. *Se questa è una città: La condizione urbana nell'Italia contemporanea.* Rome: Donzelli, ISSM-CNR, 2006.

Dente, Bruno, and Pippo Ranci, eds. *L'industria e l'ambiente*. Bologna: Il Mulino, 1992.

Diani, Mario. *Green Networks: A Structural Analysis of the Italian Environmental Movement*. Edinburgh: Edinburgh University Press, 1995.

Dickie, John, John Foot, and Frank Snowden, eds. *Disastro! Disasters in Italy since 1860: Culture, Politics, Society*. New York: Palgrave, 2003.

Dogliani, Patrizia, ed. "Ambiente, territori, parchi." *Memoria e ricerca* 1 (1998), numero monografico.

Erbani, Francesco. *L'Italia maltrattata*. Rome: Laterza, 2003.

———. *Uno strano italiano: Antonio Iannello e lo scempio dell'ambiente*. Rome: Laterza, 2003.

Fondazione Basso-Issoco, ed. *L'ambiente nella storia d'Italia*. Venice: Marsilio, 1989.

Foot, John. *Milan since the Miracle: City, Culture and Identity*. Oxford: Berg, 2001.

Frascani, Paolo. *A Vela e a Vapore: Economie, culture e istituzioni del mare nell'italia dell'ottocento*. Rome: Donzelli, 2001.

Gambi, Lucio. "I valori storici dei quadri ambientali." In *Storia d'Italia: I Caratteri Originale*, vol. 1. Turin: Einaudi, 1972.

Gambino, Roberto. *Conservare, innovare: Paesaggio, ambiente, territorio*. Turin: UTET, 1997.

Gardin, Paolo, and Massimo Pazienti. *L'ambiente in Italia: Problemi e prospettive*. Milan: Franco Angeli, 1992.

Gaspari, Oscar. *La montagna alle origni di un problema politico*. Rome: Istituto Poligrafico dello Stato, 1992.

Giansanti, Monica. "Industria e ambiente: Il caso della 'Carburo' a Collestatte e Papigno (1896–1930)." *Proposte e Ricerche* 37, no. 2 (1996): 189–215.

Gobbi, Olimpia. *Risorse e governo dell'ambiente a San Marino fra XV e XIX secolo*. Quaderni del Centro Sammarinese di Studi Storici 19. San Marino: Università degli Studi della Repubblica di San Marino, 1999.

Graf von Hardenberg, Wilko, and Paolo Pelizzari. "The Environmental Question, Employment, and Development in Italy's Left, 1945–1990." *Left History* 13, no. 1 (2008): 77–105.

Guidoboni, Emanuela. "Paesaggi seminascosti: Sismicità e disastri sismici in Italia." In *Il declino degli elementi: Ambiente naturale e rigenerazione delle risorse*, edited by Alberto Caracciolo and Gabriella Bonacchi. Bologna: Il Mulino, 1990.

Guidoboni, Emanuela, and Jean-Paul Poirier. *Quand la terre tremblait*. Paris: O. Jacob, 2004.

Hall, Marcus. *Earth Repair: A Transatlantic History of Environmental Restoration*. Charlottesville: University of Virginia Press, 2005.

————. "Restoring the Countryside: George Perkins Marsh and the Italian Land Ethic (1861–1882)." *Environment and History* 4, no. 1 (1998): 91–103.

————. "World War II and the Axis of Disease: Battling Malaria in Twentieth-Century Italy." In *War and the Environment: Military Destruction in the Modern Age,* edited by Charles Closmann, 112–31. College Station: Texas A&M University Press, 2009.

Isenburg, Teresa. *Acque e Stato: Energia, bonifiche, irrigazione in Italia fra 1930 e 1950.* Milan: Franco Angeli, 1986.

Landi, Fiorenzo. *La pianura dei mezzadri: Studi di storia dell'agricoltura padana in età moderna e contemporanea.* Milan: Franco Angeli, 2003.

Lazzarini, Antonio, ed. *Diboscamento montano e politiche territoriali: Alpi e Appennini dal Settecento al Duemila.* Milan: Franco Angeli, 2002.

Leone, Ugo. *La sicurezza fa chiasso.* Naples: Guida, 2004.

Lewanski, Rudolf, and Angela Liberatore. "The Evolution of Italian Environmental Policy." *Environment* 32, no. 5 (1990): 10–40.

Lumley, Robert, and John Foot, eds. *Italian Cityscapes: Cultures and Urban Change in Contemporary Italy.* Exeter: University of Exeter Press, 2004.

Luzzi, Saverio. *Salute e sanità nell'Italia repubblicana.* Rome: Donzelli, 2004.

————. *Il virus del benessere: Ambiente, salute, sviluppo nell'Italia repubblicana.* Rome: Laterza, 2009.

Malanima, Paolo. *Energy Consumption in Italy in the 19th and 20th Centuries: A Statistical Outline.* Naples: ISSM-CNR, 2006.

————. "La ricchezza e la povertà dell'Italia: Le risorse naturali." In *Storia economica d'Italia,* vol. 3, edited by Pierluigi Ciocca and Gianni Toniolo. Rome: Laterza, 2002.

Mazzeri, Catia, ed. *Le città sostenibili: Storia, natura, ambiente.* Milan: Franco Angeli, 2003.

McNeill, John R. *The Mountains of the Mediterranean World: An Environmental History.* New York: Cambridge University Press, 1992.

Merlin, Tina. *Sulla pelle viva: Come si costruisce una catastrofe: Il caso del Vajont.* Verona: Cierre, 2003.

Meyer, Edgar H. *I pionieri dell'ambiente: L'avventura del movimento ecologista italiano—Cento anni di storia.* Milan: Carabà, 1995.

Moreno, Diego, ed. "Boschi: Storia e archeologia 2." *Quaderni Storici* 62 (1986).

————. *Dal documento al terreno: Storia e archeologia dei sistemi agro-silvo-pastorali.* Bologna: Il Mulino, 1990.

————. "Storia e archeologia forestale." *Quaderni Storici* 49 (1982): 7–15.

Moreno, Diego, Pietro Piussi, and Oliver Rackham, eds. "Boschi: Storia e archeologia." *Quaderni Storici* 49 (1982).

Motta, Giovanna. *Paesaggio territorio ambiente: Storia di uomini e di terre.* Milan: Franco Angeli, 2004.

Nebbia, Giorgio. *Risorse, merci, ambiente.* Bari: Progedit, 2001.

Neri Serneri, Simone. "Il futuro della terra: Risorse e ambiente per le generazioni che verranno." *Parolechiave* 16 (1998): 203–31.

————. *Incorporare la natura: Storie ambientali del Novecento.* Rome: Carocci, 2005.

————. *Storia del territorio e storia dell'ambiente: La Toscana contemporanea.* Milan: Franco Angeli, 2003.

Novello, Elisabetta. *La bonifica in Italia: Legislazione, credito e lotta alla malaria dall'unità al fascismo.* Milan: Franco Angeli, 2003.

Palmieri, Walter. "Il dissesto idrogeologico: Frane e alluvioni nell'Ottocento molisano." In *Storia del Molise,* edited by Gino Massullo. Rome: Donzelli, 2006.

————. "Le frane di Sarno: Percorsi di lettura tra storia e scienze sociali." In *Libro bianco sulla gestione e messa in sicurezza del territorio a sette anni dalla catastrofe del maggio 1998,* edited by Antonio Vallario. Rome: Sigea, 2005.

Paolini, Federico. *Breve storia dell'ambiente nel Novecento.* Rome: Carocci, 2009.

————. *Un paese a quattro ruote: Automobili e società in Italia.* Venice: Marsilio, 2005.

Pedrotti, Franco. *Il fervore dei pochi: Il movimento protezionistico italiano dal 1943 ad oggi.* Trent: Temi, 1998.

Piccioni, Luigi. "La natura come posta in gioco: La dialettica tutela ambientale-sviluppo turistico nella storia della 'regione dei parchi.'" In *Storia d'Italia: Le regioni,* vol. 15, *Abruzzo,* edited by Massimo Costantini and Costantino Felice. Turin: Einaudi, 2000.

————. *Il volto amato della Patria: Il primo movimento per la protezione della natura in Italia, 1880–1934.* Camerino: Università di Camerino, 1999.

Poggio, Pier Paolo. *La crisi ecologica: Origini, rimozioni, significati.* Milan: Jaca Book, 2003.

————, ed. *Una storia ad alto rischio: L'ACNA e la Valle Bormida.* Turin: Gruppo Abele, 1996.

Porisini, Giorgio. *Bonifiche e agricoltura nella bassa Valle Padana.* Milan: Banca Commerciale Italiana, 1978.

Pratesi, Fulco. "Gli ambienti naturali e l'equilibrio ecologico." In *Storia d'Italia: Annali 8, Insediamenti e territorio,* edited by Cesare de Seta. Turin: Einaudi, 1985.

————. *Storia della natura in Italia.* Rome: Editori Riuniti, 2001.

Prosperi, Adriano, ed. *Il padule di Fucecchio: La lunga storia di un ambiente "naturale."* Rome: Edizioni di Storia e Letteratura, 1995.

Rabitti, Paolo. *Cronache della chimica: Marghera e le altre.* Naples: Cuen, 1998.

―――. *Ecoballe.* Reggio Emilia: Aliberti, 2008.

Raimondo, Sergio. *La risorsa che non c'è più: Il lago del Fucino dal XVI al XIX secolo.* Mandria: P. Lacaita Editore, 2000.

Reberschak, Maurizio, and Ivo Mattozzi, eds. *Il Vajont dopo il Vajont.* Venice: Marsilio, 2009.

Ruzzenenti, Marino. *L'Italia sotto i rifiuti: Brescia: Un monito per la penisola.* Milan: Jaca Book, 2004.

―――. *Un secolo di cloro e . . . PCB: Storia delle industrie Caffaro di Brescia.* Milan: Jaca Book, 2001.

Saba, Andrea Filippo, and Edgar H. Meyer, eds. *Storia ambientale: Una nuova frontiera storiografica.* Milan: Teti Editore, 2001.

Salzano, Eduardo. "Ambiente e urbanistica: La proposta della città sostenibile." In Salzano, *Fondamenti di urbanistica.* Rome: Laterza, 1998.

Sansa, Renato. "L'odore del contagio: Ambiente urbano e prevenzione delle epidemie nella prima età moderna." *Medicina e storia* 2, no. 3 (2002): 83–108.

―――. *L'oro verde: I boschi nello Stato pontificio tra XVIII e XIX secolo.* Bologna: CLUEB, 2003.

Sereni, Emilio. *Storia del paesaggio agrario italiano.* 1961; Bari: Laterza, 1972.

Serpieri, Arrigo. *La bonifica nella storia e nella dottrina.* 1948; Bologna: Edizioni agricole, 1957.

Settis, Salvatore. *Italia S.p.A.: L'assalto al patrimonio culturale.* Turin: Einaudi, 2002.

Sievert, James. "Abruzzo National Park: Land of Dreams." *Environment and History* 5, no. 3 (1999): 293–309.

―――. *The Origins of Nature Conservation in Italy.* Bern: Peter Lang, 2000.

Snowden, Frank. *The Conquest of Malaria: Italy, 1900–1962.* New Haven, CT: Yale University Press, 2006.

Sori, Ercole. "A proposito di ecostoria." *Proposte e Ricerche* 22 (1989): 7–27.

―――. *La città e i rifiuti.* Bologna: Il Mulino, 2001.

―――. *Il rovescio della produzione.* Bologna: Il Mulino, 1999.

Tagliolini, Alessandro. *Storia del giardino italiano: Gli artisti, l'invenzione, le forme dall'antichità al XIX secolo.* Florence: Casa Usher, 1991.

Tino, Pietro. "L'Italia meridionale e il mare: Pesca, natura e insediamenti costieri tra XVIII e XX secolo." In *Natura e società: Studi in memoria di Augusto Placanica,* edited by Piero Bevilacqua and Pietro Tino. Rome: Donzelli, 2005.

―――. "La montagna meridionale: Boschi, uomini, economie tra Otto e Novecento." In *Storia dell'agricoltura italiana in età contemporanea,* vol. 1, *Spazi e paesaggi,* edited by Piero Bevilacqua. Venice: Marsilio, 1989.

Tognotti, Eugenia. *La malaria in Sardegna: Per una storia del paludismo nel Mezzogiorno (1880–1950)*. Milan: Franco Angeli, 1990.

Tozzi, Mario. *Catastrofi: Dal terremo di Lisbona allo tsumani del sudest asiatico—250 anni di lotta tra l'uomo e la natura*. Milan: Rizzoli, 2005.

Varni, Angelo, ed. *Storia dell'ambiente in Italia tra Ottocento e Novecento*. Bologna: Il Mulino, 1999.

Varriale, Roberta. "La mano pubblica nel sottosuolo di Napoli." *Storia Urbana* 30, no. 116 (2007): 57–76.

———, ed. *Undergrounds in Naples: I sottosuoli napoletani*. Naples: ISSM-CNR, 2009.

Vecchio, Bruno. *Il bosco negli scrittori italiani del Settecento e dell'età napoleonica*. Turin: Einaudi, 1974.

Viazzo, Pier Paolo. *Upland Communities: Environment, Population, and Social Structure in the Alps since the Sixteenth Century*. New York: Cambridge University Press, 1989.

Zagli, Andrea. *Il lago e la comunità: Storia di Bientina—Un castello di pescatori nella Toscana moderna*. Florence: Edizioni Polistampa, 2001.

Zanetto, Gabriele, Francesco Vallerani, and Stefano Soriani. "Nature, Environment, Landscape: European Attitudes and Discourses in the Modern Period: The Italian Case, 1920–1970." *Quaderni del Dipartimento di Geografa, Università di Padova* 18 (1996), available online at http://wug.cab.unipd.it:8080/DigLib/DataBase/repository/1063201495/PARTE_PRIMA_DA_PAG_1_A_40.pdf.

Zanzi, Luigi. *Le Alpi nella storia d'Europa: Ambienti, popoli, istituzioni e forme di civiltà del mondo "alpino" dal passato al futuro*. Turin: CDA & Vivalda, 2004.

Zunica, Marcello, ed. *Il delta del Po: Terra e gente al di là dei monti di sabbia*. Milan: Rusconi Immagini, 1984.

Contributors

Salvatore Adorno is associate professor of contemporary history at the University of Catania, Italy. He is a member of the editorial board of *Mestiere di Storico: Annale della Società Italiana per lo Studio della Storia Contemporanea* and on the board of directors of the Associazione Italiana di Storia Urbana. His research deals with the history of urban and agrarian elites and the relationship between technical cultures and territory changes. He is the coeditor (with Simone Neri Serneri) of *Industria, ambiente e territorio: Per una storia ambientale delle aree industriali italiane* (2009), and he has published *Gli Agrari a Parma* (2007) and *La produzione di uno spazio urbano: Siracusa tra Otto e Novecento* (2004).

Marco Armiero (PhD in economic history) is a senior researcher at the National Research Council, Italy. In recent years, he has worked at the Program in Agrarian Studies, Yale University; the Environmental Science, Policy and Management Department, University of California–Berkeley; and the Bill Lane Center for the Study of the North American West, Stanford University. He has just been awarded two grants from CNR-NEH and from the European Union. He has written two books and several articles on the environmental-social history of natural resources, on environmental conflicts, and on environmental historiography. With Stefania Barca, he is the author of the first Italian university textbook on environmental history, *Storia dell'ambiente: Una introduzione* (2004). In English, he has published several essays and edited the book *Views from the South: Environmental Stories from the Mediterranean World* (19th–20th Cent.) (2006). He is currently working on two projects: a book on landscape and nation in modern Italy and a research program on the environmental history of migrations.

Stefania Barca holds a PhD in economic history and is currently senior researcher at the Center for Social Studies of the University of Coimbra,

Portugal. Her dissertation on the electrification of Apulia was published (in Italian) in 2001. She is coauthor of *Storia dell'ambiente: Una introduzione* (2004), a textbook of world environmental history. She has been a visiting scholar at the Program in Agrarian Studies of Yale University (2005–06) and a Ciriacy Wantrup Fellow at the University of California–Berkeley (2006–08). She has published numerous articles and book chapters and is now working on a book about water enclosures and the making of industrial capitalism. Her secondary research project is on labor-environment relationships in the petrochemical industry in Italy and Africa.

Piero Bevilacqua is professor of contemporary history at the University of Rome "La Sapienza." He has written extensively on the history of southern Italy, agriculture, and the history of Italian territory. In the field of environmental history, he has published *La mucca è savia: Ragioni storiche della crisi alimentare europea* (2002); *Venezia e le acque: Una metafora planetaria* (1995, 1998, 2000)—translated in French (in 1996), in German (in 1998), and in English (in 2009); *La terra è finita: Breve storia dell'ambiente* (2006); and *Miseria dello sviluppo* (2008). In 1986, he founded, with other scholars, the Istituto Meridionale di Storia e Scienze Sociali, of which he is chair. He codirects *I Frutti di Demetra: Bollettino di Storia e Ambiente,* the Italian environmental history journal.

Laura Centemeri (PhD in economic sociology, University of Brescia, Italy) is a researcher in the Observatory on Risk (OSIRIS) of the Center for Social Studies, University of Coimbra, Portugal. She is the author of *Ritorno a Seveso: Il danno ambientale, il suo riconoscimento, la sua riparazione* (2006).

Roberta Cevasco is contract professor in historical ecology and in geography of local products at the University of Piemonte Orientale "Amedeo Avogadro." She has collaborated since 1996 with the Laboratory of Environmental Archeology and History at Genoa University. She is the author of *Memoria verde: Nuovi spazi per la geografia* (2007) and has published articles in the *Bollettino della Società Geografica Italiana, Rivista Geografica Italiana,* and international geographic journals. She is also on the staff of the editorial board of *Quaderni Storici.* Her research interests are in geography and historical ecology and their applications to the identification and valorization of the living rural heritage.

Gabriella Corona is senior researcher at the Institute of Studies on Mediterranean Societies of the National Research Council in Naples (CNR-ISSM). She is codirector of the journals *I Frutti di Demetra: Bollettino di Storia e*

Ambiente and *Global Environment: A Journal of History and Natural and Social Sciences.* Her work mainly focuses on the economic, social, and environmental history of Italy. Recent publications include: "La propriété collective en Italie," in Marie-Danielle Demelas and Nadine Vivier, eds., *Les propriétés collectives face aux attaques libérales (1770–1914)* (2003), and "Sustainable Naples: The Disappearance of Nature as a Resource," in Dieter Schott, Bill Luckin, and Geneviève Massard-Guilbaud, eds., *Resources of the City: Contributions to an Environmental History of Modern Europe* (2005).

Emanuela Guidoboni, a historian by training, is a senior scientist and head of the Historical Seismology and Vulcanology Unit at the Istituto Nazionale di Geofisica e Vulcanologia in Bologna, Italy. From 1983 to 2007, she served as director of SGA-Storia Geofisica Ambiente, a company specializing in the study of the earthquakes and environmental history. She is a leading expert in the historical seismicity of the Mediterranean region and the author of a number of historical earthquake catalogs, important for seismic hazard evaluations, and more than a hundred scientific publications.

Marcus Hall (PhD, University of Wisconsin, 1999) is senior lecturer of environmental history at the University of Zurich. Before moving to Europe, he was assistant professor of history at the University of Utah, where he held the Environmental Humanities Research Professorship. In Italy, he has held fellowships at the University of Turin, University of Bologna, European University Institute, and the American Academy of Rome. In his research projects, Hall is pursuing various transatlantic questions that involve malaria, warfare, exotic species, conservation salvage, and environmental restoration, on which he published *Earth Repair* (2005) and edited *Restoration and History* (2010). He currently serves on the executive committee of the American Society for Enviromental History and on the editorial board of *Environment and History.*

Wilko Graf von Hardenberg holds a postdoctoral fellowship at the University of Trento, Italy. His research interests are environmental and social conflict in twentieth-century Europe, the history and practice of sustainable mobility, the impact of post–World War II reconstruction on the natural world, and the position of the Italian social-communist Left on the environmental question. Currently, he is working on the impact of modernization processes on access rights to natural resources in Trentino. He received his PhD from the Cambridge University in 2007, with a dissertation entitled "Fascist Nature: Environmental Policies and Conflicts in Italy, 1922–1945."

Simone Neri Serneri is professor of contemporary history at the University of Siena, Italy. His research focuses on the urban and industrial environmental history of late nineteenth- and twentieth-century Italy. His books in environmental history are *Incorporare la natura: Storie ambientali del Novecento* (2005); *Storia del territorio e storia dell'ambiente: La Toscana contemporanea* (which he edited, 2002); and *Storia e ambiente: Città, risorse e territori nell'Italia contemporanea* (coedited with G. Corona, 2007). As regional representative for Italy, Neri Serneri is a member of the board of the European Society for Environmental History.

Walter Palmieri is researcher at the Institute of Studies on Mediterranean Societies (ISSM), Naples, Italy, belonging to the National Research Council (CNR). He is also member of the editorial board of *I Frutti di Demetra: Rivista di Storia e Ambiente*. His research focuses on southern Italy before unification, with an emphasis on territory, agrarian issues, and the economic associations of the period. A further field of investigation regards deforestation in southern Italy in the nineteenth century. He is currently working on a database on landslides and floods in southern Italy during the last centuries and their historical significance.

Luigi Piccioni teaches economic history and history of tourism at the University of Calabria, Italy. His publications include many essays on the social and economic history of southern Italy and on the history of Italian environmental movements. He is the author of *Il volto amato della patria: Sul primo movimento italiano per la tutela della natura (1883–1934)* (1999) and "La natura come posta in gioco: La dialettica tutela ambientale-sviluppo turistico nella storia della regione dei parchi" (2000).

Bruno Vecchio is professor of geography at the University of Florence. His book on the perceptions of forest problems in early nineteenth-century Italy, published in 1974, was a landmark contribution to Italian historiography on the environment. Currently, he is the director of the *Rivista Geografica Italiana*.

Donald Worster (PhD, Yale University, 1971) is Joyce and Elizabeth Hall Professor of U.S. History and Environmental Studies and Director of the Graduate Program at the University of Kansas. His most recent book, *A Passion for Nature: The Life of John Muir*, was published in 2008. Earlier books include *A River Running West: The Life of John Wesley Powell; The Wealth of Nature; Under Western Skies; Rivers of Empire; Dust Bowl;* and *Nature's Economy* (now available in five languages). He is former president of the American Society for Environmental History.

Index

DATE DUE

HIGHSMITH